满语中的条件句式——语义、形态句法、语用与类型学多角度研究

Conditional Constructions in the Manchu Language: A Study from the Perspectives of Semantics, Morphosyntax, Pragmatics and Typology

陈 辰 著

山东大学出版社

图书在版编目(CIP)数据

满语中的条件句式:语义、形态句法、语用与类型学多角度研究:英语/陈辰著.—济南:山东大学出版社,2020.7

ISBN 978-7-5607-6682-9

Ⅰ.①满… Ⅱ.①陈… Ⅲ.①满语－研究－英文 Ⅳ.①H221

中国版本图书馆 CIP 数据核字(2020)第 161861 号

责任编辑:张申华

封面设计:牛　钧

出版发行:山东大学出版社

社　址　山东省济南市山大南路 20 号

邮　编　250100

电　话　市场部(0531)88364466

经　销:山东省新华书店

印　刷:济南新科印务有限公司

规　格:720 毫米×1000 毫米　1/16

15.5 印张　261 千字

版　次:2020 年 7 月第 1 版

印　次:2020 年 7 月第 1 次印刷

定　价:59.00 元

前　言

本书从语义、形态句法、语用和类型学等角度考察满语的条件句式。在本书中，“条件句式”(conditional constructions)是基于满足语义和形态句法标准的“原型”(prototypes)来定义的。一方面，语义标准规定原型的条件句式把两个事态(state of affairs)关联起来，其中一个事态是另外一个事态的原因，而任何一个事态都不能认为是已经实现的。另一方面，形态句法标准规定原型的条件句式应当频繁地、首要地表达条件意义。那些仅满足部分标准的句式则为“条件句式”这个范畴的“非原型”。条件句式的原型与非原型均为本书关注的对象。

本书分析的数据(例句)来自一个由清朝满语文本组成的自制语料库。选取的例句或者表达条件意义，或者在其从句中含有条件副动词 V-*ci* 组成的结构(此副动词结构是表达条件关系的首要方式)。根据前述定义，符合语义和句法形态标准的例句可视为“候选”原型条件句式。其他例句则视作条件句式的非原型。

在确定原型条件句式的形态句法类型时，本书的依据是语料库中语言的实际用例，以及清朝的满人所描写的语法中所记录的条件句。在讨论非原型条件句时，将其与原型句式联系起来。本书借鉴其他学者的研究方法，涉及多个“域”(domain)，包括“(命题)内容域”(the content domain)、“言语行为域”(the speech-act domain)、“认识域”(the epistemic domain)与“感知域”(the perceptual domain)，因为条件关系的某些方面就在这些不同的域中展现出来。

此外，本书比较了满语的条件句式与其他在亲缘关系或类型学上相近的阿尔泰(或类阿尔泰)语言的条件句式，将满语置于更大的类型学图景中，以期对将来类似的研究提供一些借鉴。

以上是本书的内容梗概。本书是在我博士论文的基础上略加删改而成的。删去的部分涉及满语助动词 *bi-*(有,是)的完整体分词(perfective participle)*bihe* 以及满语的条件连接词 *aika* 与 *aikabade*(如果)。一方面,在博士论文写作之时,力图面面俱到,唯恐论证不力,因此原文相关部分的讨论更加详细。然而如今回顾起来,对其中细节乃至部分结论颇感不足,毕竟囿于当时的认识水平与资料数量,不可能更加全面考察。另一方面,鉴于此部分对于中心论点并非不可或缺,我决定将其从原文中删除,希望将来考虑成熟之后可以专门撰文讨论。

工作几年以来,我始终没有潜心研究些什么。虽然也不时参加一些学术会议,但每次都是为了开会本身而浅尝辄止地临时"关注"某个问题,开完会又把准备的报告抛之脑后,而不是努力整理成文章。这样的事情做过多次以后,竟渐渐迷惘起来。每当想起留学期间的两位导师 Liliya Gorelova 与 Frank Lichtenberk,总觉十分愧对他们的教诲。然而自怨自艾不会有什么用处,终究是"悟已往之不谏,知来者之可追"。我希望以此书的出版为契机,自己在学术可以更加勇猛精进。即使一事无成,至少做到问心无愧。

在此,我要感谢我所在的山东大学外国语学院。正是因为时常受到学院领导的关怀和鼓励,也正是因为学院的学术著作出版资助项目,我才有决心、也有机会将自己的博士论文整理成书。感谢山东大学出版社:如果没有各位编辑老师不厌其烦的指导帮助,我也决不可能完成出版中最关键的一步(本书内容若有任何舛误,责任均在我本人)。感谢我的父母、同事和朋友们,他们的不断督促是我前行的重要动力。

陈　辰

2020 年 1 月

List of Abbreviations

1	first person
2	second person
3	third person
ABIL	abilitative
ABL	ablative
ACC	accusative
ADJ	adjective
APRH	apprehensive
AUX	auxiliary verb
CAUS	causative
CONC	concessive
COND	conditional
COOP	cooperative
COP	copula
CVB	converb
DAT	dative
DIM	diminutive
DIRN	directional
DS	different-subject
DUR	durative
EMPH	emphatic
EPN	epenthesis
EVID	evidential
EXCL	exclusive
EXH	exhaustive
EXS	existential
FIN	finite
FUT	future
GEN	genitive
HON	honorific
IDR	indirect
IMP	imperative
INCH	inchoative
INCL	inclusive
INS	instrumental
IPFV	imperfective
N-	non-
NEG	negative
NMLZ	nominaliser
OPT	optative
PASS	passive
PFV	perfective
PL	plural
PN	proper noun
POSS	possessive
POT	potential

PRED	predicative
PRF	perfect
PROG	progressive
PROL	prolative
PST	past
PTCP	participle
PTL	particle
Q	question particle/marker
QUOT	quotative
RECP	reciprocal
SBJV	subjunctive
SG	singular
SS	same-subject
TERM	terminative
TOP	topic

Table of Contents

Chapter 1 Introduction

The present study stems from an interest in the morphosyntactic structures of the counterfactual conditionals of Manchu. Employing verb forms expressing pastness, these conditionals bear certain resemblance to counterfactual conditionals in European languages such as English and French. Later, this interest extended to Manchu conditional constructions in general, motivating a study aiming at the intersection between two fields: conditionality (in natural languages) and Manchu linguistics. The present study defines "conditional constructions" in Manchu using the prototype approach (see Chapter 2), and investigates them from multiple perspectives: semantics, morphosyntax, pragmatics and typology. It aims to answer the following research questions: What types of conditionals exist in Manchu in terms of reality status (factual, hypothetical or counterfactual) and how are they represented? What are the morphosyntactic characteristics of the prototypes of conditional constructions in Manchu? What functions do conditional constructions perform other than expressing a conditional relation? In what ways are the prototypes interrelated with the non-prototypes of conditional constructions?

This chapter is organised in the following way: Section 1.1 provides some basic facts about the Manchu language; Section 1.2 describes the Manchu materials that constitute the corpus of the present study; and Section 1.3 introduces the contents of the other chapters of this book.

1.1 The Manchu Language

The Manchu language (*manju gisun* in Manchu) is the native language of the Manchu people, an ethnic minority of the People's Republic of China. A confederation of numerous tribes, the Manchus originally inhabited Northeast Asia, including today's northeast Chinese provinces (Liaoning, Jilin and Heilongjiang), as well as Amur Oblast, Primorsky Krai and part of Khabarovsk Krai in Russia. After the Manchus conquered China and established the Qing Dynasty, Manchu naturally became the most important of all the five languages (the other four being Chinese, Mongolian, Tibetan and Chagatai) used in government and enjoyed this status until the fall of the Qing Dynasty. However, the Manchu language has been in decline ever since the latter half of the Qing Dynasty due to their people's assimilation with the Chinese (Han) people, who constituted the majority of the Qing population. In Manchuria today, only a handful of Manchu people, most of them over 70 years old, living in rural areas such as Ilanboo (Sanjiazi), Heilongjiang Province, still speak their ancestral language in addition to Chinese. Besides, the Sibe, an ethnic minority living in the Ili Kazakh Autonomous Prefecture (on the northwestern Chinese border with Kazakhstan), speak a language descended from a variety of Qing Dynasty Manchu, which the Sibe troops brought to this area when they were stationed there by Emperor Qianlong (Aisin-Gioro Hongli, r. 1736-1795) of the Qing Dynasty in the 1760s after the conquest of Jungaria.

Manchu is a member of the Tungusic language family. The other languages of this family include Even, Evenki, Negidal, Solon, Nanai (Gold), Orok, Oroch, Udeghe and Ulcha. Although scholars hold different views regarding how to classify these languages, Manchu is generally thought to belong to a separate branch (together with Sibe) within the family. The Tungusic languages, together with the Mongolic languages (Mongolian, Kalmyk, Monguor, Khamnigan, Buryat, and so forth) and the Turkic languages (Turkish, Azerbaijani, Uzbek, Uyghur,

Kazakh, and so forth), form the controversial Altaic language family. (Janhunen 1996; Vovin 2005) Even more controversial is the inclusion of Korean and Japanese as members of the Altaic Family. Despite the uncertainty about the genetic relationship within the family, the so-called Altaic languages do share salient typological characteristics: they are agglutinative, they have a basic SOV word order, and they exhibit vowel harmony (to different degrees). As far as Manchu is concerned, it is moderately agglutinative. It has a number of cases that are expressed via postpositional markers,[①] which are applicable not only to nominals but also to participles. Manchu verbs (see Chapter 3) morphologically distinguish the categories of aspect-tense, mood, and voice, but in contrast to most other Tungusic languages (and many other Altaic languages, in particular the Turkic languages) do not exhibit agreement of person.

1.2 Manchu Materials Used in the Present Study

The present study draws data (i. e. , example sentences) from a corpus of written Manchu that I have built myself. The Qing Dynasty left an abundant legacy of Manchu texts of various genres. These include, but are not limited to: historical records (especially concerning the Manchus' own history), official documents (both memorials submitted by ministers and imperial edicts), original Manchu literary works, Manchu translations of works of other languages, Manchu conversation books for teaching, Manchu grammar books (in particular descriptions of the usages of functional words), and so forth. In theory, all such materials could qualify as the source of research data, but in practice only a relatively small proportion of them has been chosen. The reason is that not all the Manchu materials are accessible, especially the official documents, the majority of which still remain in storage. In addition, it would require an overwhelming amount of work to build a corpus out of the Manchu

① The cases in Manchu and the corresponding markers are: nominative (ø), genitive-instrumental (*i*/*ni*), dative-locative (*de*), accusative (*be*), and ablative (*ci*, *deri*).

materials that are accessible. In view of this, the selection of materials is intended to include various genres.

The materials I have chosen for the corpus are available in different formats: some of them are annotated and published by modern editors, while others remain in their original Qing editions, stored in libraries and archives. I have purchased or photocopied some materials in modern publications, and have also managed to gain scanned copies (converted to PDF) of some library and archive materials. Since no ready-made research corpus was available, I have transcribed these Manchu texts into the Latin alphabet, following the transcription method devised by Von Möllendorff (1892). The following are the transcribed books that comprise my corpus (also see Bibliography):

(i) ***Manjui yargiyan kooli*** (*Veritable Records of the Manchus*, abbreviated as MYK)

This consists of eight volumes (MYK1, 2, ..., 7 and 8) and is the first part of *Qing Shilu* (*Veritable Records of the Qing Dynasty*, Zhonghua Shuju 1985). The whole text was compiled in the 18th century during the reign of the Emperor Qianlong. MYK records the (mythical) origin of the Manchus and details the military events centring around the life and death of Nurhachi (1559-1626), the chieftain (later to assume the title "khan") who forged the mutually warring tribes into a united, powerful Manchu state. The transcribed text contains approximately 52,300 words.

(ii) ***Nišan saman-i bithe*** (*The Tale of Nishan Shaman*, abbreviated as NSB)

The Tale of Nishan Shaman is an original Manchu literary work that recounts the adventures of a powerful shaman (Nishan), who travelled to the underworld in order to revive a young man. There exist various versions of the NSB, [for instance, Stary (1985) includes three unedited manuscripts; Zhao (2014) includes six versions]; the version I have chosen is a PDF version of a manuscript that Russian scholar Alexander V. Grebenshchikov (1880-1941) obtained from an ethnic Manchu, Dekdengge, in 1913 (Gorelova 2002: xxiii).[1] The transcribed text of NSB contains approximately 8,500 words.

(iii) ***Manju gisun i oyonggo jorin i bithe*** (*Essentials of the Manchu Language*, abbreviated as OJ1) and ***Sirame banjibuha nikan hergen kamcibuha manju gisun i oyonggo jorin i bithe*** (*Recompiled Essentials of the Manchu Language Supplemented with Chinese Translations*, abbreviated as OJ2)

The two volumes comprise a single work, which was originally printed in 1809. It contains 101 excerpts of Manchu dialogues, covering various topics of Manchu life: schooling, archery, ethical values, trading, travelling, and so forth. It was used for teaching ethnic Manchus their native language, which at that time was starting to give way to Chinese. The version that I have adopted for research is a modern publication of the two books by Taiwanese scholar Chang Hwa-ker in 2005. The transcribed text of the whole volume contains approximately 17,400 words.

(iv) ***An i gisun de amtan be sara bithe*** (*The Book for Knowing the Taste of the Ordinary Language*, abbreviated as AGA)

This work, consisting of four volumes (AGA1, 2, 3 and 4), was printed in 1802, roughly at the same time as OJ (1809). In terms of content AGA is also similar to OJ, as it is intended as a textbook teaching the Manchus to speak their own language proficiently. However, it is larger in size, containing 319 dialogue excerpts altogether. AGA has no recently published version, and the version that has been used in the present study is a scanned copy of the original book (in PDF). The transcribed text (of all four books) contains approximately 21,400 words.

(v) ***Nikan gisun kamciha manjurara fiyelen i gisun*** (*Passages of Spoken Manchu Supplemented with Chinese Translation*, abbreviated as MFG)

MFG is the second volume of *cing wen ki mung bithe* (*The Manchu Language for Beginners*), which was printed in 1730. It contains 51

---

[1] The Manchu text of this version is translated into Russian by Volkova (1961), who gives an introduction in its publication. Other publications based on this version of Manchu text also exist.

passages of Manchu dialogues. The version used for the present study is the scanned copy of the original book (as a PDF). The transcribed text contains approximately 6,800 words.

(**vi**) ***Qing yu laoqida*** (*The Manchu Translation of Laoqida*, abbreviated as LQD)

The book *Laoqida*, or *No-geol-dae* (in Korean), was originally written as a textbook of the Chinese language for Korean speakers. Consisting of eight chapters, it recounts the travels of a Korean businessman to China. It was later translated into other languages including Manchu, the text of which was published in 1765 in Korea. The Manchu version, which was given a new Chinese translation by Chuang Chifa, was republished in Taiwan in 1976 and 1984. The 1984 edition of LQD has been adopted for the present study. The transcription of the whole text has been made available on the Internet, and contains approximately 12,000 words (excluding the Chinese translation).

(**vii**) ***Orin emu julen*** (*Twenty-one Stories*), ***aka Sidit Hüür*** (Mongolian; traditionally: *Siditü Kegür*) (*The Bewitched Corpse*), or ***Shiyu Gushi*** (Chinese) (*Stories of the Bewitched Corpse*, abbreviated as SG in the present study).

This book was composed in the 17th century (Ji 2002), and is a Manchu adaptation of ancient Indian Buddhist stories. As suggested by its Manchu name, it consists of 21 stories. One version of these stories is provided by Lebedeva and Gorelova (1994), which is based on an oral account of a native Sibe speaker, recorded by V. V. Radlov in the years 1868 and 1869. Though at the time the Sibes spoke a language almost identical to that of the Manchus, I have decided not to adopt this version of the text in order to concentrate on written Manchu materials of Manchu in the present study. The version that I have adopted is a Chinese annotation and translation by Ji Yonghai (published in Beijing, 2002), which contains a photocopy of the original Manchu text, amounting to approximately 20,000 Manchu words.

Apart from the abovementioned transcribed materials that constitute the corpus, other types of materials are used as references and data sources, although they have not been transcribed. These mainly include some Qing Dynasty grammars and modern publications on Manchu. The Qing Dynasty Manchu grammars include *manju bithei gisun de aisilara mudan i hergen* (*Functional Words in the Manchu Language* 1730, abbreviated as AMH), which is Book Three of *cing wen ki mung bithe* (*An Elementary Textbook of Manchu*); and *dasame foloho manju gisun i untuhen hergen i temgetu jorin bithe* (*Essentials of the Functional Words in Manchu*, A Reprint, 1894, abbreviated as UH). The two books are quite similar to each other in terms of content, focusing on verb suffixes and functional words. It seems that during the Qing Dynasty the state never published a standard grammar of Manchu (though it did make efforts to standardise orthography and lexicon), which makes private publications such as UH and AMH valuable reference grammars. The general grammatical rules provided by these works are taken into consideration, and some example sentences are also included in the data for the present study.

As for the modern publications on Manchu, *ice manju nikan gisun kamcibuha buleku bithe* (*A New Manchu-Chinese Dictionary*, 1994, abbreviated as IMN), is used to aid in glossing and translation (of the example sentences), and also provides example sentences. Another useful work, *A Concise Manchu-English Lexicon* (1978), also proves indispensable for glossing. Li (2010), a textbook of Manchu, provides a few sentences.

Also, one example sentence (4.1-27) is taken from the Manchu translation (Jakdan 1848) of a Chinese novel collection, *liaozhai zhiyi* (*Strange Stories of Liaozhai*, abbreviated as LJ). The whole Manchu text is not transcribed due to its large size, which would exceed that of all the transcribed texts mentioned above. In addition, its genre—a Manchu translation of a Chinese literary work—determines that it would not be ideal corpus material, since the Manchu translation may have been strongly influenced by the Chinese-language original.

The example sentences of conditional constructions in Manchu all consist of a subordinate clause and a main clause. They are selected in accordance with at least one of two criteria: (i) the subordinate clause ends with a conditional-converb structure (V-*ci*); or (ii) there exists a conditional relation between the two clauses (Chapter 2 will elaborate on the definition of "conditional constructions"). Thus, in this process, I have excluded those very lengthy (and indeed supercomplex sometimes) sentences that do contain conditional-converb structures and express conditionality, in order to eliminate structural details irrelevant to my investigation of conditionals.

Table 1.1 summarises the information concerning the corpus texts and the number of example sentences from each source. These sentences are analysed in Chapter 4.

Table 1.1 Information on Corpus Texts and Example Sentences

Corpus Text	Genre	Year (Original Text)	Word Count	Number of Example Sentences
MYK	Historical record	The 18th century	52,300	25
NSB	Original literary work	The 19th century	8,500	7
OJ	Conversation book	1809	17,400	69
AGA	Conversation book	1802	21,400	32
MFG	Conversation book	1730	6,800	37
LQD	Manchu translation	1765	12,000	1
SG	Manchu adaptation	The 17th century	20,000	9
UH	Qing Dynasty grammar	1894	Not applicable	5
IMN	Modern dictionary	not applicable	Not applicable	1
Li 2010	Modern textbook	not applicable	Not applicable	2
LJ	Manchu translation	1848	Not applicable	1

Table 1.1 shows that the texts that make up my corpus cover a period of more than two centuries, during which the Manchu language may reasonably have undergone changes. This means that in principle it would be inappropriate to treat the materials as representing a homogeneous language variety. However, it turns out that Manchu remained quite stable in general in terms of grammar: for instance, MFG (1730) and AGA

(1802), which are of the same genre but are seventy years apart, do not appear to be distinguishable from each other in terms of language. In the case of conditional constructions in particular, there seems to be virtually no structural difference between example sentences from different periods. On the other hand, if the corpus were to include only texts from a relatively short period, there would not be sufficient data and the genres of the texts would also be restricted. Therefore, I have made a compromise between linguistic homogeneity and genre diversity by including the texts as described above.

1.3 Contents of the Book

Chapter 2 reviews previous studies on conditionality in the fields of logic and linguistics, as well as on Manchu linguistics. Specifically, this chapter discusses several issues essential to the present study. The first issue concerns the definition of "conditional", both as a logical function and as a construction in natural language, but more so the latter. Since the object of study is a natural language, the present study regards "conditional" as a linguistic category that can be defined in terms of prototype versus non-prototype. The second issue concerns the nature of the conditional relation. The present study adopts the view that (prototypical) conditionality entails causality between two unrealised states of affairs. Following Sweetser (1990) and Dancygier (1998), it also holds that the conditional relation—or a certain aspect of it (temporality, causality)—can be presented in any of multiple domains, such as the content domain, the epistemic domain, or the speech-act domain. Another issue concerns the reality status of conditionals (or degree of hypotheticality) and how they are expressed in natural language. In accordance with Dahl (1997), and Van linden and Verstraete (2008), the present study takes into account the aspect-tense forms and modal markers. In addition, contextual factors are also deemed relevant. Thus, through examining issues that have been previously discussed, this chapter outlines the theoretical framework of the study.

Chapter 3 deals with the verb system of Manchu due to the importance of verbs for the present study. This chapter describes the conjugation of Manchu verbs (mainly converbs and participles) and provides information concerning the categories of aspect-tense (imperfective, perfective, and so forth), modality (indicative, imperative, optative, and apprehensive) and voice (active, passive, causative, cooperative, and so forth). Also, the functions of three special verbs (*bi-* "to exist/be", *o-* "to become/be" and *se-* "to say") are discussed. These verbs can function both as lexical verbs and as auxiliary verbs. In particular, the perfective participle of *bi-*, i. e. *bi-he*, which plays an important role in the morphosyntax of counterfactual conditionals, is discussed in detail (Section 3. 2. 2).

Chapter 4 is the core of this book, analysing the collected data (example sentences) from multiple perspectives: morphosyntactic pattern, interclausal relation, the domain of semantic representation and so forth. The example sentences are divided into ten categories (not necessarily mutually exclusive) in terms of semantics, syntax and pragmatics, each of which is analysed in one section. Section 4. 1 concerns the basic patterns of conditional constructions in Manchu, i. e., the most common sentence patterns in which a conditional relation is evident. These include both factual and counterfactual conditionals. Section 4. 2 analyses less common patterns of sentences which nonetheless express a conditional relation. Section 4. 3 concerns itself with conditional-like sentences (that is, those containing conditional-converb [V-*ci*] structures in the subordinate clauses) that express a temporal relation. Section 4. 4 discusses a group of conditionals whose use is determined by the pragmatic environment: the protasis in fact serves as a politeness strategy. Section 4. 5 analyses conditional-like sentences that function as concessives (proper) or concessive conditionals. Section 4. 6 concerns several types of conditional-like sentences that express contrast, comparison or disjunction. Section 4. 7 discusses evaluative conditionals, while Section 4. 8 analyses sentences in which conditional-converb structures serve as topics. Section 4. 9 focuses on a group of frequently used conditional-like sentences that contain verbs denoting perception, obtaining of information or cognition. Section 4. 10, the last section of this chapter, analyses two types of conditionals (i. e., inferential conditionals and performative conditionals) that do not fall neatly into the previous categories.

Chapter 5 discusses the issue of identifying the prototypes of Manchu conditionals (both factual and counterfactual) and summarises the relation between the prototypes and the non-prototypical constructions analysed in Chapter 4. In particular, Section 5. 2 serves as a review of the analysis of Chapter 4, specifying the aspects of prototypical conditionality shared by the non-prototypical constructions, and the domains in which these aspects are presented.

Chapter 6 concludes this book. Section 6. 1 compares the functions of conditionals in other Altaic (or Altaic-like) languages with the functions of Manchu conditionals, viewing Manchu conditionals in a larger typological picture. Section 6. 2 sums up the contribution of the present study from two perspectives—that of research on linguistic conditionality, and that of Manchu linguistics. From the former perspective, the present study investigates new linguistic data—conditionals of Manchu—in a similar way to previous studies (Dancygier 1998; Declerck and Reed 2001; Xrakovskij 2005). From the latter perspective, the present study makes use of a sizeable corpus and systematically looks at conditional constructions in Manchu, which constitute an important aspect of the language. Each section also discusses what possible future research can be conducted on the basis of the present study.

Chapter 2 Literature Review

This chapter first reviews previous studies on conditionality in the fields of formal logic and linguistics, with particular emphasis on linguistic conditionality. Various issues involved in the research are discussed: the definition of "conditional", the nature of the conditional relation, the morphosyntax of conditional constructions, and so forth. This is followed by a review of the (linguistic) studies and publications on the Manchu language since the 17th century. The chapter concludes by summarising the theoretical framework of the present study.

2.1 Review of Studies on Conditionals

This section starts with a general discussion of how to define "conditional" in natural language—the approach that the present study adopts. The section then reviews the research of conditionals as a logic function before coming to review the previous studies on conditional constructions in natural language.

2.1.1 Defining Conditional

Defining "conditional" is a prerequisite for any discussion of conditionals to proceed. One possible way is to give a definition in terms of what conditions should be satisfied. It seems to be the case that both logico-philosophical and linguistic studies on conditionals (in the English language) usually treat this concept as self-evident by identifying it with *the if*-construction. For example, Bennett (2003: 4) offers a preliminary account of conditionals, which he defines as "items expressible in a sentence of the form 'If [sentence A], then [sentence C]'", while Dancygier (1998: 1) confines her research primarily to "sentences so labelled[①] by grammarians", that is, a main clause and a subordinate clause with the latter having the conjunction *if*. Yet many other studies simply dispense with an explicit definition of conditional, while actually regarding the *if*-construction as the default form for conditionals. Besides, even those who do attempt to define what a conditional is often concede that the definition is defective. For instance, Bennett (2003) points out that his preliminary definition would only address the matter of conditionals in English, and that defining such constructions in other languages would therefore depend on their translation into English. Besides, according to Bennett (2003), even in English, not all the sentences that meet the defining criterion can be properly qualified as conditionals, for structures of this kind may also give rise to other meanings.

Therefore, it does not appear to be an easy task to provide a clear-cut definition for conditional. The difficulty, however, does not necessarily amount to impossibility to conceive of it rationally. A different approach should be adopted. To start with, it is vital that the nature of a linguistic category should be clarified. According to Taylor (1995), any linguistic construction consists of a group of structures that are brought together under a category through "family resemblance"—a concept proposed by Wittgenstein (1958). In a category like this, each member shares a certain characteristic (or several characteristics) with some, but not all, of the other members, so that considered as a whole the category has no single characteristic that is shared by all its members. Specifically, as Taylor (1995) argues, no linguistic construction as a category has a characteristic shared by all the instances of the construction. He further argues that not every member of a category of linguistic constructions has the same status, with some of them being more prominent, and others less so. The former

① Labelled as "conditional".

are considered central members, or, prototypes, while the latter, peripheral members (non-prototypes). Thus, all the members of a category are connected in a network through its central members.

This line of thought is also reflected in Comrie (1986: 77), who proposes an approach to defining conditional constructions "in terms of a prototype rather than in terms of necessary-and-sufficient conditions", which is adopted in the present study. This approach is simply justified by the precarious nature of linguistic constructions in general as stated above. The next step then is to establish the criteria for identifying the prototype of the conditional construction. The criteria should cover two aspects: meaning and form, described by semantics and morphosyntax, respectively. Specifically, a prototypical conditional necessarily expresses the conditional relation (see Section 2. 1. 3. 1) on the one hand, and correspondingly has a distinguishing morphosyntax on the other. Only when both meaning and form are considered can a prototype be identified. Take an English example, "If you go out without the umbrella, you'll get wet" (Comrie 1986: 78). This sentence can be qualified as a prototype of conditional because first, the state of affairs expressed in the *if*-clause serves as a condition for the state of affairs expressed in the other clause, and second, the *if* (*-then*)-structure is accepted as a standard form for the expression of conditionality. When applying this method in practice, the descriptive grammar of a language (ideally authored by native speakers) can be used as a tool for identifying prototypical patterns of conditionals. The reason is that, if a grammar describes how to express the conditional relation at all, the examples provided would presumably be the most salient, prototypical ones in this language. One exception would be the case where in a language the conditional meaning is usually expressed by structures identical to those used for other meanings. In such cases it would not be possible to define conditional constructions as a *distinct* category within the language, even if it is still possible to discuss conditionality.

Once the prototype(s) of conditional constructions has (have) been identified, the next step will be to expand the category from the central members to peripheral ones through "family resemblance". The process of expansion involves two dimensions, which are exactly the two aspects considered during the identification of prototypes—semantics and morphosyntax. On the one hand, constructions which (partly) share the morphosyntax with the prototypes may not express conditionality but some other relation, such as temporality, concession, etc. For instance, the sentence "If he came late, he was punished" (Comrie 1986: 77) has a temporal interpretation, and "If we give him the VIP treatment, he won't be content" (König 1986: 237) is understood as a conditional concessive. On the other hand, constructions can express conditionality even when they are distinct from prototypes in terms of morphosyntax. For example, the sentence "Fix the car and I'll give you \$100" (Fillenbaum 1986: 186) has a conditional interpretation although it is a co-ordinate clause with an imperative and a statement. Thus, the category of conditionals is broadened to constitute a semantic-morphosyntactic network, with the prototypes in the centre, where meaning and form converge, and one set of constructions each of which respectively shares meaning or form with the prototypes. The meaning-form dichotomy determines that the different sets of non-prototypes of the category defined share no common characteristic with each other, and share different characteristics with the prototypes, while also extending further to structures identifiable as constructions other than conditionals. Therefore, the category of conditional constructions (defined as above) as a whole does not have a common characteristic uniting all of its members, as is the case with any linguistic construction in general, as argued by Taylor (1995).

2.1.2 Conditional as Logic Function

An indispensable notion for human reasoning, conditionals have aroused great interest among logicians and philosophers, who in general regard conditional as a relation—a "function"—held between two propositions, that is, the proposition P expressed in the protasis (or, antecedent, which mostly begins with *if* in English) and the proposition Q in the apodosis (or, consequent, which sometimes contains *then* in

English) (Jackson 1987; et al.). Particularly, in the view of some logicians, conditional, like other classical functions in mathematical logic—conjunction ("AND"/"∧"), disjunction ("OR"/"∨") and negation ("NOT"/"~")—should be described by means of how the truth value is calculated in accordance with the truth values of its component propositions P and Q. For this aim, the truth-value table (Table 2.1) for "material implication" (or, "material conditional") in logic is established, such that the conditional is false only when P is true and simultaneously Q is false, while in the other three cases the conditional remains true.

Table 2.1　　Truth Value for Conditional

Protasis	Apodosis	Conditional
True	True	True
True	False	False
False	True	True
False	False	True

Thus, with some calculation, a (material) conditional consisting of P and Q can be interpreted as "It is not the case that P is true and Q is false", or represented with logic symbols as "~ (P ∧ ~Q)" (or its equivalent "~P ∨ Q"). Its logic representation is a compound of other basic truth-functions, and it seems that the remaining problem for a conditional to be analysed in this fashion is to discuss the circumstances under which a conditional can be equated with a material implication. It is with this line of thought that Jackson (1987) introduces the concept "robustness": if one says that Q is robust with respect to P, it means that one "accord[s] Q a fairly (very) high probability on the supposition that P is true" (Bennett 2003: 34). By means of the mathematical notion "probability", Jackson (1987) demonstrates what conditions should be satisfied for a conditional construction "If P then Q" to be effectively represented as a logic expression.

Despite the sophisticated theory attempted at describing conditionals, it should be noted that this approach is far from flawless. On one hand, describing a conditional in the form of the material implication can in some cases fail to give a convincing account of what relation holds between the protasis and the apodosis of a conditional. As a matter of fact, it is indifferent to this issue. For example, a conditional like "If Paris is the capital of France, two is an even number" (Comrie 1986: 80) qualifies as a true statement by the criterion of material implication, since both the protasis and the apodosis are true. In real life, this sentence would make little sense—although admittedly a particular context could be constructed to make it sound meaningful (Sweetser 1990: 117)—but the truth-function approach is not concerned with the relation between them. On the other hand, even if this approach attempted to explain the relation between protasis and apodosis of a conditional, the delicate nature of conditionals in general would pose a serious challenge to the rigorous logic method. For instance, the conditional "If Bismarck is the capital of North Dakota, then Pierre is the capital of South Dakota" (Comrie 1986: 81) appears to consist of two irrelevant propositions, but Comrie (1986) gives a particular context for this conditional to make good sense: the speaker is first uncertain which city is the capital of which state, but he knows for sure that the two cities correspond to the two Dakotas, and when he is told by another person that Bismarck is the capital of North Dakota, he makes this conditional inference. However, this required context would be very difficult to explicate through logic formulations, for there may not exist a clear boundary that can be drawn between relevance and irrelevance in natural language.

One can also observe the defect of evaluating the conditional sentences against the truth table. That is to say, conditionals in natural language may not fill all the four columns with indisputable truth values, especially when the protasis is false while the apodosis is true. Psychological experiments have been conducted to test people's judgement on truth values of given conditionals in different situations concerning whether proposition P or proposition Q is true, and the results have displayed variation in subjects' responses (Johnson-Laird 1986). Therefore, from the perspective of humans as language users, conditionals do not match material implications well.

Another problem exists with attempting to fit conditionals of natural language into the model of material implication, even if the other problems discussed are neglected: a conditional sentence of natural language can very likely consist of only one proposition, e. g. P in the protasis, while the apodosis is not a statement. For example, the sentence "If you buy a house, will you decorate it yourself?" (Dancygier 1998: 89) has no truth value since the Q in the apodosis is missing. Still, constructions of this kind are quite common in natural language, which are not analysable as material implications.

To summarise, the truth-functional approach attempts to encapsulate the phenomenon of conditionals in a set of logical formulas (material implications), and is more concerned about truth-values in the ontological sense. To some extent it is an approximation—and an idealisation—of conditional constructions in natural language, particularly those with the prototypical form "If P then Q". However, this approach fails to consider properly, or to address effectively, conditional sentences that require pragmatic or cognitive interpretation. As Xrakovskij (2005: 4) points out, logic and linguistics not only have different objects of research, but also different research goals. He argues that logic studies only "a portion of those language constructions that may be identified as conditional" and that, the goal of logic studies on conditionals is "to determine their role in generating new knowledge from old knowledge", while linguistics deals with conditional constructions "as purely linguistic objects with inherent semantic and grammatical properties that are to be identified and described". (Xrakovskij 2005: 4-5)

In spite of the deficiency of the truth-functional approach, there are also noteworthy merits. Adopting the perspective of formal semantics, Stalnaker (1975) regards the conditional relation as a function between two propositions, yet not as a function used to calculate truth values in the sense of material implication. He attempts, by means of the notion of "possible worlds", to build a uniform theoretical framework to account for both indicative (or, factual) and counterfactual conditionals. Specifically, by selecting a "possible world", in which the proposition of the protasis (or antecedent) is realised, yet a world that "differs minimally from the actual world", one can evaluate the truth of a conditional according to whether the proposition of the apodosis (or consequent) is realised in the possible world thus selected. Therefore, since the protasis proposition is always presumed to be true, the problem concerning the truth value of a conditional with a false protasis is in some sense removed. This is an advantage in comparison with material implication, since according to the properties of material implication, a conditional with a false protasis would always produce the value "True" regardless of the truth value of the apodosis, which does not conform to people's linguistic intuition. Stalnaker (1975) also exemplifies the differences in logic properties between the conditionals (by his definition) and material implications. Furthermore, Stalnaker (1975: 175) argues that the semantic theory of conditionals should "be viewed as... an explanation of a commonly used concept". He is aware that pragmatic factors should be considered in dealing with conditionals semantically, admitting that "logic has not advanced beyond the propositional stage".

However, Stalnaker's (1975) theory of conditionals has limitations in that it still seems to be more concerned with the truth of conditionals, although in a way different from the approach of truth-functionalists. He argues that a theory of conditionals should not be "meant as a description of linguistic usage" (Stalnaker 1975: 175), which, while guaranteeing the theory as a semantic framework as opposed to grammar, might well exclude the possibility of finding various characteristics of conditionals. This limitation is also reflected in his preference for treating conditionality "as a univocal concept", which, according to the previous discussion concerning the definition of "conditional" (Section 2. 1. 1), would be a seemingly convenient, but problematic, method. This limitation is due to the fact that Stalnaker (1975) does not provide a definition for conditional, but only chooses the prototypes of conditional as the starting point of his theory.

2.1.3 Conditional as Linguistic Construction

Comrie (1986) is one of the first linguists investigating conditionals to attach more importance to language itself than to such aspects as logical forms. He advocates, as previously mentioned, identifying conditionals through prototypes rather than sufficient and necessary conditions, since the object of study is a construction in natural language. In characterising conditionals, Comrie (1986) considers logical properties of material implications as well as the connection between the protasis and the apodosis of conditionals. The reason is that, on the one hand, prototypes of conditionals behave as predicted by material implications in terms of truth values and logic relations between protasis and apodosis, which Comrie hypothesises as a universal for any language that has a conditional construction. On the other hand, conditionals in natural language require "a stronger link" (Comrie 1986: 80), which is "in most cases causal", between the protasis and the apodosis.

Comrie (1986) lays out various formal parameters with which to investigate conditional constructions: clause order, markers of protasis and apodosis, degree of hypotheticality and time reference, which also feature as important aspects in other studies on conditionals (Dancygier 1998; Xrakovskij 2005). Comrie employs examples from various languages to illustrate different situations concerning each parameter.

2.1.3.1 The Relation between the Protasis and the Apodosis

This is an essential issue for conditionals. As previously mentioned, the logico-semantic theories either are concerned with what factors are the most important in deciding whether a conditional can be regarded as material implication, or simply state that it does not matter very much whether any relation holds between protasis and apodosis, as long as the conditional as a whole can be evaluated in terms of truth. Moreover, these theories exhibit still less interest in other aspects of conditionals such as morphosyntax, and are thus inadequate in giving an account of conditionals in natural language. This necessitates a linguistic approach that puts more emphasis on language itself.

Comrie (1986) contends that a causal relation holds between the protasis and apodosis of a conditional. The relation, however, is not always straightforward, but is demonstrated in different ways as well as on multiple levels. First, causality can be confirmed on the content level between two propositions as in the most common conditional pattern "If you go out without the umbrella, you'll get wet" (Comrie 1986: 78). Second, causality can be present on the epistemic level, as in the aforementioned conditional "If Bismarck is the capital of North Dakota, then Pierre is the capital of South Dakota" (Comrie 1986: 81). As Comrie (1986) points out, the causal relation does not lie between Bismarck being the capital of North Dakota and Pierre being the capital of South Dakota, but rather between the knowledge of the first fact and the realisation of the second fact. Third, causality is present on the speech-act level, as in the conditional "If you want to know, ten isn't a prime number" (Comrie 1986: 81), in which the addressee's intention of knowing does not cause the property of the number ten, but rather, the addressee's intention of knowing causes the speaker's speech act of uttering the fact that ten is not a prime number.

Then, in what sense and to what extent do protasis and apodosis have a causal relation between them? The explanation provided by Mackie (1975) concerning the essence of causality (as represented in natural language) may shed some light on this question. Mackie analyses the example of a fire "caused" by a short circuit in order to unveil the real status of this cause in terms of sufficiency and necessity. Specifically, the event of a short circuit, together with some other conditions, forms a set of conditions sufficient to cause the fire, while there also exist other possible sets of conditions equally sufficient to cause a fire. Thus, on one hand, within the current set of conditions, which is *sufficient* (to cause the fire), the event of a short circuit is a necessary condition; on the other hand, the current set of conditions is no more than one of various possible sets, and is *not necessary* to cause a fire. Therefore, Mackie (1975: 16) argues that the event of short-circuit, commonly labelled as the "cause" of the fire, is actually a so-called INUS condition, i. e. an "*insufficient* but *necessary* part of a condition which is itself *unnecessary* but *sufficient* for the result".

This explanation can also be applied to the causal relation between the protasis and the apodosis of a conditional. For example, in the conditional "If it rains, the match will be cancelled," the falling of rain per se is insufficient for the match to be cancelled (for instance, one may also have to assume that the match cannot proceed while it is raining, or that the location for the match cannot be changed). However, it can definitely constitute a *necessary* part of a circumstance that is *sufficient* to cause the cancellation of the match (one would only need to assume the very same conditions mentioned previously). However, this very circumstance is not necessary in the sense that an alternative circumstance (for example, the absence of one playing team, or some technical problem with the venue's facilities) could also lead to the cancellation of the match. Following this line of thought, by means of being an INUS condition, the falling of rain can cause the cancelling of the match.

Affirmation of a causal relation in conditional constructions can also be found in other studies. Sweetser (1990) states that the causal relation is realised in three domains: the content domain, the epistemic domain and the speech-act domain, which also echoes Comrie's (1986) point of view. Dancygier (1998: 14) also points out that in a prototypical conditional "what is asserted is the causal connection between p and q, not the clauses themselves". Podlesskaja (2001: 1000) contends that "[o]rdinary conditionals usually presuppose that the processes, states or events denoted by protasis and apodosis are somehow related in the speaker's mind", which normally "can be interpreted as causal". Podlesskaja (2001) further argues that the causal relation between the protasis and the apodosis is imposed by natural language "whenever it is possible", even in a conditional that would otherwise seem unlikely to contain this relation. Akatsuka (1986: 334) gives an extreme example, which she names "indicative counterfactual", one of the critics' favourite examples used for refuting the assertion that certain connection holds between the protasis and apodosis of a conditional "If you are the Pope, I am the Empress of China". Akatsuka (1986) takes into account the speaker's belief as well as the addressee's, maintaining that in the paradoxical conditional, the protasis and the apodosis are related in that both of them are ridiculously false in the belief system of the speaker, and that the point of uttering this conditional is precisely to indicate the absurdity of the protasis.

Some scholars hold a different view of the relation between the two clauses of a conditional sentence. Wierzbicka (1997) argues that the conditional relation IF is a conceptual primitive that cannot be defined without resorting to more complex concepts, such as "hypothetical" or "inference", or without avoiding circularity in definition. Thus, she argues that the conceptual primitive IF can only be illustrated by examples of usage. Also, Wierzbicka (1997) particularly rejects the idea that conditionality can be explained in terms of causality, although she concedes that a causal relation is usually involved in a conditional sentence.

Wierzbicka's (1997) argument that IF is a conceptual primitive which cannot be explained in terms of causality suffers from several weaknesses. First, the examples used by Wierzbicka in order to question the causality claim are not convincing. She argues that causality does not exist in "If he invites me to dinner, I will not go" (Wierzbicka 1997: 20) since it cannot be rewritten as a sentence using the conjunction because. This line of argument is problematic on account of the non-equivalence between the causal relation and the relation able to be expressed by "because". Since "because" is a specific lexical item in English, its usage is constrained by grammar rules and may not represent causal relation of all kinds, especially when the cause in question is not a realised event. Besides, this example also invites a concessive interpretation, rather than a conditional one, despite the conjunction "if": it could actually mean "Even if he invites me to dinner, I will not go". This probability can be seen in a similar concessive sentence using "if"—"I won't do it if you pay me". Thus, discussing the example without specifying its context could lead to a mistaken conclusion.

On similar grounds (that is, inability to be paraphrased using because)

Wierzbicka (1997: 20) also denies the existence of causality in another example "If he is asleep, I will not wake him up". One can actually identify the causal relation between the two clauses if one follows Mackie's (1975) line of thought in that the so-called "cause" represented in nature is only a link of a sophisticated chain. Thus, again, in the example, the person's being asleep is one among a set of conditions (such as the person being asleep, the speaker's awareness of his sleep, the speaker's good manners, and so forth) that sufficiently cause the speaker not to wake the person up. It is the speaker who chooses to highlight the person's being asleep by means of utterance. This analysis applies to the first example given above, when one treats it as a conditional rather than a concessive sentence: the person's inviting the speaker (which the speaker expresses linguistically), together with other unuttered conditions, such as the speaker's low opinion of the person, causes the speaker not to go to the dinner.

Furthermore, Wierzbicka's (1997) argument that IF is a conceptual primitive is problematic in view of the diverse relations that can exist in conditional sentences. On the one hand, she attempts to argue against the existence of causality, while on the other hand, failing to account for the apparent diversity of sentential relations, she provides no solution other than reducing them into a concept that refuses any analysis. This does not tackle the nature of conditionality but only evades the real problem: if a conceptual primitive could exhibit a variety of meanings, one may suspect that it is at least not an ideal primitive, or even that it is not a true primitive at all.

Xrakovskij (2005) also argues against the causal relation in conditionals. On the one hand, he admits, as does Comrie (1986), that a relation does exist between the two clauses of a conditional, which he regards as a character distinguishing conditionals in natural language from material implications. On the other hand, he argues that the causal relation between protasis and apodosis, if it can exist at all, is confined to natural situations, as is shown in the conditional "If the river freezes over, navigation will stop" (Xrakovskij 2005: 23); otherwise, the speaker builds the relation "based on pragmatic reasons" (Xrakovskij 2005: 24), as is shown in conditionals like "If Johnson garners two-thirds of the vote, he will become president" (Xrakovskij 2005: 23) and "If I have time, I'll call you" (Xrakovskij 2005: 24). Additionally, Xrakovskij (2005: 24) notes that in some other conditionals, such as "If Helen buys a new dress, she will go to London", the positions of the protasis and the apodosis are interchangeable "without compromising the semantic integrity". From these different cases, Xrakovskij (2005) concludes that the causal relation is, at least in some conditionals, subjective, determined to a large extent by the speaker of the conditional, and that the protasis-apodosis relation can only be defined for its own sake, which Xrakovskij (2005: 24) names "the 'IF relation' concept". Similar to Wierzbicka (1997), he asserts that this concept is fundamental, an irreducible conceptual primitive.

Despite Xrakovskij's (2005) affirmation of the protasis apodosis connection, his claim that "the 'IF relation' concept" is an indefinable primitive is open to question, in a similar way to Wierzbicka's (1997) view discussed above. First, Xrakovskij (2005) has reached this conclusion as the result of his attempt to extract a homogeneous concept from the sophisticated connection between protasis and apodosis. This still reflects the Aristotelian approach of defining a concept in terms of sufficient-and-necessary conditions, which, as Taylor (1995) convincingly shows, is not an appropriate method. As Dancygier (1998: 185) puts it, "meaning is extended from concrete relations such as real-world causality to more abstract 'subjective' relations such as logical and speech act interaction ones". It follows that the relations within a conditional may not necessarily be homogeneous, but the variety of relations is connected with one another in a cognitive network.

Second, Xrakovskij's (2005) claim that some protasis-apodosis relations are subjective does not justify the rejection of the causal relation. The reason is that, conditionals in natural language are utterances by speakers, which, reflecting the speakers' state of mind, more or less have a subjective nature themselves. There would be no ground for imposing purely objective relations on two parts of an utterance, which is but a product of subjective mentality. However, even if a causal relation can be rejected because of its subjectivity, the mere "natural" causal relation between protasis and apodosis by Xrakovskij's (2005) standard could also be rejected for exactly the same reason that he uses to dismiss the conditional "If I have time, I'll call you" as unqualified for indicating causality. In "If the river freezes over, navigation will stop" (Xrakovskij 2005: 23), the river's freezing can be seen as an INUS condition of the cessation of navigation, according to Mackie (1975): other potential causes or conditions are simply not stated, such as the impossibility to break the river ice, or the decision made by the person in charge to stop navigation. In this example subjectivity is also involved, since navigation is a conscious activity of human beings. Then it would be just the same case with the previous example, where the speaker's having time is an INUS condition of his calling the addressee. Therefore, in natural language there seems to be no real "natural" causal relation at all, since it is virtually impossible to describe the whole set of causes of an event.

Another important aspect is that Xrakovskij (2005) fails to observe the protasis-apodosis relation on multiple levels. The conditional "If Helen buys a new dress, she will go to London" (Xrakovskij 2005: 24) and its reversed counterpart "If Helen goes to London, she will buy a new dress"① are considered by Xrakovskij to be semantically convergent in spite of the contrary clause order. This may be why he regards the protasis-apodosis relation as subjective and therefore intangible. However, if the protasis-apodosis relation is observed on the content level and the epistemic level respectively, causality will emerge in different forms. In the original conditional, the assumption of Helen's buying a new dress causes the inference that she will go to London (the epistemic level), while in the reversed conditional, Helen's action of going to London causes her action of buying a new dress (the content level). A multi-levelled analysis can reveal the diverse forms in which the causal relation is presented. In this sense,

① In this sentence the purchase of a new dress is apparently understood as a preparation for the journey to London. Thus, an alternative interpretation that the purchase of a new dress is the aim of the journey to London is excluded.

the protasis-apodosis relation of a conditional is not an indefinable primitive.

2.1.3.2 Clause Order

Both Comrie (1986) and Xrakovskij (2005) quote Greenberg's (1963: 84-85) Universal of Word Order 14 concerning the clause order of conditionals: "in conditional statements, the conditional clause precedes the conclusion as the normal order in all languages".① Comrie (1986) points out that on the one hand, no counterexample to this principle has been identified, that is, no language seems to forbid the protasis-apodosis clause order. On the other hand, some languages (such as Altaic languages) only allow the protasis-apodosis order, while many other languages (including English), tolerate both the protasis-apodosis order and its reverse. Additionally, Xrakovskij (2005) indicates that in many languages the protasis-apodosis order is the unmarked clause order, and its reverse the marked one.

With respect to the motivation for the predominance of the protasis-apodosis clause order across languages, Comrie (1986: 84) provides several candidate explanations, which may all need more supportive evidence from further research. The first of these is that posing protasis before apodosis can prevent the latter from "being interpreted as a factual statement". The example Comrie (1986: 84) gives is "If you translate for me, I'll give you $100". He explains that, if the protasis were posed after the apodosis, the addressee might well negligently focus only on the apodosis and come to misunderstand this statement as the speaker's unconditional offer to give the money.

Comrie (1986) gives two other accounts which are similar in nature. One of them claims that the protasis-apodosis order reflects the temporal sequence of the two related events, while the other argues that this specific clause order is an indicator of the cause and effect relation. Also, just as Dancygier (1993) points out, causal relation is inseparable from the

① "The conditional clause" and "the conclusion" refer to protasis and apodosis respectively.

temporal sequence. Both explanations take into consideration the iconicity of language constructions toward the event structure of the external world.

Another explanation provided by Comrie (1986) involves discourse structure. According to Lehman (1974) [who is quoted in Comrie (1986)], the protasis of a conditional is one of the means by which participants in a discourse can "gain common ground step by step" (Comrie 1986: 86). Similarly, Haiman (1978) (as Comrie notes), perceiving the sentence-initial position occupied by both protases and topics in various languages, proposes that the protases of conditionals are actually topics, because they indicate "givenness". This view of Haiman's (1978), however, is criticised by Akatsuka (1986), who argues that the participants of a conversation do not necessarily share the same knowledge at some point, and therefore the unshared knowledge cannot be regarded as "given". Similarly, Sweetser (1990: 126) argues that the protasis is not presupposed, but "is given only relative to the apodosis", while there is a causal relation between the two.

2.1.3.3 Morphosyntax

Morphosyntax involves at least these aspects: first, what forms (lexical and/or morphological) are used in a language to mark conditional constructions; and second, in the case where verb inflections (or agglutination) are adopted, how the verbs in the language are inflected (or agglutinated) in different semantic and pragmatic situations, as regards the meanings intended.

Comrie (1986) points out that, while most languages mark either the protasis or the apodosis, or both, of conditionals, marking the protasis seems to be the more common case. Conjunctions are very commonly employed to mark the protasis, such as "if" in English and "jesli" in Russian, but in certain languages a particular (non-finite) form of the verb—usually called a "converb" (Ramstedt 1902; Haspelmath and König 1995)—exists which is used in the protasis of a conditional, and sometimes more complex structures derived from non-finite verbs also function to link the protasis and the apodosis of a conditional construction. Conjunctions and non-finite verbs can also be used in combination. Languages that contain particular (non-finite) conditional verb forms include, but are not confined to, Turkish (Göksel and Kerslake 2000), Mongolian (Chenggeltei 1991), Manchu (Gorelova 2002), Even (Malchukov 2005), Evenki (Pevnov 1980; Nedjalkov and Bulatova 2005), and Japanese (Alpatov and Podlesskaja 2005).

The marking of the protasis or the apodosis can also be realised by means of syntax, especially in non-prototypical conditionals in languages where, apart from the prototypes, at least one alternative construction is available for the expression of conditionality. For instance, "Had he done that, I would have been happy" is a conditional expressed by the verb-subject word order. Alpatov and Podlesskaja (2005) investigate three constructions in Japanese in addition to the prototypical conditional, which are used under different semantic and pragmatic circumstances. The Manchu language also possesses multiple morphosyntactic methods capable of expressing conditionality, which are explored in the present study.

One question that may arise concerns the origin of certain markers of conditional clauses, or the motivation behind some morpho-syntactic structures. Haiman (1978), in arguing that conditionals express "givenness", mentions in passing his concurrence with the hypothesis that "if" is somehow etymologically related to the verb "give". Traugott (1985) identifies various origins for the emergence of conditional markers: words for modality, copula constructions, interrogatives, markers of givenness, and temporal words. Before getting into the explanation for the motivations of their function as conditional markers, Traugott (1985) contends that iconicity plays a role in conditional markers' usually being grammatical words rather than concrete lexical items: the fact that the concept of conditionality is abstract is reflected in its lexical choice. Traugott's explanation is reasonable, shedding some light on the heterogeneous collection of conditional markers.

According to Traugott (1985), modality words and copula constructions can probably develop into conditional markers because conditionals are related to possibilities or possible worlds rather than reality. This process involves, on the one hand, the selection of a certain modality, such as the optative, which is usually used to express desire or intention. On the other hand, it also involves the selection of copula constructions, which are often used to indicate existence (such as the existence of a possible world, as far as conditionality is concerned). When Traugott (1985) accounts for interrogatives as conditional markers, she agrees with Haiman's (1978) analysis, and both quote Jespersen's (1940) example: "Is he coming? (Yes.) Well then, I will stay". According to Haiman (1978: 571), in this "mini-conversation", a silent assent (yes) is given as the background just in order for the communication to proceed. This can also be seen in the aforementioned example "Had he done that, I would have been happy", which can be counted as a conditional despite the verb-subject word order typical of a question. Similarly, it is also worth mentioning that the Russian conditional conjunction "jesli"(if) originated from the combination of the verb "jest'"(there is/are) and the interrogative particle *li*. (Lavrov 1940: 65-67; Cherkasova 1973: 54-62; Vasmer 1986: 28) According to Lavrov's (1940) explanation, a conditional clause introduced by the conjunction "jesli"(can), from a diachronic point of view, be regarded as a transformation from a question, approximately interpretable as "Is there (such a state of affairs that)...?".

Traugott (1985) also notes that topic markers can evolve into conditional markers on account of the givenness usually indicated by the former. However, a structure with the conditional function can evolve into a topic marker: among other devices, the conditional converbs in Altaic languages (i. e., Turkic, Mongolic and Manchu-Tungusic languages) can serve as topic markers, especially the conditional converb of existential verbs (Gorelova 2006).

Concerning the relationship between interrogatives and conditionals, a word form in Manchu, *aika* (as well as *aikabade*, consisting of *aika* and *bade*, the latter a dative-locative structure), which also serves as an indefinite determiner/pronoun meaning "some(thing)" or "any(thing)", frequently occurs in conditional sentences. It can be regarded as a conditional connector, a semantic and functional analogue of "if" in

English.

As regards another important origin of conditional markers, temporal constructions, Traugott (1985) points out that the notion "frame" can help clarify their emergence: the example she gives, "When Bill came home, John left", has two readings—one temporal and the other conditional—the former of which depicts a specific occasion when Bill came home, while the latter covers all occasions when Bill came home. The frames set up in the two readings are different but interrelated, which can possibly account for the common phenomenon of temporal constructions serving as conditionals.

2.1.3.4 Degree of Hypotheticality and Classification of Conditionals

Conditional constructions vary in terms of the reality status of the states of affairs described. This variation involves the degree of hypotheticality. In his discussion, Comrie (1986) does not agree with the division of the whole range of conditionals into the dichotomy between "indicative" and "counterfactual" types, but favours a continuum of hypotheticality. According to Comrie, the conventional "indicative" and "counterfactual" conditionals are at the two extremes of this continuum, the former indicating the lowest degree, and the latter, the highest degree, of hypotheticality.

Being aware of an existing controversy, Comrie (1986: 80) argues that conditionals themselves express neither factuality nor counterfactuality, because they are not part of the meaning of conditionals, but are rather "derived by implicature or from context". He provides examples with indicative and counterfactual forms, respectively, which, however, trigger alternative readings. For instance, in the sentence "Are we in Bolivia now? If Brasilia is the capital of Bolivia, then we're in Bolivia" (Comrie 1986: 90), the indicative form cannot be interpreted as stating a truth. On the contrary, it can only be understood as counterfactual according to encyclopaedic knowledge. However, in the sentence "If the butler had done it, we could have found just the clues that we did in fact find" (Comrie 1986: 90), the counterfactual form actually suggests that the statement is true in the real world. Dancygier (1998: 35) gives even more peculiar examples to illustrate the indeterminacy of factuality or counterfactuality: "If Mary were allergic to penicillin, she would have exactly the same symptoms she is showing (but in fact we know that Mary is not allergic to penicillin)". It seems that one could infer from the conditional, in a similar way as Comrie (1986) suggests, that Mary is allergic to penicillin. However, this inference would prove erroneous in the face of the parenthesised information, which can be seen as a straight assertion. Dancygier (1998: 35) argues that such a conditional cannot be interpreted either as factual or as counterfactual, due to the "contradictory pieces of evidence". These examples may appear idiosyncratic, but they testify to the dependence of factual/counterfactual interpretation of conditionals on context, rather than solely on verbal morphology.

The view that hypotheticality of conditionals is a continuum is not shared by all researchers. Wierzbicka (1997) argues that (factual) conditionals and counterfactuals (counterfactual conditionals) are discrete semantic concepts. She argues that counterfactual conditionality, like (factual) conditionality, is also a conceptual primitive, which cannot be defined by means of more fundamental concepts—especially not to be defined via the (factual) conditional relation IF and other semantic components.

Questioning Comrie's (1986) argument that there are no true counterfactual conditionals in English, Wierzbicka (1997: 51) argues that true counterfactual conditionals do exist, and the "hard core of the category" consists of those that have two negative clauses (with the syntactic structure "IF NP HAD NOT V-PAST-PART, Y WOULD NOT HAVE V-PAST-PART"). She demonstrates that such conditionals, unlike the problematic conditional sentences given by Comrie (1986), do not allow non-counterfactual interpretations. Wierzbicka (1997) also postulates that factual and counterfactual conditionals universally exist in all languages, while hypothetical conditionals, which are situated between the two in terms of reality status, are a language-specific phenomenon.

Wierzbicka's (1997) argument about the authentic, prototypical counterfactual conditionals in English is convincing, and no doubt her hypothesis about the universal existence of factual and counterfactual conditionals is worthy of investigation. However, similarly to her view concerning the conditional relation, Wierzbicka's (1997) treatment of counterfactual conditionality as a conceptual primitive is problematic. The reason is that counterfactual conditionality shares with factual conditionality the internal relation between two states of affairs. The two types of conditionality differ in their respective status in relation to the speaker's belief about reality. In fact, Wierzbicka (1997) is aware that they represent two types of states of affairs—one that the speaker thinks can happen, and the other that the speaker thinks cannot happen—but she nevertheless does not regard this analysis as a semantic decomposition of counterfactual conditionality.

In order to classify conditionals, Dancygier (1998: 61) proposes a new approach based on whether "predictive reasoning" is presented or not, so that conditionals with predictive reasoning are labelled as "predictive conditionals", while those without are labelled as "non-predictive conditionals". This way of classifying conditionals does not particularly stress whether the protasis or apodosis is factual or not, but rather regards all conditionals in general—when uttered—as statements to whose factuality the speaker is not committed with certainty. The criterion of classification lies in the domain where the protasis-apodosis relation is presented: the propositional domain (the content domain) or other domains ("the epistemic domain" or "the speech-act domain"). In this manner, the "predictive conditionals" are those having the protasis-apodosis relation in the propositional domain, and the remainder are "non-predictive conditionals". Dancygier's (1998) classification is advantageous in that it avoids the notorious and controversial dilemma of distinguishing factuality and counterfactuality, leaving it to be decided by an interpretation that considers linguistic context.

2.1.3.5 Time Reference and Expression of Hypotheticality

When Comrie (1986) addresses the matter of time reference in conditionals, he explicates two important mechanisms: tense reduction and back-shifting of tense. For example, in the protasis of an English conditional, the difference in verb forms between the present and the future is neutralised, and both the present and the future are realised by the present verb form. Also, in the protasis of a counterfactual conditional, the tense of the verb is back-shifted, with the present/future (the two reduced to one form) turning into the simple past, and the past into pluperfect; the apodosis also back-shifts its verb tense accordingly. However, Comrie (1986) has not provided an explanation for this phenomenon. Dancygier (1998) points out that in the protasis and the apodosis of (predictive) conditionals, the verb forms exhibit certain compositionality. In quoting Fleischman's (1989) idea, Dancygier explains that back-shifting of tense is a common metaphorical use, which, although usually expressing a "temporal distance", is now applied to indicate "non-temporal distance", such as non-factuality, social distance, and so forth.

Dancygier (1998: 62) also notes that, since back-shifting of tense only exists in predictive conditionals (by her definition), but not in non-predictive conditionals (e. g. "If she is in the lobby, the plane arrived early"), which allow much more flexibility in the choice of verb forms, it is a crucial distinction between the two kinds of conditionals. She further argues that the temporal reference of a conditional depends on various factors, of which back-shifting of time is only one; other factors include context, the semantic class of the verb, and the hypotheticality of the construction.

Some researchers question the view that irreality or counterfactuality is simply realised via back-shifted tenses. Dahl (1997: 100) points out that "marking of irreality/hypotheticality is rarely done by means of a past tense alone but normally by the combination of a past tense with something else". For instance, in the English sentence "If I were younger, I would study Classical Greek" (Dahl 1997: 98), the verb form "were" in the protasis is not the present tense back-shifted to the past, but the (obsolescent) past subjunctive form of the verb "be". Meanwhile, the complex verb structure "would study", where "would" can be argued to be the past tense of the auxiliary "will", occurs in the apodosis instead of the past tense "studied". Dahl (1997) also explains that counterfactual conditionals are all essentially related to certain past temporal points, which proves to be a more complicated relation than the past-as-unreal hypothesis implies. Similarly to Dahl (1997), Van linden and Verstraete (2008) point out that counterfactuality tends to be realised not by means of mere past tense, but via the *combination* of modal elements and tense/aspectual markers that denote pastness or perfectiveness.

2.1.3.6 Interpreting Conditionals and Conditionals in Use

The most common way of interpreting a conditional would be, as it literally suggests, the state of affairs of the apodosis is contingent on state of affairs of the protasis, which is exactly the case covered by "predictive conditionals" as Dancygier (1998) defines them. As regards "non-predictive conditionals", the perspective of interpretation would have to shift to another domain, taking epistemic as well as speech-act factors into account.

Xrakovskij (2005) is aware of these factors and regards a conditional as the utterance of a potential speaker. He gives two explications for conditional constructions, "assertive" and "non-assertive" (Xrakovskij 2005: 18), which roughly correspond to "predictive" and "non predictive" by Dancygier's (1998) definition:[①]

> Explication I: "When producing a CC [Conditional Construction] the speaker indicates that the state of affairs p, if realised, entails the state of affairs q". Explication II: "When producing a CC the speaker indicates that the state of affairs of p, if realised, validates the entailed speech act that represents the state of affairs q".
>
> (Xrakovskij 2005: 18)

In an elaborate analysis that follows, Xrakovskij (2005: 22) provides formulated explanations for a number of sentences. For example, "If John had got his salary yesterday, he would have bought his wife a present" is

① More accurately, "non-assertive" conditionals defined by Xrakovskij (2005) may only correspond to the conditionals in the speech-act domain.

explained as "IF concept + I say: I know: this has not taken place", where "this" refers to the events indicated by the conditional. It is noteworthy that in this explanation, the role of the speaker is salient (I say), and the cognitive state of the speaker is represented by "I know". However, such explications may fail to account for the occasions in which the factuality of the conditional is indeterminate. Also, the protasis-apodosis relation is regarded as the "IF concept", a "conceptual primitive", which is deficient according to the previous analysis (Section 2. 1. 3. 1) of the definition of conditionals. The formulaic explanation of such a kind would fail to apply to the conditional given by Dancygier (1998: 62) "If he won't arrive before nine, there is no point in ordering for him". The reason is that, according to Xrakovskij (2005), this conditional would be formulated as "IF concept + I say: I know: this is not taking place (or, this will not take place)", which would also qualify as the interpretation for a different, more common conditional "If he doesn't arrive before nine, there is no point in ordering for him". However, the two conditionals here are distinguished in meaning. The former implies that the information in the protasis (his arriving) is obtained from another conversational participant or inferred from the conversation by the speaker of the sentence and that the speaker accepts this as true. In contrast, the latter conditional only indicates that the speaker makes this assumption on his or her own, probably irrelevant to the conversation.

Since the interpretation of conditionals is largely dependent on context, conditionals are able to serve different uses accordingly. On the one hand, in the field of logic, conditionals are used for "generating new knowledge from old knowledge" (Xrakovskij 2005: 4-5), and on the other hand, in natural languages, conditionals usually function "as the basis for further discussion" (Haiman 1978: 571). There are also other specific uses, for example, highlighted by Fillenbaum (1986), who analyses the illocutionary effects of certain conditionals: conditional promises and conditional threats. Fillenbaum associates conjunctive (and) and disjunctive (or) constructions with conditional promises and threats, pointing out that the speaker's intention would require that the conditionals be interpreted in a particular way. For example, the sentence "if you don't give me your money I'll kill you" (given in Fillenbaum 1986: 184) would be interpreted as "only if you give me your money, I won't kill you", through which the addressee could understand what needs to be done to avoid the consequences that he or she finds undesirable. It should be noted that the conditional is actually interpreted in such a way as if the protasis were the sufficient-and-necessary condition for the apodosis, which stands in opposition to the material implication analysis (Section 2. 1. 2).

Van der Auwera (1986: 199) identifies one type of conditionals which he calls "conditional speech act" (e. g. "where were you last night, if you wouldn't mind telling me?"). According to Van der Auwera, in such a conditional the protasis represents a sufficient condition for the speech act (the inquiry of the speaker) denoted by the apodosis. However, in quoting Sweetser (1990), Dancygier (1998: 90) points out that the speech act in question is actually carried out, regardless of the protasis (whether the addressee permits the speaker to inquire), and that the function of the protasis is "to make the utterance more polite or appropriate".

2. 2 Review of Linguistic Studies on Manchu Language

Manchu language interested the West as early as the late 17th century, during the first few decades of the Qing Dynasty. According to Meadows (1849), a Manchu grammar book, *Elementa Linguae Tartaricae*, compiled by Verdinand Verbiest, was printed in 1696. The 18th and 19th centuries witnessed more Western publications on Manchu language, including both dictionaries and descriptive grammars. Dictionaries from that time include *Dictionnaire Tartare Mantchou François* (Amiot 1789-1790) and *Polnyj man' čžursko-russkij slovar'* (*A Complete Manchu-Russian Dictionary*) (Zakharov 1875). Descriptive grammars include *Grammaire tartare mantchou* (Amiot 1788), *Eléments de la grammaire mandchoue* (Von der Gabelentz 1832), *Grammatika man' čžurskogo jazyka* (*A Grammar of the Manchu Language*) (Zakharov 1879) and Von Möllendorff (1892).

Apart from the Western works mentioned above, dictionaries and grammars of Manchu language were also published in China during the Qing Dynasty. Such dictionaries include *daicing gurun i yooni bithe* (*A Complete Lexicon of the Qing Empire*) (1683; compiled by Shen Qiliang) and *han i araha nonggime toktobuha manju gisun i buleku bithe* (*The Imperial Dictionary of Manchu Language*) (a Supplemented Version) (1771). Manchu grammars published in China include AMH (1730), UH (1894), among others. The grammars written by Qing intellectuals are quite different from the descriptive grammars of the Western linguistic tradition in that the former do not classify linguistic items into neat categories (e.g., parts of speech) as the latter do, but rather list them in a linear order, either alphabetically (according to the Manchu order) or in a way that may facilitate memorisation. They are barely concerned with grammatical concepts or origins of language structures, but provide examples of language usage with an intuitive explanation. This character of the Qing Dynasty grammars may seem to be a demerit, but it is compensated for by the fact that constructions of similar or identical meaning are easily identifiable and the possible artificiality of categorising a certain construction is minimised. When Western linguistic works on Manchu are combined with the Qing Dynasty grammars, the description of conditional constructions can be carried out.

With the fall of the Qing Dynasty (1911), Manchu lost its status as the (most important) official language of an empire. However, researchers have not stopped publishing on the language up until the present. (Sinor 1968; Avrorin 2000; Gorelova 2002; Li 2010) During the second half of the 20th century, and especially the final quarter, works on Manchu by authors based in China also appeared. They are based on classical written Manchu texts (Ji et al. 1986), or on the field work on spoken Manchu (Zhao 1989), or combine both of them (Aisin-Gioro 2004). What these works have in common is that they all employ concepts and terminology of modern (structuralist) linguistics, describing Manchu language in terms of orthography, phonology, morphology and syntax, just as would be expected in a typical descriptive grammar.

Despite the relative abundance of research literature on Manchu language in general, very few studies or works address the conditional constructions in particular. Mostly, conditional constructions are briefly mentioned and their discussion is usually scattered in different sections. In his sketch grammar Von Möllendorff (1892: 9) mentions in passing that the suffix *-ci* "makes a Conditional Tense"—a confusing misnomer by the present-day linguistic standard—without much further explanation about its function. Sinor (1968) points out the suffix *-ci* mostly expresses the conditional relation. Avrorin (2000: 206-208) labels the verb form V-*ci* as "conditional adverbial participle" (or "conditional converb"), and explains its semantics and syntactic functions not only on its own but also in combination with other lexical items. These functions include the expression of the conditional relation (via V-*ci* alone or via framed structures), the formation of the "compound predicate of an impersonal sentence", and topicalisation. Gorelova (2006), in exploring information structures of Altaic languages, discusses the use of the verb form V-*ci* (conditional converb) of quotative and existential verbs as topic markers. This very function is also discussed in Migliorenza (2004).

Although the Qing Dynasty grammars more or less touch upon conditionals in the description of functional words, they provide rather few example sentences. One problem with this is that these example sentences are the most typical examples, while the non-typical ones, which are nonetheless numerous, are largely neglected. Moreover, the Qing Dynasty grammars do not give explanations beyond basic usage. It is these shortcomings that the present study aims to overcome, through exploring the whole range of functions of conditional constructions in the corpus, and explaining the internal motivations for these functions.

2.3 Summary: The Theoretical Framework of the Present Study

The review in the previous sections demonstrates the complexity of defining "conditional" as a category in natural language and the debate centring around the nature of conditionality as well as the reality statuses of different types of conditionals. With previous studies on conditionals and on the Manchu language in mind, the present study makes the following assumptions in investigating Manchu conditionals.

First, the prototypical conditional relation involves two states of affairs (P and Q), which, in the mind of the speaker, are both unrealised. This relation entails causality in the sense defined by Mackie (1975): P is one insufficient but necessary state of affairs among a set of unnecessary but sufficient states of affairs that causes Q.

Second, the three reality statuses of conditionals—factual, hypothetical and counterfactual—are conceptually distinct from each other, but in natural language their interpretations are closely related to context. Besides, there are also other types of reality status, such as that of the "problematic" conditional exemplified by Comrie (1986: 90) "If the butler had done it, we could have found just the clues that we did in fact find" (see Section 2.1.3.4). In this sentence the speaker makes an inference concerning one past state of affairs based on another, but does not express counterfactuality, since the latter state of affairs, represented by the apodosis, is a fact. Yet this sentence shares the same syntax as others that do have a counterfactual interpretation. Therefore, one cannot necessarily identify a one-to-one correspondence between reality statuses and morphosyntax.

Third, the conditional constructions in the general sense are defined in the present study as a semantic and morphosyntactic network. Basically, each construction consists of two clauses, one subordinate and the other main. In terms of verb morphology, the subordinate clause is non-finite and the main clause is finite. Furthermore, at least one of the following two criteria should be met: (i) semantically, a conditional relation exists between the states of affairs represented by the clauses; (ii) morphosyntactically, the predicate of the first (subordinate) clause should contain a conditional-converb (V-*ci*) structure (see Section 3. 1. 1 for the conditional converb V-*ci*). When both criteria are met, the constructions are considered as *candidates* for the prototypes. The prototypes of conditional constructions should meet a further criterion: the structures used are expected to be described by (Qing Dynasty) Manchu grammars (whose authors presumably described what they considered as the most prototypical examples) and to occur frequently in corpus.

Finally, shared morphosyntax (such as conditional-converb structures) implies certain shared aspects of meaning (such as conditionality). However, just as argued by Sweetser (1990) and Dancygier (1998), the conditional relation can be presented in any multiple domains. Such domains include (but are not necessarily limited to) the following: the content domain, concerning propositional content, in which conditionality is literally understood between two states of affairs; the epistemic domain, which concerns epistemic activities such as reasoning; the speech-act domain, which concerns speech acts (other than statement); and the perceptual domain, concerning acts of perception (the last term is not used by Sweetser 1990 or Dancygier 1998). The multi-domain analysis is particularly useful for the non-prototypes of conditional constructions.

Chapter 3 A Grammar of Manchu Verbs

This chapter provides a basic description of Manchu verbs in view of their essential role in the grammatical system of Manchu and their relevance to the present study. The description is generally based on contemporary Manchu studies (mainly Gorelova 2002; also Sinor 1968, Avrorin 2000, and Li 2010), but also takes into account the uses recorded in the Qing Dynasty Manchu grammars. Section 3. 1 describes the conjugations of Manchu verbs and the categories of aspect-tense, modality and voice. Section 3. 2 is dedicated to several verbs of Manchu that can serve as lexical verbs as well as auxiliary verbs. In Section 3. 2. 2 the perfective participle of the verb *bi-* "to be", *bi-he*, is given a particular analysis concerning its functions, since it is relevant to counterfactual conditionals.

3. 1 The Manchu Verb System

Manchu verbs distinguish aspect-tenses, voices and moods, but do not indicate the category of either person or number by means of morphology.

In terms of syntactic function, Manchu verb forms can be divided into two types: finite forms and non-finite forms. The finite forms are those which can serve as main predicates: either the predicates of simple sentences or as the main predicates of complex sentences. In contrast, non-finite forms are those which cannot serve as main predicates. It is the finite forms that embody the categories of (absolute) aspect-tense and mood.

Relative aspect-tenses are able to be expressed by non-finite forms: participles and converbs.

3.1.1 Converbs

As a special group of verb forms common to all Altaic languages, converbs primarily function to express the subordination of one verb to another. This property determines that, in contrast with the finite forms, converbs cannot serve as the main predicates in simple sentences or in the main clauses of complex sentences. However, they can serve as predicates in subordinate clauses.

Converbs are formed by attaching a converbal suffix to a verb stem. A converb can either have its own subject or take the same subject as the verb to which it is subordinate. This point is important especially because in languages like Manchu, in which the converbs do not indicate the category of person, thus leaving the identification of their subjects largely to the context in which they occur. There are eight main types of converbs in Manchu, expressing various semantic and grammatical relations, as shown in Table 3.1 (the capital letter A indicates a vowel that has more than one possible value in accordance with vowel harmony).

Table 3.1　　Manchu Converbs

Converb[①]	Suffix	Basic Meaning
Imperfective	*-me*	while doing something...
Perfective	*-fi*	after doing/having done something...
Conditional	*-ci*	if (one) does something...
Concessive	*-cibe*	although/even if (one) does something...

① Not all these converbs have a widely used designation in previous studies, and I have made my own decision in this respect. For instance, Gorelova (2002: 282) labels the converb ending in-*tAlA* as "terminal converb", while I prefer the term "terminative". Some converbs do not even have any explicit designation at all, in spite of descriptions about their functions. For instance, I am responsible for coining the designations "anticipative" and "exhaustive", though Gorelova (2002: 283-284) explains the usages of the two converbs.

Continued

Converb	Suffix	Basic Meaning
Durative	*-hAi*	having been doing something...
Terminative	*-tAlA*	until (one) does something...
Anticipative	*-nggAlA*	before doing something...
Exhaustive	*-tAi*	to the extent of doing something

Six of these converbs can express a temporal relation of one kind or another: the durative, terminative and anticipative converbs (almost) exclusively express temporal relations; the imperfective and perfective converbs primarily express temporal relations, while also functioning in many cases to express the means by which (or the manner in which) the actions of their governing verbs take place: *tata-me* [hang-IPFV. CVB] *wa-* [kill] "to hang to death"[lit. : "to kill by hanging"; *nende-fi* (be. in. front-PFV. CVB) *yabu-*(go) "to go in front"]. The conditional converb serves to express both conditional and temporal relations, depending on the specific context.

The rest of the converbs seem to express non-temporal relations. The concessive converb admits the state of affairs that it represents while drawing attention to a state of affairs that is contrary to expectation, which is represented by the following predicate. The exhaustive converb, whose usage is mostly restricted to a handful of verbs, largely serves as an adverbial of degree: *buce-tei* [die-EXH] *afa-* [fight] "to fight desperately (with readiness to die)".

The conditional converb is one of the research focuses of the present study. Apart from being used in subordinate clauses to express conditional or temporal meanings (discussed elaborately in Chapter 4), it can also build complex structures when combined with other verb forms or postpositional connectors. First, the conditional converb V-*ci* can combine with either *o-* "to become/be" or *aca-* "to suit" to express a modal meaning, as shown in Table 3. 2.

Table 3.2 Complex Conditional-converb Structures Expressing Modal Meanings

Modal Verb	Grammatical Polarity	Structure	Meaning	English Translation
o- "to become/be"	Affirmative	V-*ci o-*	Possibility or permission	can/may/be allowed to do something
	Negative①	V-*ci ojo-rakū*		cannot/may not/not be allowed to do something
aca- "to suit"	Affirmative	V-*ci aca-*	Obligation	should/be supposed to do something
	Negative	V-*ci aca-rakū*		should not/not be supposed to do something

Second, the conditional converb is used with the perfective participle (see Section 3.1.2 on participles) of the phase verb *waji-* "to finish", forming the structure V-*ci wajiha*, which means "it suffices to do something", for instance, *uttu* [like. this] *gama-ci* [deal. with] *waji-ha* [finish-PFV. PTCP] "it suffices to deal with it like this". Furthermore, the conditional converb forms a structure with the postposition *tetendere*, which serves as a sentence connector expressing the causal meaning "since", "because": *bithe* [book] *taci-ci* [study-COND] *tetendere* "since [you] study the books".

It should be noted that other components can be inserted between the conditional converb and the auxiliary verb of the complex structures mentioned above, e.g. *uthai* "then", *teni* "only then", as in *tuttu* [in. that. manner] *icihiya-ci* [handle-COND] *teni* [only. then] *aca-mbi* [suit (AUX)-IPFV. FIN] "Only if [you] handle [it] in that manner will it be appropriate", *menggun* [money] *bu-ci* [give-COND] *uthai* [then] *waji-ha* [finish-PFV. PTCP] "It just suffices to give (him) the money".

3.1.2 Participles

According to Gorelova (2002), the term "participle", when applied to

① While for the affirmative forms of the (modal) verbs, the verb stems (*o-*, *aca-*) are used, the negative forms are represented by the negative imperfective participles (*ojo-rakū*, *aca-rakū*), since negative participles are the only verb forms that express negation. Participles and their negative forms are discussed in Section 3.1.2.1.

Altaic languages (Manchu included), is in fact a "hyperform" that combines both verbal and nominal characteristics in realising different syntactic functions. There are three main such functions: attribute, main predication, and subordinate predication (all the functions are discussed in Section 3. 1. 2. 2). The attributive function embodies the nominal characteristic of the participle, while the functions as predicates (governing nominals and exhibiting aspect-tense and mood/modality) demonstrate the verbal characteristics of the participle. Gorelova (2002: 254) states that when serving as attributes of nominals and subordinate predicates, Manchu participles "reveal an aspectual meaning", while as main predicates they have "a certain temporal meaning". Concurring with Avrorin (1949), Gorelova (2002) also points out that, when serving as main predicates, Manchu participles are in a transition from expressing aspectual meanings to expressing temporal meanings. On the other hand, Sinor (1968) argues that Manchu participles only concern aspect rather than tense. The present study, taking into account the multiple syntactic functions of participles discussed by Gorelova (2002), considers that participles (of most lexical verbs) express predominantly aspectual meanings, regardless of their syntactic function. However, the present study does agree with the opinion of Avrorin (1949) and Gorelova (2002) that Manchu participles are developing temporal meanings, and actually demonstrates this point with the usage of the perfective participle *bi-he* (see Section 3. 2. 2. 1).

3. 1. 2. 1 Morphology of Participles

There are two types of participles in terms of aspectuality: the imperfective participle and the perfective participle.

The imperfective participle, used to represent ongoing or habitual states of affairs, is formed by the verb stem and the suffix-*rA*, where the vowel A is determined by the stem-final vowel of the verb (in accordance with vowel harmony when the stem-final vowel is *a*, *e* or *o*; elsewhere the suffixal vowel *A* is *e*). Table 3. 3 shows how vowel harmony operates in forming the imperfective participle.

Table 3.3 Vowel Harmony in the Imperfective Participle

The Final Stem/Root Vowel	Verb	Imperfective Participle
a	*ala-* "to tell"	*ala-ra*
	isa- "to gather"	*isa-ra*
o	*bodo-* "to consider"	*bodo-ro*
	tolo- "count"	*tolo-ro*
e, *i*, *u*, *ū*, *oo*, etc.	*gene-* "to go"	*gene-re*
	ali- "to accept"	*ali-re*
	hendu- "to say"	*hendu-re*
	kūthū- "to mingle"	*kūthū-re*
	too- "to swear"	*too-re*

Some verbs, mainly those having a monosyllabic or disyllabic root, have an irregular stem (which has one more syllable than the root) when forming the imperfective participle, as shown in Table 3.4.

The perfective participle, used to describe completed states of affairs, is formed by the verb stem and the suffix *-hA*, where the vowel is largely determined by a set of much more complex rules than that of the imperfective participle, with some exceptions (for example, *buju-ha* but *guku-he*; see Table 3.5). These rules are not discussed here, but a few examples may serve to shed light on this matter. Table 3.5 shows the perfective participle of several verbs with a disyllabic stem/root.

Table 3.4 Irregular Imperfective Participles

Verb Root	Imperfective Participle
bi- "to exist/be"	*bisi-re*
je- "to eat"	*jete-re*
ji- "to come"	*jide-re*
gala- "(of sky) to clear up"	*galanda-ra*
ba- "to be lazy"	*banda-ra*
o- "to become/be"	*ojo-ro*

Table 3. 5　　Vowel Harmony in the Perfective Participle

Stem/Root Vowels	Verb Stem/Root	Perfective Participle	Suffixal Vowel
a-a-	*ala-* "to tell"	*ala-ha*	
a-i-	*banji-* "to be born"	*banji-ha*	
a-u-	*sabu-* "to see"	*sabu-ha*	
i-i-	*ili-* "to stand up"	*ili-ha*	*a*
i-u-	*iju-* "to smear"	*iju-ha*	
i-ū-	*ikū-* "to shrink"	*ikū-ha*	
u-u-	*buju-* "to boil"	*buju-ha*	
e-e-	*gene-* "to go"	*gene-he*	
e-i-	*benji-* "to send"	*benji-he*	
e-u-	*hendu-* "to say"	*hendu-he*	*e*
i-e-	*fide-* "to dispatch"	*fide-he*	
u-i-	*ulhi-* "to understand"	*ulhi-he*	
u-u-	*guku-* "to perish"	*guku-he*	
	bodo- "to consider"	*bodo-ho*	
o-o-	*osonjo-* "to choose"	*sonjo-ho*	*o*
	tokto- "to decide"	*tokto-ho*	

Some verbs have an irregular form for the perfective participle: instead of the suffix *-hA*, they contain the alternative suffix *-kA*. Furthermore, a few verbs (mostly those having a monosyllabic stem) even change their stem (by inserting the velar or uvular nasal *ng* [ŋ]/[N] between the bare stem and the suffix *-kA*). Table 3. 6 shows the irregular perfective participles.

Table 3. 6 **Irregular Perfective Participles**

Verb Root	Perfective Participle
je- "to eat"	*je-ke*
tuhe- "to fall"	*tuhe-ke*
dosi- "to enter"	*dosi-ka*
okdo- "to welcome"	*okdo-ko*
guwe- "to tweet"	*guweng-ke*
jo- "to mention"	*jong-ko*

Both the imperfective and perfective participles have their negative counterparts. The negative participles are formed by attaching the negative particle akū to the participial suffixes, giving rise to forms such as *-rakū* (<-*rA* + *akū*) and *-hAkū* (<-*hA* + *akū*) respectively, for example, *gene-rakū*[go-IPFV. PTCP. NEG], *sabu-hakū* [see-PFV. PTCP. NEG], *ji-hekū* [come-PFV. PTCP. NEG], *je-kekū* [eat-PFV. PTCP. NEG].

3.1.2.2 Functions of Participles

As stated above, the first function of participles is to serve as the predicate in a simple sentence or as the main predicate of a complex sentence. For instance, *bi* [1SG] *ji-he* [come-PFV. PTCP] "I came/I have come", *bi sin-de* [2SG (*si/sin*)-DAT] *bithe* [book] *bene-bu-re* [send. thither-CAUS-IPFV. PTCP] "I'll (make someone) send you the book" (simple sentences); *tere* [that/3SG] *min-de* [1SG(*bi/min*)-DAT] *ala-fi* [tell-PFV. CVB] *bi uthai* [then] *gene-he* [go-PFV. PTCP] "After he told me (that thing), I went (away)" (complex sentence). In functioning as main predicates, the participles behave in the same way as finite forms. Participles also function as attributes of nominal structures, in a way similar to participles or relative clauses in European languages: *ji-he* [come-PFV. PTCP] *niyalma* [person] "the person who came"; *buce-he* [die-PFV. PTCP] *haha* [man] "a dead man"; *bi* [1SG] *sin-de* [2SG(*si/sin*)-DAT] *bene-bu-he* [send-CAUS-PFV. PTCP] *bithe* [book] "the book which I made someone send to you"; *sin-i* [2SG(*si/sin*)-GEN] *yalu-ha* [ride-PFV. PTCP] *morin* [horse] "the horse you rode".

Besides, participles can serve as predicates in subordinate clauses by taking various case markers in accordance with the type of subordination. Specifically, participial structures in the dative-locative case express the temporal relation "at the time when", for instance, *si* [2SG] *min-i* [1SG (*bi/min*)-GEN] *boo-de* [house-DAT] *ji-he-de* [come-PFV. PTCP-DAT], *muse* [1PL. INCL] *sain* [good] *gisure-ki* [speak-OPT] "Let's have a good talk when you come to my house". In the ablative case, particle structures can express the temporal relation "since", for instance, *banji-ha-ci* [be. born-PFV. PTCP-ABL] *ebsi* [hitherto] *ere* [this] *gese* [like] *beikuwen* [cold] *be* [ACC] *we* [who] *dulembu-he* [experience-PFV. PTCP] *bi-he* [be (AUX)-PFV. PTCP] "who has ever experienced such cold since [s/he] was born?". Second, participle structures in the accusative case serve as object clauses of some perception verbs or phase verbs, such as *donji-* "to hear", *sabu-* "to see", *naka-* "to stop": *age* [sir] *ji-he* [come-PFV. PTCP] *be* [ACC] *donji-hakū* [hear-PFV. PTCP. NEG] "[I] didn't hear that you came, sir"; *šun* [sun] *dosi-re* [enter-IPFV. PTCP] *hami-ka* [approach-PFV. PTCP] *be sabu-fi* [see-PFV. CVB], *teni* [only, then] *umusi* [back] *ji-mbi* [come-IPFV. FIN] "only when (we) saw that the sun was close to setting did (we start to) come back"; and suwe [2PL] *becendu-re* [quarrel-IPFV. PTCP] *be* [ACC] *naka-ø* [stop-IMP] "you, stop quarrelling!". In combination with case markers, participles exhibit nominal characteristics.

3.1.3 Finite Verb Forms

Finite verb forms serve as the predicates in simple sentences or as the main predicates of complex sentences. They display the properties of mood/modality, aspect-tense, and grammatical voice. In the following sections the marking of mood and modality of Manchu verbs is discussed first, followed by the marking of grammatical voice.

3.1.3.1 Moods/Modalities

(1) The Indicative Forms

The indicative forms are used by the speaker to describe states of affairs that happened, are happening or will happen. They subsume various aspect-tense verb forms, as shown below.

The first is the imperfective finite form V-*mbi*, which consists of the verb stem (V) and the imperfective finite suffix (*-mbi*). Gorelova (2002: 286) points out that scholars have different opinions concerning the functions of this form. Some consider it to be a present tense form (Zakharov 1879: 173), or regard it as a form describing present or future states of affairs, while according to others this form describes a state of affairs that has already started but not yet completed. Sinor (1968: 268) argues that the form V-*mbi* does not locate in time the state of affairs it describes, that is, it is not a tense form, but only makes a general assertion about a state of affairs, regardless of whether it is completed or not, and is a neutral aspect. Based on corpus data, the present study agrees with Sinor (1968) that the form V-*mbi* is not a tense form but an aspectual form. Yet, when the reference time coincides with the time of speech—which is usually the case—the form V-*mbi* behaves like a non-past tense form: *bi* [1SG] *inenggidari* [every day] *yamun* [yamen] *de gene-mbi* [go-IPFV. FIN] "I go to the *yamen* every day"; *cimari* [tomorrow] *simne-mbi* [take. exams-IPFV. FIN] "tomorrow there are exams". In cases like these the form V-*mbi* also exhibits an imperfective aspectual feature, rather than a purely neutral one, contrary to what Sinor (1968) argues.

Another finite form is the perfective finite form V-*hAbi*, which obviously originated from the combination of the perfective participle (V-*hA*) and the existential particle *bi*. It also has a negative counterpart V-*hAkūbi*, which is, however, used less frequently than the negative perfective participle V-*hAkū*. Semantically similar to the perfective participle V-*hA*, the perfective finite form serves to describe a state of affairs as completed, which is usually located in the past: *tere gene-hebi* "(she or he) has already gone".

The progressive finite form (V-*me bi*) is a combination of the imperfective converb (V-*me*) and the existential particle (*bi*), describing an "action or situation [that] is in progress" (Li 2010: 366):[①] *bithe* [letter] *be* [ACC] *aliya-me* [wait-IPFV. CVB] *bi* [EXS. PTL] "(he) is/was waiting for a letter"[②] (Li 2010: 93).

Furthermore, some complex finite forms are built by combining certain verb forms and *bi-he*, the perfective participle of the verb *bi-*. Such forms include V-*hA bi-he*, V-*me bihe*/V-*mbihe*, and their negative counterparts V-*hAkū bi-he*, V-*rakū bi-he*. Their functions are discussed in Section 3.2.2.2, which focuses on the participle *bi-he*.

(2) The Imperative, Optative and Apprehensive Forms

The imperative forms are used to express commands or requests to the addressee. They have different forms in accordance with the degree of politeness or imposition. For the sake of convenience, they are labelled here as imperative (i), (ii) and (iii) respectively.

The first or the most fundamental imperative form (imperative [i]) coincides with the bare verb stem: *hūdun* [quick] *gene-ø* [go-IMP(i)] "go quickly!", *min-de* [1SG(*bi*/*min*)-DAT] *ala-ø* [tell-IMP(i)] "tell me!", *muke* [water] be [ACC] *omi-ø* [drink-IMP(i)] "drink the water!". Some basic verbs, however, have irregular forms for the imperative, as shown in Table 3.7.

Table 3.7 Irregular Imperative (i) Forms

Verb Root	Imperative (i)
bi- "to be/stay"	*bisu*
bai- "to seek"	*baisu*
gai- "to take"	*gaisu*
je- "to eat"	*jefu*

① The term "progressive finite form" is my own creation, whereas Li (2010) gives no term for this complex structure. The description given by Li (2010) seems to entail that the structure V-*me bi* is used for the present tense; that is, the structure is actually the "present progressive (finite form)". My term, in contrast, is meant to be exclusively aspectual, with no regard to tense.

② Li (2010) only gives the translation "... is waiting". I consider the past progressive interpretation ("... was waiting") as equally possible.

Continued

Verb Root	Imperative (i)
ji- "to come"	*jio*
o- "to become"	*oso*

The second imperative form (imperative [ii]) consists of the verb stem and the suffix *-cina*, also used to express commands: (*si*) *gene-cina* [go-IMP(ii)] "you just go!". Its use is similar to that of the first stem-based imperative.

The third imperative form V-*rAo* (imperative [iii]) consists of the imperfective participle V-*rA* and the question particle *o*. It is the polite imperative form, expressing a request rather than an order, and is commonly used to address people of superior positions: *majige* [a. little] *gisure-reo* [say-IMP(iii)] "would you please say a little bit (about it) to me?", *min-de* [1SG(*bi*/*min*)-DAT] *emu* [one] *bithe* [book] *bu-reo* [give-IMP(iii)] "would you please give me a book?".

The imperative forms have a negative counterpart, which can be labelled as the prohibitive form. It consists of the negative particle *ume* "do not" and the imperfective participle V-*rA*, while the latter can either immediately follow the former or be separated by other components: e. g. *ume* [do. not] *gisure-re* [speak-IPFV. PTCP] "do not speak!", *ume* [do. not] *tere* [that] *yoro gisun* [rumour] *be* [ACC] *akda-ra* [believe-IPFV. PTCP] "do not believe that rumour!".

(3) The Optative Forms

There are two optative forms, V-*ki* and V-*kini*, both of which have more than one meaning. The first optative form V-*ki* can be used to express a polite request, which has a slightly lower degree of politeness than the imperative (iii), V-*rAo*, but a higher degree of politeness than imperative (i) (V-ø) and imperative (ii) (V-*cina*): *age* [sir] *cai* [tea] *omi-ki* [drink-OPT] "sir, please have some tea!". The optative form V-*ki* can also express the speaker's intention of carrying out an action: *bi* [1SG] *tacikū* [school] *de* [DAT] *gene-ki* [go-OPT] "I'll go to school". With this meaning it also carries an apparent future connotation of this action. It can also form a complex modal structure with the quotative verb *se-* "to say" (used as an auxiliary verb), V-*ki se-*, also expressing the speaker's intention of doing something: *bi* [1SG] *manju* [Manchu] *gisun* [language] *be* [ACC] *taci-ki* [learn-OPT] *se-mbi* [say(AUX)-IPFV. FIN] "I want to learn the Manchu language".

The second optative form V-*kini* is mainly used to express the speaker's wish that some state of affairs should take place. The verb is usually used in the 3rd person and is not confined to human beings: *tesu* [local] *ba-i* [place-GEN] *hafan* [official] *icihiya-kini* [handle-OPT] "let the local officials handle it!"; *tumen* [ten. thousand] *baita* [matter] *ijishūn* [smooth] *o-kini* "may everything" (lit.: "ten thousand matters") go smoothly!". When the subject is human, as in the first example, the form V-*kini* can express an indirect command.

(4) The Apprehensive Forms

The apprehensive modality, expressing the speaker's concern that something might happen, has several forms, which usually combine with the quotative verb *se-*, but not necessarily. The first form consists of the verb stem and the apprehensive suffix, V-*rahū* (*se-*), for instance, *tere* [that] *niyalma* [person] *jide-rahū* [come-APRH] (*se-mbi* [say(AUX)-IPFV. FIN]) "(I) fear that that man may come". The second apprehensive form consists of the imperfective participle (affirmative and negative) and the apprehensive particle *ayoo*: *tere* [that] *jaka* [thing] *efuje-re* [be. broken-IPFV. PTCP] *ayoo* (*se-mbi* [say(AUX)-IPFV. FIN]) "(I) worry that that thing might be broken", *si* [2SG] *gene-rakū* [go-IPFV. PTCP. NEG] *ayoo* (*se-mbi* [say(AUX)-IPFV. FIN]) "I'm worried that you might not go".

3.1.3.2 Voices

The grammatical category of voice in Manchu can exhibit itself in both finite and non-finite verb forms. There are various voices in Manchu in terms of the argument structure of verbs: active, passive, causative, cooperative and reciprocal. Of all these voices, the active voice serves as the morphological base from which other voices are derived.

(1) The Passive and Causative Voices

The passive and causative verb stems share the same form, both consisting of the active verb stem and the suffix-*bu*: *wa-bu-* [kill-PASS] "to be killed"; *gene-bu-* [go-CAUS] "to make [someone] go". Despite the shared morphology, the passive and causative voices can be distinguished in specific sentences. First, semantically, only transitive verbs can have both the passive and causative voices, while intransitive verbs can only have the causative voice. For example, the verb *jafa-* "to hold/grasp" can have both the passive and causative voices *jafa-bu-* "to make [someone] hold/grasp" or "to be held/caught". On the other hand, *gene-bu-* can only be understood as the causative "to make [someone] go", since *gene-* "to go" cannot take an object. Second, the passive and causative voices usually form different syntactic structures due to their internal semantic distinction. Specifically, the causee of the causative structure is generally governed by the accusative marker *be*, while the agent of the passive structure is—if indicated at all—governed by the dative-locative marker *de*: *bi* [1SG] <u>*im-be*</u> [3SG(*i/in*)-ACC] *bithe* [book] (*be* [ACC]) <u>*hūla-bu-mbi*</u> [read-CAUS-IPFV. FIN] "I make him read books", *hecen* [city] *bata* [enemy] <u>*de*</u> [DAT] <u>*gai-bu-ha*</u> [take-PASS-PFV. PTCP] "The city has been/was taken by the enemy".

(2) The Cooperative and Reciprocal Voices

These two voices share the feature that the action in question involves more than one participant: the cooperative voice indicates that "the action is performed by several participants together" (Gorelova 2002: 250),[①] while the reciprocal voice indicates "an action performed through a mutual interaction of one subject with another" (Gorelova 2002: 251).

The cooperative voice suffix *-cA* is attached to the basic active voice verb stem: *daha-ca-* [follow-COOP] "to follow together"; *inje-ce-* [laugh-COOP] "to laugh together"; *te-ce-* [sit-COOP] "to sit together".

① Gorelova (2002) uses the term "associative" instead of "cooperative". I regard "cooperative" as a more appropriate term.

Sometimes it is used with adverbials that indicate the joint nature of the action, for example, *gucu-i* [friend-GEN] *emgi* [together] *leole-ce-mbi* [chat-COOP-IPFV. FIN] "chat with one's friends". The reciprocal voice stem is formed by adding the suffix *-nu/-ndu* to the basic active voice verb stem, e. g. *aisila-ndu-* [help-RECP] "to help each other", *tanta-nu-* [beat-RECP] "to beat one another". There is also an adverb that is commonly used with the reciprocal voice, *ishunde* "mutually", for example in *ishunde* [mutually] *afa-ndu-mbi* [fight-RECP-IPFV. FIN] "wage wars against each other".

3.2 Verbs that Can Function as Auxiliary Verbs

In Manchu there are no pure auxiliary verbs as such, but some verbs can function either as lexical verbs or as auxiliary verbs. These verbs mainly include the verbs *o-* "to become/be", *bi-* "to exist/be", and *se-* "to say".

3.2.1 The Verb *o-*

The verb *o-* can serve as a copular verb meaning "to become/be" and occurs in every conjugated form. Table 3. 8 shows some commonly used forms (it should be noted that the imperfective participle *ojoro* and the imperative [i] *oso* are irregular forms).

Table 3.8 Some Conjugated Forms of *o-* (as a Copular Verb):

Conjugation	Verb Form	Example
Imperfective Finite	*o-mbi*	*sain* [good] *o-mbi* "(one) becomes/will become good"
Imperfective Participle	*ojo-ro*	*han* [khan] *ojo-ro niyalma* [person] "the man to become the khan"
Perfective Participle	*o-ho*	*halhūn* [hot] *o-ho* "(it) became/has become hot"
Imperative (i)	*oso*	*ekisaka* [quite] oso "be quiet!"

Continued

Conjugation	Verb Form	Example
Conditional Converb	*o-ci*	*tere* [that] *haha* [man] *tondo* [honest] *o-ci* "if that man is honest..."
Perfective Converb	*o-fi*	*gaitai* [suddenly] *halhūn* [hot] *o-fi* "(it) suddenly becoming hot..."

As an auxiliary verb, *o-* forms complex structures with other (lexical) verbs: it combines mainly with the imperfective converb V-*me* and the negative participles V-*rakū*/V-*hAkū* in different syntactic environments. First, with the converb V-*me*, the perfective participle *o-ho* takes the dative-locative marker *de* and serves to express the conditional meaning. Similarly the perfective converb *o-fi* expresses the causal meaning with a preceding imperfective converb V-*me*. Second, the negative participles can combine with various forms of the verb *o-*, forming negative counterparts of those V-*me o-* combinations. With the negative participles (especially the imperfective one), other forms of the verb *o-*, either finite or non-finite forms, can also build complex structures. Table 3. 9 shows the complex structures discussed so far.

It should be noted in particular that when *o-* (as an auxiliary verb) follows a negative participle (such as V-*rAkū*), forming a complex structure that serves as the main predicate of a sentence, the original meaning of *o-* as a basic lexical verb indicating change of state is still perceivable. For instance, in *saburakū o-ho* "(one) can't/couldn't see (it) any more" (see Table 3. 9 for gloss), the verb *o-* marks the change from one state in which people can or could still see the thing to another state in which people can/could no longer see it, the latter state itself represented by the negative participle (*sabu-rakū*). Similarly in *tere cimari generakū ombi* "(now) he won't go tomorrow" (see Table 3. 9 for gloss), the verb *o-* marks the change from one state, in which he is probably expected to go tomorrow, to another state, in which it turns out that he will not go. The difference between the use of *o-* as an auxiliary verb and its use as a lexical verb lies in whether the state in question is represented by a negative participle or a nominal structure (such as *han* "khan", *halhūn* "hot / heat").

Table 3.9　Some Combinations of the Verb *o-* (as an Auxiliary Verb) and Lexical Verbs

Form of Lexical Verb		Combination	Example
Affirmative	V-*me*	V-*me o-ho de*	*si* [2SG] *kice-me* [strive-IPFV. CVB] *taci-me* [study-IPFV. CVB] *o-ho-de* [become(AUX)-PFV. PTCP-DAT] "if you study hard"
		V-*me o-fi*	*tere* [3SG/that] *ji-me* [come-IPFV. CVB] *o-fi* [become(AUX)-PFV. CVB] "because he comes"
	V-*rA*	V-*rA o-ci*	*bithe* [book] *hūla-ra* [read-IPFV. PTCP] *o-ci* [become(AUX)-COND] "if (one) reads books"
Negative	V-*rakū*	V-*rakū o-ho de*	si [2SG] *taci-rakū* [study-IPFV. PTCP. NEG] *o-ho-de* [become(AUX)-PFV. PTCP-DAT] "if you don't study"
		V-*rakū o-fi*	*tere* [3SG/that] *jide-rakū* [come-IPFV. PTCP. NEG] *o-fi* [become(AUX)-PFV. CVB] "because he won't come"
		V-*rakū o-ci*	*si* [2SG] *taci-rakū* [study-IPFV. PTCP. NEG] *o-ci* [become(AUX)-COND] "if you don't study"
		V-*rakū o-mbi*	*tere* [3SG/that] *cimari* [tomorrow] *gene-rakū* [go-IPFV. PTCP. NEG] *o-mbi* [become(AUX)-IPFV. FIN] "he won't go tomorrow"
		V-*rakū o-ho*	*sabu-rakū* [see-IPFV. PTCP. NEG] *o-ho* [become(AUX)-PFV. PTCP] "[one] cannot/could not see (it) any more"
	V-*hAkū*	V-*hAkū o-fi*	*tere* [3SG/that] *ji-hekū* [come-PFV. PTCP. NEG] *o-fi* "because he did not come..."

3.2.2 The Verb *bi-* and the Functions of Its Perfective Participle *bi-he*

When functioning as a lexical verb, *bi-* mainly expresses the meaning of existence (or location). Table 3.10 demonstrates some commonly used conjugated forms of the verb *bi-* "to exist/be" (it should be noted that the imperfective participle *bisi-re* and the imperative [i] *bisu* are irregular forms).

Table 3.10 Conjugated Forms of the Verb *bi-*

Conjugation	Verb Form	Example
Imperfective Finite	*bi-mbi*	*bele* [grain] *kemuni* [still] *hecen* [city] *de* [DAT] *bi-mbi* [be-IPFV. FIN] "there is still grain in the city"
Imperfective Participle	*bisi-re*	*ula-i* [river-GEN] *talga* [surface] *de* [DAT] *bisi-re* [be-IPFV. PTCP] *jahūdai* [boat] "the boat (being/existing) on the surface of the river"
Perfective Finite	*bi-hebi*	*tere* [that] *gurun* [country] *de* [DAT] *emu* [one] *amba* [great] *han* [khan] *bi-hebi* [be-PFV. FIN] "in that country there was/lived a great khan"
Perfective Participle	*bi-he*	*sain* [good] *ahūn deo* [brothers] *bi-he* [be-PFV. PTCP] "(they) used to be good brothers"
Imperative (i)	*bisu*	*boo-de* [house-DAT] *bisu* [be. IMP] "stay at home!"
Conditional Converb	*bi-ci*	*baita* [matter] *bi-ci* [be-COND] "if there are matters"

It should be noted that the imperfective finite form *bi-mbi* is not very frequently used, but the existential particle *bi* (which is most likely related to the verb *bi-* etymologically) is used instead in many contexts, for instance, *bira* [river] *de* [DAT] *nimaha* [fish] *bi* [EXS. PTL] "there are fish in the river". The perfective participle of the verb *bi-*, *bi-he*, has multiple functions and is of particular relevance to the present study. These functions are discussed in the rest of Section 3.2.2.

3.2.2.1 The Perfective Participle *bi-he*

When *bi-* is a lexical verb, the participle *bi-he* can serve to express: (i) existence [(3. 2-1) and (3. 2-2)]; (ii) identification (3. 2-3); and (iii) evaluation (3. 2-4):

(3. 2-1)

sin-i	*dergi-de*	*emu*	*ahūn*	*bi-he*	*tofohon*
2SG(*si/sin*)-GEN	top-DAT	one	elder. brother	be-PFV. PTCP	fifteen
se	*de*	*beye*	*dube-he*		
year(-old)	DAT	body	end-PFV. PTCP		

beye dube-: "to die", lit.: "(of the body) to end"

You had an elder brother before you [were born] (lit.: "above you"). (He) died at the age of fifteen. (NSB: 2)

(3. 2-2)

min-i	*eje-he-ngge*,	*sin-de*	*inu*	*emke*
1SG(*bi/min*)-GEN	memorise-PFV. PTCP-NMLZ	2SG(*si/sin*)-DAT	also	one
bi-he				
be-PFV. PTCP				

min-i eje-he-ngge: "as I remember", lit.: "what I have memorised"

As I remember, you also had one (of those). (OJ2: 46)

(3. 2-3)

ilan	*aniya-i*	*onggolo*,	*muse-i*	*uba-de*,	*tere*
three	year-GEN	before	1PL. INCL-GEN	this. place-DAT	that/3SG
geli	*we*	*bi-he*	*fungsan*	*yadahūn*	*kai*
again	who	be-PFV. PTCP	impoverished	poor	PTL

fungsan yadahūn: "very poor"

And what was he like (lit.: "who was he") in our neighbourhood three years ago? He was indeed very poor (back then)! (OJ1: 93)

(3. 2-4)

antaka	*senggime*,	*antaka*	*haji*	*bi-he*
how	intimate	how	dear	be-PFV. PTCP

How intimate and how dear (they) were (to each other)! (OJ1: 70)

All the examples above describe past states of affairs (prior to the time of speech, or to a certain state of affairs in the past), usually with a connotation that the states of affairs once existed but ceased to exist. In (3. 2-1) the addressee had a brother who nevertheless had already died (before the addressee was born), and in (3. 2-4) the people in question no longer feel intimate with each other.

3.2.2.2 The Perfective Participle *bi-he* in Complex Structures

As mentioned in (1) in Section 3.1.3.1, when *bi-* serves as an auxiliary verb, its participle *bi-he* builds complex structures with lexical verbs. Table 3.11 demonstrates some of these structures.

The meanings of the listed complex structures are discussed in the following passages. Since most attested examples in my corpus are those in which these structures serve as main predicates (rather than attributes or subordinate predicates), the following discussion will be restricted to their meanings under such syntactic circumstances.

Table 3.11 Complex Structures Built by Lexical Verbs and the Participle *bi-he*

	Lexical Verb Form		Complex Structure
Affirmative	Perfective Participle	V-*hA*	V-*hA bi-he*
	Imperfective Converb	V-*me*	V-*me bi-he*/V-*mbihe*
	Imperfective Participle	V-*rA*	V-*rA bi-he* (rather rare)
Negative	Perfective Participle	V-*hAkū*	V-*hAkū bi-he*
	Imperfective Participle	V-*rakū*	V-*rakū bi-he*

(1) The Complex Structure V-*hA bi-he*

Scholars tend to consider the structure V-*hA bi-he* as the counterpart of the Indo-European pluperfect/past perfect, presumably due to its morphology, that is, the perfective participle of a lexical verb (V-*hA*) combined with the perfective participle of an auxiliary verb (*bi-he*). Avrorin (2000: 192) points out that the structure V-*hA bi-he* has the meaning of "remote past". Gorelova (2002: 292) labels it as "past perfect", and translates it accordingly: *gisure-he* [say-PFV. PTCP] *bi-he* [be(AUX)-PFV. PTCP] "(one) had said". Similar translations are also given by Li (2010: 72), for instance, *harangga* [subject] *o-ho* [become-PFV. PTCP] *bi-he* [be(AUX)-PFV. PTCP] "he had become a subject". The following are some examples.

(3.2-5) *bi* *im-be* *solina-ha* *bi-he.* *indahūn*
1SG 3SG(*i/in*)-ACC invite-PFV. PTCP be(AUX)-PFV. PTCP dog
inu *emke* *takūra-ha* *ba* *akū*
even one send-PFV. PTCP NMLZ NEG
V-*hA ba akū*: [one] did not V, lit.: "there is no such thing as one's having V-ed"
I had invited/did invite him, (but he) didn't even (so much as) send a dog [to my house]! (OJ1: 44)

(3.2-6) *bi* *cen-i* *hala* *be* *fonji-ha*
1SG 3PL(*ce/cen*)-GEN family. name ACC ask-PFV. PTCP
bi-he. *min-de* *emte* *justan* *gebu* *jergi*
be(AUX)-PFV. PTCP 1SG(*bi/min*)-DAT one. each stripe name rank
ara-ha *bithe* *weri-hebi*
write-PFV. PTCP letter leave-PFV. FIN
I did (indeed) ask/had asked their family name. (They) left one letter each, on which were written (their) name and rank (OJ1: 58)

(3.2-7) *jakan* *sihin-i* *fejile* *sišana-ha* *bi-he.* *yasa*
just. now eave-GEN below hang. down be(AUX)-PFV. PTCP eye
habtala-ha *andan-de,* *in-i* *cisu-i* *tuhe-kebi*
blink-PFV. PTCP instant-DAT 3SG(*i/in*)-GEN self-GEN fall-PFV. FIN
yasa habtala-ha andan-de: in the blink of an eye
in-i cisu-i: naturally, by itself
Just now (the icicles) were hanging down below the eaves, (but) in the blink of an eye, (the icicles) naturally fell (onto the ground). (AGA2: 107)

(3.2-8) *sucungga* *bi* *hono* *cem-be* *hūwaliyambu-me*
initial 1SG still 3PL(*ce/cen*)-ACC reconcile-IPFV. CVB
acabu-ki *se-me* *gūni-ha* *bi-he.*
harmonise-OPT say(AUX)-IPFV. CVB think-PFV. PTCP be(AUX)-PFV. PTCP
amala *tuwa-fi* *joo-ø*
afterwards look-PFV. CVB stop-IMP
V-*ki se-*: complex structure expressing intention/desire
At first I was still wishing to reconcile them, (but) afterwards, looking (at the situation), (I told myself) "(just) give (it) up!" (AGA4: 70)

In (3. 2-5)-(3. 2-8), while the point of reference to which the structure V-*hA bi-he* is anchored is another past state of affairs (represented by another verb), a temporal adverbial may also occur, such as *amala* "afterwards" in (3. 2-8). Similar to the cases where the participle *bi-he* has lexical meanings [(3. 2-1)-(3. 2-4)], some of the sentences above (3. 2-5)-(3. 2-8), where *bi-he* is an auxiliary verb, also tend to carry the connotation that the states of affairs represented by the structure V-*hA bi-he* have ceased to exist (or are followed by states of affairs that are in a sense contrary to expectation). For instance, in (3. 2-5) the speaker's invitation was met with ingratitude; in (3. 2-7), the icicles fell to the ground, and thus no longer hung down from the eaves.

(2) The Complex Structure V-*me bi-he*

The most important, but not the sole, syntactic function of the structure V-*me bi-he* is to serve as the main predicate of a sentence. Semantically, it expresses the meaning of "progressive (process) in the past" and "habitual past" (Li 2010: 365). A structure with similar functions is V-*mbihe*. Some scholars suggest that V-*mbihe* originated from V-*me bi-he* (e. g., Zakharov 1879: 174), while others do not distinguish the two forms but consider them to be orthographic variants of the same structure (Avrorin 2000: 192; Li 2010: 365). Meanwhile, in the corpus for this study in actual usage the structures V-*me bi-he* and V-*mbihe* do not exhibit semantic distinction. Based on this observation and in view of the orthographic inconsistencies common in Manchu texts (especially concerning ligature), the present study considers the two verb forms as variants of one and the same structure, both of which consist of the imperfective converb (V-*me*) and the perfective participle *bi-he*. The following are examples.

(3. 2-13) *leose-i* *dele* *tafu-fi* *afa-ra* *be*
tower-GEN top ascend-PFV. CVB fight-IPFV. PTCP ACC
tuwa-me *bi-he-ngge*, *hecen* *gai-bu-ha*
watch-IPFV. CVB be(AUX)-PFV. PTCP-NMLZ city take-PASS-PFV. PTCP
be *sa-fi* *uthai* *leose* *be* *tuwa* *sinda-fi*

ACC know-PFV. CVB then tower ACC fire set-PFV. CVB

buce-he

die-PFV. PTCP

(He) came to the top of the (city gate) tower and was watching the battle, (and then) knowing that the city was taken (by the enemy), (he) set the tower on fire and died. (MYK7: 8)

(3.2-14) *sucungga tanta-ra de hono too-me*

initial beat-IPFV. PTCPDAT still swear-IPFV. CVB

<u>*sure-mbihe*</u>, *amala kudeše-hei*, *nidu-re*

shout-PST. IPFV afterwards beat. back. with. hands-DUR. CVB groan-IPFV. PTCP

jilgan gemu akū o-ho

sounds all NEG become-PFV. PTCP

At first when (people) beat (him), (he) was still swearing and shouting. Afterwards, (while people kept) beating him on the back with both hands, all (his) groaning sounds were (heard) no more. (OJ2: 78)

(3.2-15) *bi daruhai* <u>*sidere-mbihe*</u>, *enenggi onggo-fi*

1SG often tie-PST. IPFV today forget-PFV. CVB

sidere-hekū

tie-PFV. PTCP. NEG

Usually I would tie (the horse), (but) forgetting it today, (I) didn't tie (the horse) (LQD3: 60)

(3.2-16) *duleke aniya ilan jiha menggun de emu*

pass-PFV. PTCP year three tael silver DAT one

ginggin <u>*baha-mbihe.*</u> *te sunja jiha menggun de emu*

jin get-PST. IFPV now five tael silver DAT one

ginggin hono baha-rakū

jin still get-IPFV. PTCP. NEG

dule-ke aniya: last year

Last year (people) used to get one jin (of ginseng) for three taels of silver, (but) now (people) don't get one jin even for five taels of silver. (LQD: 164)

(3.2-17) *Daiming Gurun sin-de atanggi ere gese šang ambula*

Ming empire 2SG(*si*/*sin*)-DAT when this like reward greatly

<u>*bu-mbihe*</u>

give-PST. IPFV

šang bu-: to reward

When did the Ming Empire ever generously reward you like this? (MYK6: 26)

One can see from (3. 2-13)-(3. 2-17) that the structure V-*mbihe*/V-*me bi-he* is similar to the structure V-*hA bi-he* in that the structure V-*mbihe*/V-*me bi-he* has a salient tense feature and emphasizes the occurrence of a past state of affairs. It is different from the structure V-*hA bi-he* in that the state of affairs represented by V-*mbihe*/V-*me bi-he* is depicted as ongoing, repetitive or habitual (imperfective in terms of aspect)—rather than completed (perfective in terms of aspect). Thus, in parallel with the structure V-*hA bi-he*, the structure V-*mbihe*/V-*me bi-he*, when serving as a main predicate, can be interpreted as follows: "It did indeed occur that a state of affairs was taking place/usually took place."

3.2.2.2.3 The Complex Structures V-*rakū*/-*hAkū bi-he*

These structures consist of negative participles (imperfective V-*rakū*, perfective V-*hAkū*) and the form *bi-he*, and mainly serve as main predicates. Semantically they do not exhibit new patterns except for the negation of their affirmative counterparts: V-*hAkū bi-he* is the negation of the form V-*hA bi-he*, and the structure V-*raku bi-he* is the negation of both V-*mbihe* and V-*rA bi-he* (however, it should be noted that the structure V-*rA bi-he* is very rare in Manchu). The following are some examples.

(3. 2-18) *bi* *seibeni* *niyalma-i* *muke* *tata-ra* *be*
1SG formerly people-GEN water pull-IPFV. PTCP ACC
tuwa-ha *bi-cibe* *taci-hakū* *bi-he*
watch-PFV. PTCP be(AUX)-CONC learn-PFV. PTCP. NEG be(AUX)-PFV. PTCP
Though I have watched people drawing water (out of a well) before, I have never learnt (to do it myself). (LQD: 80)

(3. 2-19) *juwe* *biya* *gucule-fi* *ishunde* *dere*
two month befriend-PFV. CVB mutually face
fularja-hakū *bi-he*
redden-PFV. PTCP. NEG be(AUX)-PFV. PTCP
dere fularja-: to argue, to be angry, lit.: "the face to redden"

Being friends for two months, (we) have never been angry with each other. (LQD: 292)

(3.2-20)

tere	*juwen*	*bu-rakū*	*bi-he*	*bi*
that/3SG	loan	give-IPFV. PTCP. NEG	be(AUX)-PFV. PTCP	1SG
dahūn dahūn i		*bai-re*	*de*	*hami-rakū*
repeatedly		request-IPFV. PTCP	DAT	bear-IPFV. PTCP
o-fi		*arkan seme*	*bu-he*	
become(AUX)-PFV. CVB		reluctantly	give-PFV. PTCP	

juwen bu-: to lend

dahūn dahūn i: repeatedly

arkan seme: reluctantly

(At first) He wouldn't lend (it to me), (and then) unable to bear my nagging him again and again, (he finally) gave (it to me) reluctantly. (LQD: 44)

(3.2-21)

nunggala-ha	*lalanji*	*booha*	*be*	*bi*	*hihala-rakū*	
stew-PFV. PTCP	soft	dish	ACC	1SG	like-IPFV. PTCP	
bi-he.	*te*	*urui*	*angga*	*de*	*nilukan*	*haihū*
be(AUX)-PFV. PTCP	now	just	mouth	DAT	smooth	soft
ningge	*be*	*buye-mbi*				
NMLZ	ACC	love-IPFV. FIN				

I didn't like soft stewed dishes (before), (but) nowadays (I) just love smooth, soft things in (my) mouth. (AGA2: 115)

3.2.2.3 Non-temporal Meanings Expressed by Structures Containing *bi-he*

Apart from aspectual-temporal meanings, structures containing *bi-he* can also express a variety of non-temporal meanings, or at least contribute to expressing them. Such meanings are related to knowledge state, including uncertainty, mirativity, and counterfactuality.

First, the perfective participle *bi-he* can reflect the speaker's uncertainty. When expressing this meaning, the participle *bi-he* appears in combination with interrogatives, which themselves also reflect the speaker's uncertainty (about the situation). The following are examples.

(3.2-22)	*agu-sa*	*ere*	*aiba*	*bi-he*
	sir-PL	this	what. place	be-PFV. PTCP

Sirs, what is this place? (NSB: 68)

(3.2-23)	*si*	*ai*	*niyalma*	*bi-he?*	*bi*	*ainu*	*taka-rakū*
	2SG	what	person	be-PFV. PTCP	1SG	why	know-IPFV. PTCP. NEG

Who (on earth) are you? Why don't I know you? (NSB: 72)

It is clear from the contexts that despite the presence of the participle *bi-he*, (3.2-22) and (3.2-23) do not describe past states of affairs [cf. (3.2-1)-(3.2-4)] but only concern the present ("what this place is" and "who the addressee is"). *On the other hand*, to describe present states of affairs, no verb or copula is necessary to express identification (or evaluation).① Therefore, the participle *bi-he* would be expected to express a certain type of non-temporal meaning. Since it can be seen that in both (3.2-22) and (3.2-23) the speaker attempts to reason but is unable to find the answer, the participle *bi-he* would be expected to mark—or at least to contribute to marking—the speaker's uncertainty.

Second, the participle *bi-he* is also used in some sentences where the speaker has come to a sudden realisation of certain state of affairs—expressing the mirative/admirative meaning. (Friedman 1986; Jacobsen 1986; DeLancey 1997) The participle *bi-he* occurs in combination with a particle *ni*,② and in some cases with the particle *dule* "in fact" in addition. Examples (3.2-24)-(3.2-27) below can be seen as mirative constructions in Manchu (though there are also structures which can express mirativity

① Usually, Manchu can simply juxtapose two nominal structures, one as the subject, and the other as the predicate, e.g., *ere* [this] *min-i* [1SG(*si/sin*)-GEN] *fiyanggū* [youngest. child] "this [is] my youngest child" (OJ2: 40); *inenggi* [day] *šun* [sun] *foholon* [short] "the days [are] short" (OJ1: 27).

② The particle *ni* does not have a conveniently glossable counterpart in English. Li (2010: 374) states that it is an "interrogative particle [... which] is used in questions that are contrary to the speaker's belief". One can see that what Li (2010: 374) characterises as "contrary to the speaker's belief" is close to the mirative meaning.

without the participle *bi-he*). ①

(3.2-24) *si* *emu* *sain* *niyalma* *bi-he* *ni*
you one good person be-PFV. PTCP PTL
So you are a good person (and I didn't know that)! (NSB: 51)

(3.2-25) *dule* *emu* *tondokon* *niyalma* *waka* *bihe* *ni*
in. fact one honest person not be-PFV. PTCP PTL
In fact (he) is not an honest man (which I have just realized)! (OJ1: 100)

(3.2-26) *ai* *buce-he* *yali* *geli* *bi-he* *ni*
what die-PFV. PTCP meat even be-PFV. PTCP PTL
buce-he yali: garbage (as a swearing word), lit.: "dead meat"
[I have just realized that] There is even such garbage (in the world)! (AGA3: 91)

(3.2-27) *dule* *emu* *butu* *hūlha*, *jortai* *hutu* *ara-me*
in. fact one secret thief on. purpose ghost pretend-IPFV. CVB
niyalma *be* *gelebu-mbihe* *ni*
people ACC frighten-PST. IPFV PTL
butu hūlha: thief [who sneaks]
(I have just realized that) it was a thief sneaking around and frightening people by pretending to be a ghost! (OJ2: 68)

It should be noted that the main predicate of (3.2-27) is a complex structure containing *bi-he*—the past imperfective V-*mbihe* [see (2) in Section 3.2.2.2]. It expresses the aspectual-temporal meaning of past progressive, apart from contributing the meaning of mirativity.

Third, when the verb *aca-* forms a complex structure (V-*ci aca-*) that expresses the modal meaning "to be obligated to", takes the form—*mbihe* and serves as the predicate of a simple sentence, it functions to describe a

① For instance: *dule* [in. fact] *teisu* [matching] *akū* [NEG] *ni* [PTL]. "(So) in fact there is no matching (between them)! (I have just realized this)" (UH: 61) uses the particles *dule* and *ni*, but not the participle *bi-he*. Also, when a lexical verb serves as the main predicate, mirativity can be expressed by these two particles alone without a complex structure of *bi-he*: *si* [2SG] *dule* [in. fact] *taka-rakū* [know-IPFV. PTCP. NEG] *ni* [PTL] *kai* [PTL] "So you actually don't know (it) (which I have just realized)!" (OJ2: 118).

counterfactual state of affairs in the past. The original modal meaning of obligation is also retained. Here are two examples.

(3.2-28) *sikse* *uthai* *ere* *emu* *jurgan* *emu* *hontoho* *be*
yesterday then this one line one half ACC
wacihiyabu-ci *aca-mbihe*
finish-COND suit(AUX)-PST. IPFV
V-*ci aca-*: complex structure expressing obligation
(You) should have finished this one line and a half (of the text) yesterday. (AGA1: 66)

(3.2-29) *sim-be* *guile-ci* *aca-mbihe.* *sin-de*
2SG(*si/sin*)-ACC invite-COND suit(AUX)-PST. IPFV 2SG(*si/sin*)-DAT
mejige *isibu-hakū-ngge*, *ere-i* *dorgi-de*
message send-PFV. PTCP-NEG-NMLZ this-GEN inside-DAT
sin-de *aca-rakū* *niyalma* *bi-fi* *kai*
2SG(*si/sin*)-DAT suit-IPFV. PTCP. NEG people be-PFV. CVB PTL
sinde acarakū niyalma: people who do not get along with you, lit.: "people not suiting you"
bi-fi kai: indeed because there is/are/was/were
(I) should have invited you. (That I) did not send you a message (is) because there were people among them who don't get along well with you. (OJ2: 92)

Furthermore, in conditional constructions of Manchu, the perfective participle *bi-he* and the structures it forms (e.g. V-*mbihe*) can also express a counterfactual meaning. These structures can be formed by lexical verbs, and are not limited to complex structures expressing modality as in (3.2-28) and (3.2-29). The structures containing *bi-he* occur at least in one clause of a conditional construction. Counterfactual conditionality is thus expressed by the combination of the conditional converb (V-*ci*) and structures containing *bi-he*. Here are two examples. The main predicate of (3.2-30) is a complex verb structure expressing a modal meaning, as in (3.2-28) and (3.2-29), while the main predicate of (3.2-31) is a lexical verb. ①

① See Section 4.1.2.1 for more examples of counterfactual conditionals.

(3.2-30) *donji-mbihe* *bi-ci*, *urgun* *i* *doro-i*
hear-PST. IPFV be(AUX)-COND happiness GEN rite-GEN
acana-me *gene-ci* *aca-mbihe*
go. to. meet-IPFV. CVB go-COND suit(AUX)-PST. IPFV
urgun i doro: congratulations, lit.: "the rite of happiness"
V-*ci aca*-: complex structure expressing obligation
If (I) had heard (about your good news), (I) should have gone to meet (you and offer my) congratulations. (MFG: 7)

(3.2-31) *tere* *inenggi* *baha* *bi-ci*, *sim-be*
that day get. PFV. PTCP be(AUX)-COND 2SG(*si/sin*)-ACC
wa-mbihe
kill-PST. IPFV
If (I) had captured (you) that day, (I) would have killed you. (MYK2: 46)

To sum up, the meanings discussed above include the following: uncertainty [(3. 2-22) and (3. 2-23)]; mirativity [(3. 2-24)-(3. 2-27)]; counterfactuality in simple sentences [(3. 2-28) and (3. 2-29)]; and counterfactuality in complex sentences—conditional constructions [(3. 2-30) and (3. 2-31)]. All these meanings are (at least partly) realised by structures containing the perfective participle *bi-he* (either *bi-he* by itself or the complex structures it forms). One thing that these meanings share with the temporal meaning (i. e. past state of affairs) is their distinction from what the speaker always knows (for certain) as the present reality. It should also be noted that this is not to claim that these meanings are realised exclusively by the structures containing *bi-he*, nor even to claim that to express these meanings, structures containing *bi-he* are needed at all—in fact for each meaning there are alternative structures without the participle *bi-he*. Nevertheless, when the structures containing *bi-he* do occur, they undoubtedly play an important role in representing the cognitive distance between the state of affairs described and what the speaker knows as the reality.

3.2.3 The Two Perfective Participles *bi-he* and *o-ho*: A Contrast in Meaning

As shown in Section 3. 2. 1 and (3) in Section 3. 2. 2. 2, the perfective participles of the two verbs *bi-* and *o-*, i. e. , *bi-he* and *o-ho*, are similar in terms of syntactic functions. For instance, in forming predicates, both can combine with nominal structures (N+*bi-he*; N+*o-ho*) when *bi-* and *o-* function as lexical verbs, or with the negative imperfective participle (V-*rakū bi-he*; V-*rakū o-ho*) when *bi-* and *o-* function as auxiliary verbs. However, they should be semantically distinguished from each other. First, when serving as the predicate of a sentence, the participle *bi-he* usually implies that the state which it represents (had) existed for a certain period of time but no longer existed or exists, or the state was somehow affected. For instance, *tere* [3SG/that] *hafan* [official] *bi-he* [be-PFV. PTCP] "He had been/used to be an official" implies that he was or is no longer an official. In contrast, when serving as the (main) predicate of a sentence, the participle *o-ho* only indicates that the state in question was or has been realised, potentially implying that the realised state would afterwards exist for a certain period of time. For instance, *tere* [3SG/that] *hafan* [official] *o-ho* [become-PFV. PTCP] "He became/has become an official" indicates that his becoming an official was realised, and implies that he would remain an official afterwards for a certain period.

Second, one can also observe a similar difference between the complex structures V-*rakū bi-he* and V-*rakū o-ho*. In the case of *bi-he*, the state represented by the preceding negative participle (V-*rAkū*) usually ceased/ceases to exist. For instance, *sabu-rakū* [see-IPFV. PTCP. NEG] *bi-he* [be (AUX)-PFV. PTCP] "(one) couldn't see (it)" implies that the state of affairs that people were unable to see ceased or has ceased to exist, and therefore people became or have become able to see the thing after a certain temporal point (in the past). In the case of *o-ho*, by contrast, the state represented by the negative participle was realised at a certain temporal point (in the past). For instance, as explained in Section 4. 2. 1, *sabu-rakū* [see-IPFV. PTCP. NEG] *o-ho* [become(AUX)-PFV. PTCP] "(one) could not see any more" indicates the change into a state in which people could not see the thing, and implies that this state would exist for a certain period.

3.2.4 The Verb *se-*

When used as a lexical verb, the verb *se-* is a quotative verb, serving to quote the content of speech (either direct speech or indirect speech). It may be used alone or together with other verbs of speech. For instance, *tere* [that/3SG] *bi* [1SG] *ji-he* [come-PFV. PTCP] *se-he* [say-PFV. PTCP] "He said, 'I've come.'" (direct speech, *se-* used alone); *tere* [that/3SG] *hendu-me* [speak-IPFV. CVB], *si* [2SG] *ebsi* [hither] *jio* [come. IMP] *se-he* [say-PFV. PTCP] "He said, 'You, come here!'" (direct speech, *se-* combining with verb of speech *hendu-* "to speak"). In the course of time the quotative verb *se-* has also formed structures which, though related metaphorically to its original function, express other meanings such as intention, expectation or wish. In such structures the verb *se-* functions as an auxiliary verb. From (3) in Section 3. 1. 3. 1 (on optative forms) we can see that the complex structure V-*ki se-* expresses the modal meaning of intention, which presumably originated from a first-person direct-speech use and later on fossilised as a fixed structure. For instance, it is likely that at an earlier stage the modal sentence *bi* [1SG] *yabu-ki* [go-OPT] *se-mbi* [say(AUX)-IPFV. FIN] "I want to go" literally meant "I'm saying, '[I] would like to go'". As a matter of fact, such direct-speech use of the structure V-*ki se-* exists in parallel with its modal use in Manchu, which can be contextually distinguished, for example, *emu* [one] *gašan* [village] *de* [DAT] *aca-fi* [get. together-PFV. CVB] *te-ki* [live-OPT] *se-me* [say-IPFV. CVB] *gisure-me* [discuss-IPFV. CVB] *waji-ha* [finish-PFV. PTCP] "saying 'let's live together in one village!', (they thus) finished discussing (the matter)."

The quotative verb is also used to "quote" the content of one's thought or hearsay, e. g. *aga-me* [rain-IPFV. CVB] *deribu-he* [begin-PFV. PTCP] *dere* [PTL] *se-me* [say-IPFV. CVB] *gūni-habi* [think-PFV. FIN] "(I) thought, 'it may have begun to rain'", *antaha-sa* [guest-PL] *gemu* [all] *isinji-ha* [arrive-PFV. PTCP] *se-re* [say-IPFV. PTCP] *be* [ACC] *donji-ha* [hear-PFV. PTCP] "(I) heard that all the guests had arrived". In particular, when the verb *se-*, in the form of the imperfective converb *se-me* or the participles *se-re/se-he*, is governed by cognition or perception verbs (such as *gūni-* "to think", *donji-* "to hear"), it is comparable to the complementiser *that* in English as in "I think that". It is also important to note that the verb *se-*, in its various forms, takes finite forms as its subordinate clauses; that is, these clauses can stand on their own as simple sentences: *uyun* [nine] *hala-i* [clan-GEN] *gurun* [tribe] *aca-fi* [get. together-PFV. CVB] *ilan* [three] *jugūn-i* [route-GEN] *cooha* [troops] *ji-mbi* [come-IPFV. FIN] *se-me* [say(AUX)-IPFV. CVB] *donji-fi* [hear-PFV. CVB] "hearing that (these) nine tribes had got together and (their) troops were coming in three routes..."

The basic function of the verb *se-* enables it to form topic structures or cleft structures in various forms (Gorelova 2006: 157-159; also see Section 4.8), such as the nominalised participles *se-re-ngge*, *se-he-ngge*, and the conditional converb *se-ci*, for example, *gurun-i* [nation/state-GEN] *gisun* [language] *se-re-ngge* [say-IPFV. PTCP-NMLZ] *muse-i* [1PL. INCL-GEN] *ba-i* [place-GEN] *gisun* [language] "what is called the national language is our dialect" (AGA1: 1) and *nure* [wine] *se-ci* [say-COND], *horon-i* [poison-GEN] *okto* [medicine] *geli* [even] *waka* [not] "speaking of wine, (it is) not even poison" (MFG: 47).

The above is an outline of the grammar of Manchu verbs, which are most relevant to the present study. The next chapter is the core of this book, analysing the collected data, which are divided into distinct, yet related, categories.

Chapter 4 Data Analysis

This chapter categorises and analyses the example sentences from the corpus. The sentences are divided into ten groups, each of which is analysed in one section. The categorisation takes morphosyntax, semantics and pragmatics into consideration, and the categories are not meant to be mutually exclusive, particularly in terms of morphosyntax.

The example sentences are glossed on a morpheme-by-morpheme basis and translated. Extra glosses are provided after the sentences wherever I deem necessary, such as some set phrases as well as complex verb structures. Each section of data analysis first demonstrates the morphosyntactic properties of sentences, which are arranged in order of increasing complexity of the predicate. Then the meanings of the sentences are discussed in association with their morphosyntax.

4.1 Basic Patterns of Conditional Constructions

This section analyses the basic patterns of conditional constructions, which are the most common constructions and are uniform in morphosyntax—containing conditional-converb (V-*ci*) structures (both simple and complex).[1] Therefore, they are the candidates for the prototypes of conditional constructions. The basic conditionals are analysed in two groups: factual conditionals and counterfactual conditionals (see Sections 4.1.1.2 and 4.1.2.2 respectively for the definition of each type of conditional), both of which exhibit distinctive morphosyntactic characteristics.

4.1.1 Basic Factual Conditionals

4.1.1.1 Morphosyntax

The simplest form of a factual conditional has the conditional converb of a lexical verb V-*ci* serving as the predicate of the subordinate clause (protasis). Other morphosyntactic patterns of conditionals can be regarded as derived from it. The following are some examples. The predicate of the main clause (apodosis) can be the imperfective finite form V-*mbi* [(4.1-1) and (4.1-2)], an imperative form (4.1-3), an optative form (4.1-4), or a nominal structure [(4.1-5) and (4.1-6)].

(4.1-1)	*inenggi-dari*	*hūla-ci*,	*gisun*	*eje-mbi*
	day-every	read-COND	words	remember-IPFV.FIN

If (one) reads every day, (one) will remember words. (OJ1: 24)

(4.1-2)	*muse*	*dobori*	*farhūn*	*de*	*cooha*	*jura-ci*,	*gurun*
	1PL.INCL	night	dark	DAT	troops	set.out-COND	people
	durge-mbi						
	be.disturbed-IPFV.FIN						

If we march the troops during the night, the people (in the city) will be disturbed. (MYK2: 37)

---

[1] Conditional-converb (V-*ci*) structures frequently and primarily express conditionality. For instance, a rough count of conditional-converb structures in MYK (see Section 1.2) reveals that 289 of all 411 occurrences (excluding fixed expressions containing the conditional converb; see Section 3.1.1) express conditionality, while 122 express temporality (see Section 4.3). On the other hand, only 28 occurrences of dative-locative participial structures (V-*hA de*) express conditionality (see Section 4.2.1), an absolute minority in comparison with the 289 occurences of conditional-converb structures expressing conditionality.

(4.1-3)

gene-ci,	*uthai*	*hūdun*	*jio*
go-COND	then	quick	come. IMP

If (you) go (there), then come (back) quickly! (UH: 17)

(4.1-4)

suwe	*te-de*	*acana-ci*,	*mim-be*	*guile-fi*
2PL	3SG-DAT	go. to. meet-COND	1SG(*bi/min*)-ACC	invite-PFV. CVB
sasa	*yo-ki*			
together	go-OPT			

If you go to meet him, take me (and) let's go together. (MFG: 16)

(4.1-5)

age	*si*	*mim-be*	*wakaša-ci*,	*bi*	*yala*	*sui mangga*
sir	2SG	1SG(*bi/min*)-ACC	blame-COND	1SG	really	wronged

sui mangga: wronged, done injustice to; *sui*: guilt, sin; *mangga*: difficult

Sir, if you blame me, I (will be) really wronged. (OJ2: 116)

(4.1-6)

ere	*juwe*	*amban*	*be*	*wa-ci*,	*min-i*
these	two	high. official	ACC	kill-COND	1SG(*bi/min*)-GEN
beye	*inu*	*buce-he*	*gese*	*kai*	
self	also	die-PFV. PTCP	like	PTL	

If (you) kill these two generals (of mine), (I will) also (be) as dead myself. (MYK3: 24)

When a factual conditional has a negative protasis, its subordinate predicate is a complex structure. When it contains a verb, the subordinate predicate consists of the negative imperfective participle (V-*rakū*) and *o-ci*, the conditional converb (V-*ci*) of the verb *o-* "to become/be", used as an auxiliary verb. When no verb is involved, the subordinate predicate consists of the negative particle, *akū*, and the conditional converb of the verb *o-*. Examples (4.1-7)-(4.1-10) below contain lexical verbs in the subordinate clauses, while (4.1-11) and (4.1-12) do not. The forms of the main predicates include the imperfective finite form [(4.1-7) and (4.1-11)], the imperfective participles [negative in (4.1-8), affirmative in (4.1-9)], and the imperatives (4.1-10) and (4.1-12)].

(4.1-7)

daha-rakū	*o-ci*,	*be*	*afa-mbi*
surrender-IPFV. PTCP. NEG	become(AUX)-COND	1PL. EXCL	attack-IPFV. FIN

If (you) do not surrender, we shall attack (you). (MYK6: 10)

(4.1-8) *min-i* *ere* *uniyen* *tukšan* *banji-rakū*
1SG(*bi/min*)-GEN this cow calf give.birth-IPFV.PTCP.NEG
o-ci, *ayara* *nimenggi* *baha-rakū*
be(AUX)-COND sour.milk fat obtain-IPFV.PTCP.NEG
nimenggi: "fat", here referring to butter.
If this cow of mine does not give birth to calves, (I shall) not (be able to) obtain sour milk or butter. (SG: 266)

(4.1-9) *turgun* *be* *tucibu-me* *ala-rakū* *o-ci*,
reason ACC reveal-IPFV.CVB tell-IPFV.PTCP.NEG become(AUX)-COND
ainambaha-fi *sa-ra*
how.can-PFV.CVB know-IPFV.PTCP
If (you) do not reveal the reason (to me), how can (I) know (it)? (OJ1: 104)

(4.1-10) *giyan* *de* *acana-rakū* *o-ci*, *uthai*
principle DAT suit-IPFV.PTCP.NEG become(AUX)-COND then
naka-ø
stop-IMP
If (the matter) does not suit (our) principles, then stop (handling it)! (MFG: 11)

(4.1-11) *jete-re* *jeku* *akū* *o-ci*,
eat-IPFV.PTCP provisions NEG become(AUX)-COND
muse-i *jušen* *gemu* *ubaša-mbi* *kai*
1PL.INCL-GEN subjects all rebel-IPFV.FIN PTL
If there are no provisions, our subjects will all rebel (against us). (MYK1: 47)

(4.1-12) *min-i* *hese* *akū* *o-ci*, *ume*
1SG(*bi/min*)-GEN order NEG become(AUX)-COND do.not
tucibu-re
release-IPFV.PTCP
ume V-rA: negative imperative (or, prohibitive) structure
If (you) do not (have) my order, do not release (her)! (NSB: 92)

Apart from the factual conditionals with negative protases discussed above, the subordinate predicate can also have a complex structure even when a factual conditional has an affirmative protasis. Semantically, there is no difference between such a conditional and a conditional with a simple predicate in the protasis. The complex subordinate predicate in question consists of the imperfective participle (V-*rA*) and the conditional converb of the auxiliary verb *o*-. The following are examples.

(4.1-13)

jiha	*menggun*	*i*	*uda-fi*	*etu-re*
money	silver	GEN	buy-PFV.CVB	wear-IPFV.PTCP
o-ci,	*niyalma*	*oforo*	*deri*	*suk seme*
become(AUX)-COND	people	nose	ABL	snorting
inje-mbi	kai			
laugh-IPFV.FIN	PTL			

suk seme inje-: to laugh through the nose while trying to hold a straight face

If (you) buy (the clothes) with money and wear them, people will laugh at you (through the nose). (OJ2: 54)

(4.1-14)

ali-me	*gaisu*	*manggi*	*geli*	*angga*	*aifu-re*
accept-IPFV.CVB	take.IMP	after	then	mouth	break.word-IPFV.PTCP
o-ci,	*niyalma*	*jai*	*adarame*	*sin-i*	
become(AUX)-COND	people	again	how	2SG(*si/sin*)-GEN	
gisun	*be*	*akda-mbi*			
words	ACC	believe-IPFV.FIN			

ali-me gai-: to accept, to make a promise

angga aifu-: to break one's word

If (you), after making a promise, break (your) word, how can people believe your words again? (OJ2: 60)

Factual conditionals can also have another type of complex predicate in the subordinate clause, which consists of the verb *se-* "to say" (as an auxiliary verb) and a preceding verb structure that it governs (usually the optative form V-*ki*), as shown in the following examples. The forms of the main predicate [the imperfective participle V-*rA* in (4.1-15) and the imperative in (4.1-16)] also occurred in previous examples [(4.1-9) and (4.1-10), respectively].

(4.1-15)

age	*tuwa-ki*	*se-ci,*	*bi*	*bene-bu-re*
sir	look-OPT	say(AUX)-COND	1SG	send-CAUS-IPFV.PTCP

V-*ki se-*: complex structure expressing desire or intention

Sir, if you want to read (this book), I'll have someone send (it to you). (OJ2: 110)

(4.1-16)

min-i	*emgi*	*banji-ki*	*se-ci,*	*juwe*	*juse*
1SG(*bi/min*)-GEN	together	live-OPT	say(AUX)-COND	two	children

be *bošo-ø*!
ACC expel-IMP
If (you) want to live together with me, expel (those) two children! (SG: 417)

Besides the syntactic patterns of factual conditionals shown by all the previous examples, there also exist numerous factual conditionals that contain the conditional connector *aika/aikabade*[1] in the protases. It occurs before the conditional converb, either in the sentence-initial position or following some other components (such as the subject or the object, the adverbial, and so forth). This connector, which approximately corresponds to the English conjunction *if*, forms a framed structure with the subordinate predicate. The following are some examples.

(4.1-17) *aikabade* *in-i* *baru* *emu* *gūnin* *mujilen-i*
if 3SG(*i/in*)-GEN toward one thought mind-GEN
baita *be* *hebdene-ci*, *damu* *oilori deleri*
matter ACC go.to.discuss-COND only superficial
se-me *jabu-mbi*
say(AUX)-IPFV.CVB reply-IPFV.FIN
oilori deleri se-me: superficially, perfunctorily
If (you) go to discuss something (that is) on your mind, (he) will only reply to you perfunctorily. (MFG: 7)

(4.1-18) *age* *si* *enenggi* *aikabade* *min-i* *boo-de*
sir 2SG today if 1SG(*bi/min*)-GEN house-DAT
dosi-rakū *o-ci*, *bi* *yargiyan-i*
enter-IPFV.PTCP.NEG become(AUX)-COND 1SG real-GEN
sim-be *usha-mbi*
2SG(*si/sin*)-ACC be.angry-IPFV.FIN
yargiyan i: really
Sir, if you don't come into my house today, I will be really angry with you. (MFG: 49)

---

① The conditional connector aika can also function as an indefinite determiner (some, (a) certain) or pronoun "something" and *aikabade* < *aika* + *ba-de* [place-DAT], can also function as an indefinite adverbial, literally meaning "at a certain place".

(4.1-19)	*aika*	*icakū*	*ba*	*bi-ci*,	*majige*	*joriša-me*
	if	inappropriate	place	be-COND	a. little	point. out-IPFV. CVB
	tuwancihiya-ø					
	correct-IMP					

If there is anything inappropriate (in my shooting posture), please point (it) out a little bit and correct (me)! (OJ1: 40)

(4.1-20)	*sin-i*	*boo-de*	*aika*	*mihan*	*yali*	*niongniyaha*
	2SG(*si/sin*)-GEN	house-DAT	if	young. pig	meat	goose
	yali	*bi-ci*,	*bi*	*dosi-fi*	*je-ki*	
	meat	be-COND	1SG	enter-PFV. CVB	eat-OPT	

If there is the meat of young pigs or of geese in your house, I would like to go in and eat. (MFG: 49)

From a comparison of (4.1-1)-(4.1-16) with (4.1-17)-(4.1-20), one can see that in order to express the conditional meaning, the connector *aika/aikabade* seems to be dispensable in the protasis. However, the presence of *aika/aikabade* in the frame structures that contain the conditional converb V-*ci* reinforces the conditional interpretation of the sentences.

Factual conditionals containing *aika/aikabade* are in a sense similar to factual conditionals in European languages, though there are also important differences. First, the subordinate predicates of Manchu conditionals contain the conditional converb (V-*ci*) and are therefore not finite forms, while conditionals in European languages mostly contain finite verb forms in the protases. Second, the syntactic position of the conditional connector *aika/aikabade* within the protasis is rather flexible [see (4.1-17)-(4.1-20)], while the conditional conjunctions in European languages (English *if*, French *si*, and German *wenn*) are always clause-initial.

Table 4.1 is a summary of the morphosyntactic patterns of factual conditionals as shown in examples (4.1-1)-(4.1-20). "Subj1" and "Pred1" represent the subject and the predicate in the subordinate clause (protasis), while "Subj2" and "Pred2" stand for the subject and the predicate in the main clause (apodosis). Despite different numbering, "Subj1" and "Subj2" do not necessarily refer to different entities. Both of them are put in parentheses since Manchu allows the omission of subjects. It should also be noted that these syntactic patterns do not necessarily exhaust all the possibilities of combination between the subordinate and the main clauses.

Table 4.1 Basic Morphosyntactic Patterns of Factual Conditionals

Subordinate Clause (Protasis)	Main Clause (Apodosis)	Example
{(Subj1+) Pred1 [V-*ci*]}	{(Subj2+) Pred2 [V-*mbi*]}	(4.1-1) and (4.1-2)
	{(Subj2+) Pred2 [V-IMP]}	(4.1-3)
	{(Subj2+) Pred2 [V-OPT]}	(4.1-4)
	{(Subj2+) Pred2 [N]}	(4.1-5) and (4.1-6)
{(Subj1+) Pred1 [V-*rakū o-ci*]}	{(Subj2+) Pred2 [V-*mbi*]}	(4.1-7)
	{(Subj2+) Pred2 [V-*rakū*]}	(4.1-8)
	{(Subj2+) Pred2 [V-*rA*]}	(4.1-9)
	{(Subj2+) Pred2 [V-IMP]}	(4.1-10)
{(Subj1+) Pred1 [*akū o-ci*]}	{(Subj2+) Pred2 [V-*mbi*]}	(4.1-11)
	{(Subj2+) Pred2 [V-IMP]}	(4.1-12)
{(Subj1+) Pred1 [V-*rA o-ci*]}	{(Subj2+) Pred2 [V-*mbi*] (+*kai*)}	(4.1-13) and (4.1-14)
{(Subj1+) Pred1 [V-*ki se-ci*]}	{(Subj2+) Pred2 [V-*rA*]}	(4.1-15)
	{(Subj2+) Pred2 [V-IMP]}	(4.1-16)
{(Subj1+) aika/*aikabade* +Pred1 [V-*ci*]}	{(Subj2+) Pred2 [V-*mbi*]}	(4.1-17)
	{(Subj2+) Pred2 [V-IMP]}	(4.1-19)
	{(Subj2+) Pred2 [V-OPT]}	(4.1-20)
{(Subj1+) *aika*/*aikabade* +Pred1[V-*rakū o-ci*]}	{(Subj2+) Pred2 [V-*mbi*]}	(4.1-18)

4.1.1.2 Interpretation

Despite the term, a factual conditional does not describe a fact known by the speaker. Rather, the speaker of a factual conditional generally indicates that the states of affairs are not realised yet and suggests that the states of affairs are still realisable. What the speaker does confirm is the relation between two states of affairs, one of which serves as a precondition or cause for the other state of affairs. For instance, in (4.1-7), the protasis state of affairs—the addressee's refusal to surrender—will be the cause for the apodosis state of affairs—the speaker's launching an attack on the addressee.

While the protases always have propositional content, the apodoses do not necessarily constitute propositions, but are speech acts other than statements: the apodosis of (4.1-9) is a question, the apodosis of (4.1-20) expresses a wish, and the apodoses of (4.1-3), (4.1-4), (4.1-10), (4.1-12), (4.1-16) and (4.1-19) are requests. Nevertheless, the conditional relation is present in these cases as well. For instance, in (4.1-9), the protasis state of affairs—the addressee's not revealing the reason—will be the cause for the speaker's speech act of asking a question. In (4.1-10), the protasis state of affairs—the matter's violation of principles—will be the cause for the speaker's speech act of requesting the addressee to stop handling the matter.

The predicate structures of both clauses of all the constructions [(4.1-1)-(4.1-20)]—especially the structures of the main predicates, due to the relative nature and dependence of the subordinate predicates—contribute to their interpretation as factual conditionals. The structures of the main predicates tend to describe states of affairs that take place at present or in the future by default. Specifically, the imperfective finite form (V-*mbi*), the imperfective participles [affirmative V-*rA* as in (4.1-9), and negative V-*rakū* as in (4.1-8)] or imperative in the apodosis of a conditional would be expected to describe a general state of affairs or an ongoing action (in the case of the imperfective finite form), or a state of affairs that is yet to start (in the case of the imperative). On the other hand, in the case of an apodosis with a non-verbal—more exactly, nominal—main predicate [e.g., in (4.1-5)], the protasis would describe a state of affairs that does not trigger an interpretation about the past unless indicated by a past temporal adverbial.

However, it should be stressed that the morphosyntactic characteristics of predicate structures as discussed above do not necessarily guarantee a (factual) conditional interpretation. In Manchu there exist various constructions which share morphosyntactic characteristics with factual conditionals, but express different meanings (such as temporality or concession) or realise different functions (such as comparison, topicalisation, and so forth).[①] Therefore, although all of the examples analysed so far are the most common factual conditionals in Manchu, the identification of their prototypes requires more constraints from semantics as well as the context. Section 5.1 will point out that the conditional connector *aika/aikabade* is also important in establishing the morphosyntactic criteria for prototypes of factual conditionals.

4.1.2 Basic Counterfactual Conditionals

4.1.2.1 Morphosyntax

The protases of counterfactual conditionals always have complex predicates containing the conditional converb of the verb *bi-* "to exist/be" (as an auxiliary verb), *bi-ci*, which can follow a variety of verb forms (as can be seen in the examples below). Such verb forms themselves vary in complexity, but in general they can be divided into two types according to their grammatical polarity: affirmative and negative. The least complex type of all subordinate predicates consists of the perfective participle of a lexical verb (V-*hA*) and *bi-ci*. The following are some examples [(4.1-22) was also discussed in Section 3.2.2.3].

(4.1-21) *donji-ha* *bi-ci*, *inu* *tuwanji-mbihe*
hear-PFV.PTCP be(AUX)-COND also come.to.see-PST.IPFV
If (I) had heard (your news), (I) would also have come to see (you).
(OJ1: 89)

(4.1-22) *tere* *inenggi* <u>*baha*</u> <u>*bi-ci*</u>, *sim-be*
that day get.PFV.PTCP be(AUX)-COND 2SG(*si/sin*)-ACC
<u>*wa-mbihe*</u>

① Such constructions are analysed in other sections of this chapter.

kill-PST. IPFV

If (I) had captured (you) that day, I would have killed you. (MYK2: 46)

(4. 1-23) *gūwa niyalma o-ho bi-ci, aina-ha*

other person become-PFV. PTCP be(AUX)-COND do. what-PFV. PTCP

se-me tuwa-rakū bi-he

say(AUX)-IPFV. CVB look-IPFV. PTCP. NEG be(AUX)-PFV. PTCP

ainaha seme: absolutely, by any means (always used with negation)

tuwa-: here meaning "to prophesy", lit: "to look [into someone's destiny]"

If (he) were anybody else, (I) would absolutely not prophesy (for him). (NSB: 27)

(4. 1-24) *weri i jombu-ha be majige gai-ha*

other. people GEN advise-PFV. PTCP ACC a. little take-PFV. PTCP

bi-ci, inu e-de tuhene-rakū bi-he

be(AUX)-COND also this-DAT fall-IPFV. PTCP. NEG be(AUX)-PFV. PTCP

If (you) had taken even a little advice from other people, (you) would not have fallen into this (trap). (AGA3: 35)

(4. 1-25) *sa-ha bi-ci, aifini sim-be*

know-PFV. PTCP be(AUX)-COND long. ago 2SG(*si*/*sin*)-ACC

tuwanji-rakū bi-he-o

come. to. see-IPFV. PTCP. NEG be(AUX)-PFV. PTCP-Q

If (I) had known (that you lived here), wouldn't (I) have come to see you long ago? (OJ1: 24)

The main predicates of counterfactual conditionals, as shown by (4. 1-21)-(4. 1-25), have one type of structure each for either polarity. The predicate of an affirmative apodosis [see (4. 1-21) and (4. 1-22)] consists of the past imperfective form V-*mbihe*, which, as argued in (2) in Section 3. 2. 2. 2, is a complex form consisting of the imperfective converb (V-*me*) and the perfective participle of the verb *bi-* ("to exist/be"), *bi-he*. The predicate of a negative apodosis [see (4. 1-23)-(4. 1-25)][①] consists of the negative imperfective participle (V-*rakū*) and *bi-he*.

---

① Though the main clause of (4. 1-25) is a question, it is formed by attaching the sentence-final question particle *o-* directly to the main predicate—a negative verb structure, V-*rakū bi-he*. Thus, the analysis here of negative apodosis also applies to (4. 1-25).

When the protases of counterfactual conditionals are affirmative, they can also use structures that are still more complex, but are derived from the structure V-*hA bi-ci*. One such type of predicate structure consists of the past imperfective form V-*mbihe* (=V-*me bi-he*) and *bi-ci*. In (4.1-26) (also discussed in Section 3.2.2.3), the main predicate is a complex structure (V-*ci aca-*) expressing modality "to be obligated to", where the auxiliary verb *aca-* is in the past imperfective form V-*mbihe*.

(4.1-26)

donji-mbihe	*bi-ci*,	*urgun*	*i*	*doro-i*
hear-PST. IPFV	be(AUX)-COND	happiness	GEN	rite-GEN

acana-me	*gene-ci*	*aca-mbihe*
go. to. meet-IPFV. CVB	go-COND	suit(AUX)-PST. IPFV

urgun i doro: congratulations, lit.: "the rite of happiness"

V-*ci aca-*: complex structure expressing obligation

If (I) had heard (your good news), (I) should have gone to meet (you and give my) congratulations. (MFG: 7)

Another such type of predicate structure consists of the imperfective participle (V-*rA*), followed by *bi-he*, which in turn is followed by *bi-ci*. Compared with the complex structure V-*hA bi-ci*, this structure is rarely used in protases. In the following example, the main predicate is a complex verb structure expressing the modal meaning "to be possible", which is formed by the verb *o-* in the past imperfective form.

(4.1-27)

aika	*muduri*	*gurung*	*ni*	*amdun*	*baha-ra*
if	dragon	palace	GEN	glue	obtain-IPFV. PTCP

bi-he	*bi-ci*,	*giranggi*	*jalan*	*be*
be(AUX)-PFV. PTCP	be(AUX)-COND	bone	joint	ACC

jalga-fi,	*yali*	*sukū*	*banjibu-ci*
put. together-PFV. CVB	flesh	skin	generate-COND

o-mbihe

become(AUX)-PST. IPFV

V-*ci o-*: complex structure expressing permission or possibility

If (you) had obtained the glue of the Dragon Palace, and (using it) put together the joints of bones, (you) could have regenerated (your) flesh and skin. (LJ11: 75)

It should be noted that (4. 1-27) uses the conditional connector *aika* in its protasis, forming a framed structure with its subordinate predicate, just as in numerous factual conditionals discussed in Section 4. 1. 1. 1. However, it seems that the connector *aika* occurs less frequently in counterfactual conditionals than in factual conditionals.

When counterfactual conditionals have negative protases, there are a variety of structures that are used for the subordinate predicates. First, the least complex structure consists of a negative participle [either imperfective V-*rakū* as in (4. 1-28), or the perfective V-*hAkū* as in (4. 1-29)] and *bi-ci*. The following are two examples. The main predicate of (4. 1-28) consists of the negative imperfective participle of *o*- "to be/become" [just as in (4. 1-27)] and *bi-he*. In (4. 1-29), the main predicate is the past imperfective form V-*me bi-he*. Both structures of the main predicate also occurred in previous examples of counterfactual conditionals [(4. 1-21)-(4. 1-28)].

(4. 1-28) *bi moo-i funghūwang ara-rakū bi-ci,*
1SG wood-GEN phoenix make-IPFV. PTCP. NEG be(AUX)-COND
fujin be boo leose ci tucibu-ci
lady ACC house building ABL rescue-CAUS-COND
ojo-rakū bi-he
become(AUX)-IPFV. PTCP. NEG be(AUX)-PFV. PTCP
V-*ci ojo-rakū*: here meaning "not to be able to do something", the negation of the structure V-*ci o*-, expressing permission/likelihood
If I had not made the wooden phoenix, (we) could not have rescued the lady out of the building. (SG: 245-246)

(4. 1-29) *min-i jui be dahūme aitu-hakū*
1SG(*bi/min*)-GEN child ACC again save-PFV. PTCP. NEG
bi-ci, fulehe lakca-me bi-he
be(AUX)-COND root be. severed-IPFV. CVB be(AUX)-PFV. PTCP

dahūme aitu-: to revive, lit.: "to save (one to let one live) again"
If you had not revived my child, the root (of my family) would have been severed. (NSB: 87)

Second, other counterfactual conditionals with negative protases have predicate structures that are more complex, consisting of a negative participle [either imperfective as in (4.1-30) and (4.1-31), or perfective as in (4.1-32)], followed by *bi-he*, and then the conditional converb of *bi-*. Their main predicates, both affirmative (4.1-30) and negative [(4.1-31) and (4.1-32)], also repeat the structural patterns discussed in previous examples.

(4.1-30) *Nomina* *Naikada* *alana-rakū* *bi-he*
PN PN go.to.tell-IPFV.PTCP.NEG be(AUX)-PFV.PTCP
bi-ci, *Nikan Wailan* *be* *baha-mbihe*
be(AUX)-COND PN ACC get-PST.IPFV
If Nomina and Naikada had not gone to inform (him), (we) would have caught Nikan Wailan. (MYK1: 36)

(4.1-31) *bi* *jakan* *giyalame giyalame* *sin-de*
1SG just.now intermittently 2SG(*si*/*sin*)-DAT
jombu-rakū *bi-he* *bi-ci*, *si*
remind-IPFV.PTCP.NEG be(AUX)-PFV.PTCP be(AUX)-COND 2SG
kemuni *wacihiyame* *šejile-me* *mute-rakū*
still completely recite-IPFV.CVB be.able-IPFV.PTCP.NEG
bi-he
be(AUX)-PFV.PTCP
If I had not reminded you from time to time, you would still have been unable to recite (it) completely. (ASA1: 54)

(4.1-32) *taci-hakū* *bi-he* *bi-ci*, *inu*
learn-PFV.PTCP.NEG be(AUX)-PFV.PTCP be(AUX)-COND also
ulhi-me *mute-rakū* *bi-he*
understand-IPFV.CVB be.able-PFV.PTCP.NEG be(AUX)-PFV.PTCP
If (I) hadn't learnt it, (I) wouldn't have been able to understand it. (UH: 30)

Table 4. 2 is a summary of the morphosyntactic patterns of counterfactual conditionals as shown in examples (4. 1-21)-(4. 1-32). Some complex structures expressing modal meanings, such as V-*ci o-* "to be likely to", V-*ci aca-* "to be obligated to", and V-*me mute-* "to be able to", are indicated due to their frequent occurrence in the main clauses. Table 4. 2 does not necessarily exhaust all the possibilities of combination between the subordinate and the main clauses.

Table 4. 2 Basic Morphosyntactic Patterns of Counterfactual Conditionals

Subordinate Clause (Protasis)	Main Clause (Apodosis)	Example
{(Subj1+) Pred1 [V-*hA bi-ci*]}	{(Subj2+) Pred2 [V-*mbihe*]}	(4. 1-21), (4. 1-22)
	{(Subj2+) Pred2 [V-*rakū bi-he*]}	(4. 1-23)-(4. 1-25)
{(Subj1+) Pred1 [V-*mbihe bi-ci*]}	{(Subj2+) Pred2 [V-*mbihe*]}	(4. 1-26)
{(Subj1+) (*aika/aikabade*+) Pred1 [V-*rA bi-he bi-ci*]}	{(Subj2+) Pred2 [V-*ci o-mbihe*]}	(4. 1-27)
{(Subj1+) Pred1 [V-*rakū bi-ci*]}	{(Subj2+) Pred2 [V-*ci ojo-rakū bi-he*]}	(4. 1-28)
{(Subj1+) Pred1 [V-*hakū bi-ci*]}	{(Subj2+) Pred2 [V-*me bi-he*]}	(4. 1-29)
{(Subj1+) Pred1 [V-*rakū bi-he bi-ci*]}	{(Subj2+) Pred2 [V-*mbi*he]}	(4. 1-30)
{(Subj1+) Pred1 [V-*rakū bi-he bi-ci*]}	{(Subj2+) Pred2 [V-*me mute-rakū bi-he*]}	(4. 1-31)
{(Subj1+) Pred1 [V-*hAkū bi-he bi-ci*]}	{(Subj2 +) Pred2 [V-*me*+V*mute-rakū bi-he*]}	(4. 1-32)

4.1.2.2 Interpretation

In each of sentences (4. 1-21)-(4. 1-32) the speaker imagines a world different from his or her own in that the states of affairs realised in his or her own world (the "real" world) were or are not realised in this imagined world, and vice versa. Such states of affairs can concern the past, the present or the future, depending on the specific context. For instance, in

(4.1-21), the (unreal) protasis state of affairs (that is, the speaker's hearing about the news), and the (unreal) resulting apodosis state of affairs (that is, the speaker's coming to visit the addressee), are both set in the past (of the imagined world). On the other hand, in (4.1-23), the (unreal) state of affairs in the protasis (that is, the addressee's being someone else), is set in the present (of the imagined world), and the (unreal) apodosis state of affairs (that is, the speaker's not prophesying for the addressee) is set in the present/near future (of the imagined world). In all the counterfactual conditionals, the conditional relation per se is no different from that in factual conditionals.

A question naturally arises as to how the counterfactual meaning emerges from these constructions. Since the apodoses of all the counterfactual conditionals, as well as the protases of some [(4.1-26), (4.1-27), (4.1-31) and (4.1-32)], contain *bi-he* in their complex predicates, it is important to shed light on the meaning of *bi-he*, and of the structures it forms. As stated in Section 3.2.2.1, *bi-he* is the perfective participle of the verb *bi-* "to exist/be" is closely related to the temporal meaning pastness. The complex structures formed by *bi-he*, such as V-*mbihe* (V-*me bi-he*), V-*rAkū bi-he*, and V-*hAkū bi-he*, also integrate pastness into their meaning, when they serve as predicates in simple sentences. On the other hand, in conditionals (4.1-21)-(4.1-32), the counterfactual meaning is expressed. It is then reasonable to assume that the combination of complex structures formed by *bi-he* and conditionality (represented by the conditional converb V-*ci*) gives rise to counterfactual conditionality.

Comrie (1986) notes that the back-shifting of tense is used to indicate hypotheticality in European languages. The English examples "If he came, I would run away" and "If he had come, I would have run away"(Comrie 1986: 94) suffice to illustrate this mechanism. Similarly in Manchu, the complex structures containing *bi-he* can also be seen as the back-shifting of tense, since *bi-he* is associated with past temporality. The phenomenon can be understood in a broader framework proposed by Fleischman (1989), who explores the cross-linguistic usage of temporal distance for indicating modality, social distance, evidentiality, and so on. Thus, the past marker *bi-he* in Manchu can be considered as an indicator of the modal distance of counterfactuality from reality.

Furthermore, Van linden and Verstraete (2008), investigating simple counterfactual constructions in some 40 languages, note that counterfactuality is usually expressed by a combination of modal markers and tense or aspect markers, and that the counterfactual meaning itself is derived from a scalar implicature triggered by the contrast between modal and corresponding non-modal constructions. The mechanism works in the following way. When one utters a modal sentence, for example, "John should have come yesterday", one usually implies that John did not come, where the implicature is triggered by the contrast between this modal sentence and the non-modal sentence "John came yesterday". Van linden and Verstraete (2008) argue that the speaker usually knows about the past with certainty; therefore, according to the Gricean maxim of quantity, if it were the speaker's belief that John did come yesterday, the speaker would produce the non-modal sentence "John came yesterday" instead, which is epistemically stronger than the modal sentence "John should have come yesterday". Assuming that the speaker has given enough information about the past state of affairs, and since he or she chooses the modal sentence, the speaker must have a reason for not uttering the non-modal (indicative) sentence. The implicature that John did not come is thus triggered. ①

Returning to the counterfactual conditionals in Manchu, one can see the same pattern as explained by Van linden and Verstraete (2008), since conditionality is a type of irrealis modality. First, the perfective participle *bi-he*, which is used primarily as a past marker when attached to a verb structure, occurs in the main clause of a conditional construction. With the subordinate clause expressing supposition (via structures of V-*ci*), the

① Van linden and Verstraete (2008) also point out that there is an additional layer to the implicature in that when one says John should have come, the original (deontic) modal meaning of obligation is still present: one thinks that John was supposed to come, though he actually did not. However, this additional meaning is less related to the current discussion of counterfactuality.

whole construction would be expected to exhibit weaker certainty than does a simple sentence not expressing supposition. Second, in some constructions, complex verb structures expressing obligation (4. 1-26) or possibility [(4. 1-27) and (4. 1-28)] are used in the main clauses, further weakening the certainty of the utterances. Therefore, these constructions tend to imply the counterfactual conditional meaning.

In addition, the morphosyntactic contrast between the complex structures of the subordinate predicates V-*hA bi-ci* [in (4. 1-21)-(4. 1-25)], V-*rakū/hAkū bi-ci* [in (4. 1-28) and (4. 1-29)], V-*rakū/hAkū bi-he bi-ci* [in (4. 1-30)-(4. 1-32)] and so forth on the one hand, and the structures of subordinate predicates such as V-*ci* or V-*rakū o-ci*, on the other, also contributes to expressing the counterfactual meaning. The reason is that the latter type of predicate structures is common among factual conditionals, and the morphosyntactic contrast would be expected to bring about a contrast in meaning. Thus, the conditionals using the former type of predicate structures would be distinct from factual conditionals; in Manchu, they present themselves as counterfactual conditionals.

This morphosyntactic dichotomy seems to exclude the existence of hypothetical conditionals from Manchu, which are located between factual and counterfactual conditions on the axis of the speaker's belief about reality. In fact, however, Manchu is able to conceptualise a low possibility of future states of affairs occurring, which is typical of hypothetical conditionals. Yet, such constructions are indistinguishable from factual conditionals in terms of morphosyntax, but are only interpretable as expressing hypothetical conditions via the context. For instance, in its context, (4. 1-6) also allows a hypothetical interpretation, which can be translated as "if (you) killed these two generals (of mine), (I would) also (be) as dead myself." The following are sentence (4. 1-6) repeated here and another example that allows the hypothetical interpretation.

(4.1-6)

ere	*juwe*	*amban*	*be*	*wa-ci*,	*min-i*
these	two	high.official	ACC	kill-COND	1SG(*bi/min*)-GEN
beye	*inu*	*buce-he*		*gese*	*kai*
self	also	die-PFV.PTCP		like	PTL

If (you) kill these two generals (of mine), (I will) also (be) as dead myself. (MYK3: 24)

(4.1-33)

niyalma	*gemu*	*sin-i*	*adali*	*o-me*
people	all	2SG(*si/sin*)-GEN	like	become-IPFV.CVB
mute-ci,		*ai*	*bai-re*	
be.able-COND		what	request-IPFV.PTCP	

If people can/could all become (excellent) like you, what (else will/would one) request (of them)? (OJ1: 40)

However, examples such as (4.1-6) and (4.1-33) are not numerous in Manchu, and as pointed out, their interpretation is always dependent on the context. Therefore, hypothetical conditionals in Manchu do not constitute a distinctive morphosyntactic category, and are therefore unlikely to have identifiable prototypes.

Returning to the morphosyntax of counterfactual conditionals, both complex structures of the subordinate predicate containing *bi-ci* and those containing *bi-he* prove to have distinctive characteristics. However, in Section 4.3 it will be shown that the complex structure V-*hA bi-ci* also occurs commonly in temporal constructions. On the other hand, the occurrence of the structures formed by *bi-he* in conditionals qualifies as a morphosyntactically sufficient (but not necessary; see Section 4.2) condition for the counterfactual interpretation. This naturally leads to the identification of the prototypes for counterfactual conditionals. As pointed out in Section 4.1.2.1, in counterfactual conditionals the conditional connector *aika/aikabade* is not used as frequently as in factual conditionals. Identifying the prototypes for counterfactual conditionals would require the occurrence of complex structures containing *bi-ci* in the subordinate clauses and those of *bi-he* in the main clauses. This issue will be addressed in Section 5.1 along with the prototypes of factual conditionals.

4. 2 Non-prototypical Conditional Constructions

Apart from the basic patterns of conditional constructions analysed in Section 4. 1, various other constructions serve to express the conditional relation. These constructions differ morphosyntactically from the basic patterns in one respect or another and occur less frequently in comparison to the basic patterns. They are regarded as "non-prototypical conditional constructions", although the very prototypes of conditionals are yet to be identified (see Section 5. 1). The reason is that the prototypes are selected from the basic "candidate" patterns as shown in Section 4. 1; since the conditional constructions in question are distinct from those basic patterns, they are not likely to be considered to be prototypes of conditionals. This section analyses these constructions in two groups—factual and counterfactual conditionals—according to their meanings.

4. 2. 1 Factual Conditionals

4. 2. 1. 1 Morphosyntax

Generally speaking, the factual conditionals grouped here all use structures formed with the perfective participle in dative-locative (V-*hA de*) in the protases, instead of structures containing the conditional converb (V-*ci*). The following are some examples in which V is a lexical verb. Note that (4. 2-4) has the conditional connector *aikabade*, highlighting the conditional meaning.

(4. 2-1) *da* *sekiyen* *be* *tucibu-he-de*, *geli* *mim-be*
root source ACC reveal-PFV. PTCP-DAT again 1SG(*bi/min*)-ACC
fetereku *se-mbi*
fastidious say-IPFV. FIN
da sekiyen: fundamental things, lit.: "root and source"
If (I) reveal everything (about him), (he) will think I am fastidious (about him). (OJ2: 138)

(4.2-2) *beise-i* *beye* *emke* *juwe* *tuhe-ke* *de*, *tere* *cooha*
leaders-GEN self one two fall-PFV. PTCP DAT those troops
uthai *burula-mbi* *kai*
then flee-IPFV. FIN PTL
If one or two of (their) leaders fall, then those troops will surely flee.
(MYK2: 43)

(4.2-3) *si* *tuttu* *te-he-de*, *bi* *absi* *te-mbi*
2SG like. that sit-PFV. PTCP-DAT 1SG how sit-IPFV. FIN
If/When you sit down like that, how will I sit? (OJ1: 25)

(4.2-4) *si* *aikabade* *daila-ha* *de*, *bi*
2SG if wage. war-PFV. PTCP DAT 1SG
sim-be *tookabu-mbi*
2SG(*si*/*sin*)-ACC destroy-IPFV. FIN
If you wage war (against me), I will destroy you. (MYK6: 25)

While in (4.2-1) and (4.2-2) the lexical verbs in the structure V-*hA de* are used in the subordinate clauses and serve as affirmative predicates, the verb *o*- (as an auxiliary verb) can also be used in the structure *o-ho-de* to constitute complex predicates. They can be either affirmative or negative, depending on the verb form preceding the auxiliary *o*-: the imperfective converb (V-*me*) is used in an affirmative protasis (4.2-5), while the negative imperfective participle (V-*rakū*) is used in a negative protasis [(4.2-6) and (4.2-7)] as shown below. Similarly to (4.2-4), (4.2-5) also uses a conditional connector [*aikabade* in (4.2-4), and *aika* in (4.2-5)].

(4.2-5) *bi* *aika* *sin-de* *emu* *baita* *fonji-me*
1SG if 2SG(*si*/*sin*)-DAT one matter ask-IPFV. CVB
o-ho-de, *si* *uthai* *sa-rkū*
become(AUX)-PFV. PTCP-DAT 2SG then know-IPFV. PTCP. NEG
se-re, *donji-hakū* *se-re*
say-IPFV. PTCP hear-PFV. PTCP. NEG say-IPFV. PTCP
sarkū < *sa-rakū* < *sa-ra* [know-IPFV. PTCP] + *akū* [NEG]
If I ask you (about) something, then you will say you don't know or you haven't heard (about that). (MFG: 6)

(4.2-6)

bi	*eici*	*gene-rakū*	*o-ho-de*,
1SG	or	go-IPFV. PTCP. NEG	become(AUX)-PFV. PTCP-DAT
si	*geli*	*mim-be*	*wakala-mbi-o*
2SG	still	1SG(*bi/min*)-ACC	blame-IPFV. FIN-Q

Or if I do not go, will you then blame me? (MFG: 39)

(4.2-7)

ere	*cooha*	*be*	*gida-rakū*	*o-ho-de*,
this	army	ACC	defeat-IPFV. PTCP. NEG	become(AUX)-PFV. PTCP-DAT
mim-be	*wa*			
1SG(*bi/min*)-ACC	kill-IMP			

If (I) can't defeat this army, kill me! (MYK2: 41)

In some other constructions expressing the conditional meaning, the quotative verb *se-* "to say" (as an auxiliary verb; see Section 3.2.4) also occurs in the structure V-*hA-de*. The verb *se-* (in the form *se-he-de*) in turn takes a finite clause as its complement, whose predicate is in the form of the perfective participle (of a lexical verb). The following are some examples.

(4.2-8)

tere-i	*hūbin*	*de*	*dosi-ka*
that/3SG-GEN	trap	DAT	enter-PFV. PTCP
se-he-de,	*sarba-tala*	*o-mbi*	
say(AUX)-PFV. PTCP-DAT	writhe-TERM	become-IPFV. FIN	

hūbin de dosi-: to fall into a trap

sarba-tala o-: to end up writhing (with pain)

If (you), say, fall into his trap, (you) will end up writhing (in pain). (OJ1: 101)

(4.2-9)

ere-ci	*tara afara*	*manggašacuka*	*baita*	*teisulebu-he*
this-ABL	troublesome	difficult	matter	encounter-PFV. PTCP
se-he-de,	*adarame*	*elehun*	*i*	*gama-me*
say(AUX)-PFV. PTCP-DAT	how	ease	GEN	handle-IPFV. CVB
hoo hio	*se-mbi*?			
decisively	say(AUX)-IPFV. FIN			

hoo hio se-: to act decisively

If (you), say, are faced with a matter (more) troublesome and difficult than this one, how (will you) handle (it) with ease and act decisively? (AGA1: 69-70)

(4.2-10)

talude	*ufara-ha*	*se-he-de*,	*aliya-ha*
by. chance	lose-PFV. PTCP	say(AUX)-PFV. PTCP-DAT	regret-PFV. PTCP
se-*me*	*amcabu-rakū*	kai	
say(AUX)-IPFV. CVB	chase-IPFV. PTCP. NEG	PTL	

V-*hA seme*: complex structure expressing concession, meaning "even if/though one does something"

amcabu-: to chase, to (be able to) catch up

If (you), say, by any chance lose (it), (you) won't (be able to) catch up (to get it back), even if (you) feel regretful (for losing it). (UH: 51)

(4.2-11)

talude	*baita*	*be*	*sartabu-ha*	*se-he-de*,
by. chance	matter	ACC	delay-PFV. PTCP	say(AUX)-PFV. PTCP-DAT
ainahai	*ali-me*	*mute-re*		
how	take-IPFV. CVB	be. able-IPFV. PTCP		

If (I), say, by any chance delay the (important) matter, how can (I) take (responsibility)? (AGA3: 81)

Throughout (4.2-1)-(4.2-11), although the subordinate predicates vary in terms of components or complexity, the main predicates invariably have structures that represent uncompleted states of affairs. Such structures include the imperfective finite form V-*mbi* [(4.2-1)-(4.2-4), (4.2-6), (4.2-8) and (4.2-9)], the affirmative and negative imperfective participles V-*rA* [(4.2-5) and (4.2-11)] and V-*rakū* (4.2-10), and the imperative (4.2-7). It was shown in Section 4.1 that these predicate structures also occur frequently in factual conditionals that contain the conditional converb V-*ci* in the protases. Table 4.3 below summarises the morphosyntactic patterns of the non-prototypical factual conditionals [(4.2-1)-(4.2-11)].

Table 4.3 Morphosyntactic Patterns of Non-prototypical Factual Conditionals

Subordinate Clause (Protasis)	Main Clause (Apodosis)	Example
{(Subj1+) Pred1 [V-*hA de*]}	{(Subj2+) Pred2 [V-*mbi*]}	(4.2-1)-(4.2-3)
{(Subj1+) *aika* + Pred1 [V-*hA de*]}	{(Subj2+) Pred2 [V-*mbi*]}	(4.2-4)

Continued

Subordinate Clause (Protasis)	Main Clause (Apodosis)	Example
{(Subj1+) *aika* + Pred1 [V-*me o-ho de*]}	{(Subj2+) Pred2 [V-*rA*]}	(4. 2-5)
{(Subj1+) Pred1 [V-*rakū o-ho de*]}	{(Subj2+) Pred2 [V-*mbi*]}	(4. 2-6)
	{(Subj2+) Pred2 [V-IMP]}	(4. 2-7)
{(Subj1+) Pred1 [V-*hA se-he de*]}	{(Subj2+) Pred2 [V-*mbi*]}	(4. 2-8) and (4. 2-9)
	{(Subj2+) Pred2 [V-*rakū*]}	(4. 2-10)
	{(Subj2+) Pred2 [V-*rA*]}	(4. 2-11)

4. 2. 1. 2 Interpretation

The structure of the participle in dative-locative (V-*rA*/-*hA*-*de*) usually serves to express temporal relations, and such usage is common in Manchu. The following are some examples [imperfective participle in (4. 2-12) and (4. 2-13), perfective participles in (4. 2-14) and (4. 2-15)].

(4. 2-12) *ecimari* *ebsi* *jide-re-de*, *jugūn* *giyai* *de*
this. morning hither come-IPFV. PTCP-DAT road street DAT
yabu-re *urse* *gemu* *ili-me*
go-IPFV. PTCP people all stand-IPFV. CVB
mute-rakū
be. able-IPFV. PTCP. NEG
When (I) was coming here this morning, (I saw that) people going along the street were all unable to stand (upright). (OJ2: 10)

(4. 2-13) *teike* *min-i* *emhun* *ubade* *te-re-de*,
just. now 1SG(*bi*/*min*)-GEN alone that. place-DAT sit-IPFV. PTCP-DAT
fa-i *duthe* *de* *emu* *cecike* *do-habi*
window-GEN wooden. lattice DAT one small. bird alight-PFV. FIN
When I was sitting there by myself just now, a small bird alighted by the wooden lattice of the window. (OJ2: 96)

(4. 2-14) *tuktan* *bi* *abala-me* *gene-he-de*, *emu* *suru* *morin*
at. first 1SG hunt-IPFV. CVB go-PFV. PTCP-DAT one white horse
yalu-mbihebi

ride-PST. IPFV. FIN

At first, when I went to hunt, (I) was riding a white horse. (OJ2: 2)

(4.2-15) *ecimari* *ili-fi* *tuci-ke-de*, *waburu* *sa* *gemu* *ji-he*

this. morning get. up-IPFV. CVB go. out-PFV. PTCP-DAT damned PL all come-PFV. PTCP

This morning when (I) got up and was going out, all (those) damned (servants of mine) came (to see me). (OJ2: 166)

However, under some circumstances the temporal meaning is weakened, which gives rise to a conditional interpretation, as shown by (4.2-1)-(4.2-11). In fact, the semantic—and sometimes morphosyntactic—overlap between temporality and conditionality is also observed in many other languages. For instance, the German conjunction *wenn* can be used in either conditional or temporal constructions, corresponding to the English conjunctions *if* (conditional) and *when* (temporal), respectively. In the case of these Manchu examples, it seems that the temporal relation is not conspicuous and that there exists a causal relation between the states of affairs represented in both clauses,① while the temporal plane of states of affairs is non-past. All of these factors induce the conditional interpretation, which automatically fills the semantic space caused by the rarefaction of the temporal meaning. However, the temporal interpretation is still compatible in some of these examples: the conditional meaning is not absolute and in a sense it constitutes an equilibrium with the temporal meaning.

Apart from the general features, more explanation needs to be provided for sentences that contain the quotative verb *se-* "to say", which takes as its complement a clause that can stand as a simple sentence (see Section 3.2.4). Sentence (4.2-8) is used for illustration: literally, either

① The causal relation in (4.2-8) and (4.2-11) is not straightforward in the content domain but is present between the complement clause within the subordinate clause and the main clause. See discussion below.

by conditionality or by temporality, it can be paraphrased as "if (you)[1] say/when (you) say that (one) has fallen into his trap, (one) will end up writhing in pain". However, this lengthy, even though more faithful, interpretation can actually be re-paraphrased in a way that dispenses with the verb *se-*, as is seen from the translation of (4. 2-8). The translation can be justified by the Qing Dynasty grammars, which clearly state that the structure *se-he-de* has the function of expressing supposition (UH: 17; AMH: 13). Furthermore, even if one puts aside the description (or prescription) of these grammars and focuses on the semantic relation between the two clauses of the sentence, it can be concluded that the subordinate predicate represented by the verb *se-* "to say" hardly bears any logical relation to the main predicate represented by *sarba-tala o-* "to end up writhing (with pains)". Rather, it is the predicate of the complement clause of the quotative verb *se-*, i. e. , *terei hūbin de dosi-* "to fall into his trap" that can be conceived of as the cause or condition of the apodosis state of affairs. In light of the twofold evidence (the description of Qing Dynasty grammars and semantic analysis), it is reasonable to conclude that in (4. 2-8)-(4. 2-11) the quotative verb *se-*, in the form *se-he-de*, is grammaticalised in a way that it can be interpreted as a marker of supposition, and it is not part of the conditional relation. Specifically, it embodies a speech act on the part of the speaker of asking the addressee to make a supposition. Thus (4. 2-8) can be represented by the following pseudo-formula: let's suppose: IF (one) falls into his trap, (one) will end up writhing (in pain).

On a final note, the analysis and representation of conditionals containing the structure *se-he-de* clearly demonstrate that conditionals like (4. 2-8)-(4. 2-11), though bearing some apparent similarity to conditional constructions containing the structure *o-ho-de* [(4. 2-5)-(4. 2-7)] are of a morphosyntactic type that is distinct from the latter. The reason is that in the latter constructions, the auxiliary *o-* comprises part of a complex predicate (Section 3. 2. 1), and referentially shares a subject with the verb

---

① "You" here is used to refer to people in general, not particularly the addressee of the utterance.

(regardless of its specific form) that precedes the auxiliary *o-*. By contrast, in the former constructions, the quotative verb *se-* does not necessarily share a subject with the preceding verbs—it can have its own subject, though implicit—and the preceding verb form is actually the predicate of its complement clause, as pointed out in the previous paragraph. However, it should be noted that the predicate structure in the complement clause of the verb *se-* is not arbitrary in these examples. In fact, it can be observed in (4. 2-8)-(4. 2-11) that the predicate of this complement clause seems to be invariably the perfective participle.

4. 2. 2 Counterfactual Conditionals

4. 2. 2. 1 Morphosyntax

The counterfactual conditionals that differ in morphosyntax from the basic patterns can be divided into three types according to their basic patterns. The first type is defined as including constructions in which the protasis has a complex predicate formed by the conditional converb *bi-ci*, but the apodosis does not contain complex structures formed with the perfective participle *bi-he*. The second type includes constructions in which the protasis is different from those of the basic pattern, but the apodosis appears to be characteristic of the basic pattern. The third and final type consists of constructions that might otherwise not be considered as counterfactual conditionals in any respect, except for having a counterfactual meaning inferred from the context in which they occur. The following are constructions of the first type as defined above (see "Type I" in Table 4. 4). While (4. 2-18) contains the conditional connector *aika* in the protasis, which forms a framed structure together with the subordinate predicate, the predicate structure is analysed in the same way as the other two constructions.

(4. 2-16)	*sin-i*	*tere*	*nionio*	*waliya-rakū*			
	2SG(*si*/*sin*)-GEN	that/3SG	child	abandon-IPFV. PTCP. NEG			
	bi-he	*bi-ci*,		*inu*	*uyun*	*juwan*	*se*
	be(AUX)-PFV. PTCP	be(AUX)-COND		also	nine	ten	year(old)

o-hobi
become-PFV. FIN
nionio: pupil of the eye, here an endearment for the child
waliya-: to abandon, here an euphemism for "to die"
If that adorable child of yours weren't dead, (he) would also be nine or ten years old (by now). (OJ2: 42)

(4. 2-17) *gosi-rakū* *bi-ci*, *aina-ha* *se-me*
love-IPFV. PTCP. NEG be(AUX)-COND do. what-PFV. PTCP say(AUX)-IPFV. CVB
ere *gese* *gosihon* *gisun* *i* *tafula-rakū*
this like bitter words GEN advise-IPFV. PTCP. NEG
aina-ha se-me: absolutely, by any means (always used with negation), lit.: "no matter doing what"
gosihon gisun i tafula-: to advise someone in bitter words, to take the trouble to give someone good advice
If (you) didn't love (me as your good friend), (you) absolutely wouldn't have taken the trouble to give (me) good advice. (MFG: 53)

(4. 2-18) *bi* *aika* *ere* *lengseki* *šabtungga* *mahala* *be*
1SG if this clumsy ear. flap-ADJ hat ACC
bucile-fi *cak seme* *hūwaita-hakū* *bi-he*
put. down-PFV. CVB neatly tie-PFV. PTCP. NEG be(AUX)-PFV. PTCP
bi-ci, *min-i* *šan* *i* *hešen* *haribu-hai*,
be(AUX)-COND 1SG(*bi/min*) GEN car GEN margin freeze-DUR
kemuni *funce-mbi-o*
still remain-IPFV. FIN-Q
šabtungga mahala: a hat with protective ear flaps
cak seme: neatly
If I hadn't put down the ear flaps of this clumsy hat and tied it up neatly, would my ears, suffering from frostbite, still remain now? (AGA2: 90-91)

As seen from the above, in the protasis of (4. 2-16), the subordinate predicate consists of the negative imperfective participle *gosi-rakū* "not loving" and the conditional converb *bi-ci*, whereas (4. 2-16) and (4. 2-18) have more complex predicates in the protasis, formed with *bi-he*, just as in (4. 1-30)-(4. 1-32) of Section 4. 1. On the other hand, the structure of the main predicate is a perfective finite form, *o-hobi* "became/has become" in (4. 2-16), while the other constructions contain imperfective forms in the main clause, either the imperfective form V-*mbi* in (4. 2-18) or the negative imperfective participle V-*rakū* in (4. 2-17), which are common in the apodosis of factual conditionals.

Since the structure of the main predicate is distinct from what would be expected of a counterfactual conditional, it is reasonable to assume that the counterfactual meaning of the constructions arises—partly at least—from the structure of the subordinate predicate: the verb *bi-* (as an auxiliary verb) in the form of the conditional converb *bi-ci* as part of a complex structure in the protasis is conducive to a counterfactual interpretation. The reason is that, if the subordinate predicate containes a simple lexical verb in the form V-*ci*, or a complex structure formed by the conditional converb *o-ci*, then, all else being equal, one would interpret the uttered conditional as a factual one. In particular, the perfective participle *bi-he*, which carries with it a strong past or irrealis connotation, adds to the probability of a counterfactual interpretation.

In counterfactual conditionals of the second type (see "Type II" in Table 4. 2. 2), the predicate structures in the protases are practically the same as those found in the basic patterns of factual conditionals (either simple as V-*ci* or compound as V-*rakū o-ci*), while the main predicates invariably consist of a variety of structures containing the perfective participle *bi-he*.

(4. 2-19) *emu* *niyalma-i* *baita* *o-ci*, *kemuni* *ja* *bi-he*

one person matter become-COND still easy be-PFV. PTCP

If (it) were one person's matter, it would still be easy. (MFG: 8)

(4. 2-20) *min-i* *jili* *majige* *hahi* *o-ci*, *sin-i*

1SG(*bi*/*min*)-GEN temper a. little fierce be-COND 2SG(*si*/*sin*)-GEN

baita *faijuma* *bi-he*

matter tricky be-PFV. PTCP

If my temper had been (even) a little fierce, your matter would have been tricky. (OJ1: 48)

(4.2-21) *unenggi* *sa-ci*, *yala* *onggolo* *ji-ci*
really know-COND indeed previously come-COND
aca-mbihe
suit(AUX)-PST. IPFV
V-*ci aca-*: complex structure expressing obligation
If (I) had really known, (I) indeed should have come at an earlier time.
(OJ1: 78)

(4.2-22) *age* *si* *ere* *baili* *cashūla-ha* *niyalma* *be*
sir 2SG this kindness be. ungrateful-PFV. PTCP person ACC
jono-rakū *o-ci*, *bi* *inu*
mention-IPFV. PTCP. NEG be(AUX)-COND 1SG also
fanca-rakū *bi-he*
get. angry-IPFV. PTCP. NEG be(AUX)-PFV. PTCP
baili be cashūla-ha niyalma: an ungrateful person who fails to show appreciation for other people's kindness
Sir, if you didn't mention that ungrateful man, I wouldn't get angry (at thinking of him). (MFG: 54)

(4.2-23) *majige* *niyalma-i* *gūnin* *bi-ci*, *inu* *sere-ci*
a. little human-GEN mind be-COND also feel-COND
aca-mbihe
suit(AUX)-PST. IPFV
V-*ci aca-*: complex structure expressing obligation
If there were even a little bit (of a normal) human mind (in him), (he) should have felt (that), too. (OJ1: 103)

(4.2-24) *i* *aika* *emu* *usun* *seshun* *niyalma* *o-ci*,
3SG if one bothersome disgusting person be-COND
bi *inu* *gisure-rakū* *bi-he*
1SG also speak-IPFV. PTCP. NEG be(AUX)-PFV. PTCP
If he were someone bothersome and disgusting, I wouldn't make any (further) remark. (OJ2: 112)

It should be noted that (4.2-24) contains the conditional connector *aika*, forming a framed structure. Additionally, in (4.2-21) and (4.2-23) the verb *aca-*, expressing a modal meaning "to be obligated to" in a complex verb structure, takes the past imperfective (V-*mbihe*) in forming the main predicate with the preceding verb.

The second type of construction reflects a similar situation to that of the first type in that one clause of the construction determines the counterfactual meaning. Different from the first type, in the second type it is the structure of the main—rather than the subordinate—predicate that contributes to expressing the counterfactual meaning.

The third type of counterfactual conditional (see "Type III" in Table 4.4), as pointed out at the beginning of Section 4.2.2.1, has the same morphosyntax as factual conditionals. The following are some examples.

(4.2-25) *gele-ci*, *bi* *ainu* *amga-mbi*
fear-COND 1SG why sleep-IPFV. FIN
If (I) were afraid, why would I sleep? (MYK2: 38)

(4.2-26) *bi* *dosi-ki* *se-ci*, *aifini* *uthai* *dosi-mbi*
1SG enter-OPT say(AUX)-COND long. ago then enter-IPFV. FIN
kai
PTL
V-*ki se*-: complex structure expressing desire or intention
If I (really) wanted to enter (your house), then indeed (I) would have entered a long time ago. (MFG: 48)

Table 4.4 summarises the morphosyntactic patterns of the non-prototypical counterfactual conditionals (4.2-16)-(4.2-26).

Table 4.4 Morphosyntax of Non-prototypical Counterfactual Conditionals

	Subordinate Clause (Protasis)	Main Clause (Apodosis)	Example
Type I	{(Subj1+) Pred1 [V-*rakū bi-he bi-ci*]}	{(Subj2+) Pred2 [N+ *o-hobi*]}	(4.2-16)
	{(Subj1+) Pred1 [V-*rakū bi-ci*]}	{(Subj2+) Pred2 [V-*rakū*]}	(4.2-17)
	{(Subj1+) *aika*+P [V-*hAkū bi-he bi-ci*]}	{(Subj2+) Pred2 [V-*mbi*]}	(4.2-18)

Continued

	Subordinate Clause (Protasis)	Main Clause (Apodosis)	Example
Type II	{(Subj1+) Pred1 [N+*o-ci*]}	{(Subj2+) Pred2 [N+*bi-he*]}	(4. 2-19) and (4. 2-20)
	{(Subj1+) Pred1 [V-*ci*]}	{(Subj2+) Pred2 [V-*ci aca-mbihe*]}	(4. 2-21) and (4. 2-23)
	{(Subj1+) Pred1 [V-*rakū o-ci*]}	{(Subj2+) Pred2 [V-*rakū bi-he*]}	(4. 2-22)
	{(Subj1+) *aika* + Pred1 [N+*o-ci*]}	{(Subj2+) Pred2 [V-*rakū bi-he*]}	(4. 2-24)
Type III	{(Subj1+) Pred1 [V-*ci*]}	{(Subj2+) Pred2 [V-*mbi*]}	(4. 2-25)
	{(Subj1+) Pred1 [V-*ki se-ci*]}	{(Subj2+) Pred2 [V-*mbi*] (+*kai*)}	(4. 2-26)

NOTE: The shaded areas represent the morphosyntactic characteristics shared with the basic patterns of counterfactual conditionals.

4.2.2.2 Interpretation

Although the counterfactual reading (rather than the factual reading) is inferred from the context, lexical items can also contribute to the meaning. For instance, in (4.2-26), *aifini* "long ago", which is usually used with perfective verb forms (participle V-*hA* or finite V-*hAbi*), explicitly refers to a state of affairs prior to the time of utterance. Thus, the speaker makes a supposition about the past.

The counterfactual conditionals of all three types above [(4.2-16)-(4.2-27)] differ in the extent to which they deviate morphosyntactically from the basic patterns of counterfactual conditionals. The first type [(4.2-16)-(4.2-18)] and the second type [(4.2-19)-(4.2-24)] share some features with the basic patterns, while the third type is the most distinct, and is indistinguishable from factual conditionals. Even within the first group, (4.2-16) is morphosyntactically closer to the basic patterns than (4.2-17) and (4.2-18) are, due to the presence of a perfective finite form, V-*hAbi*, as the main predicate, since it describes completed states of affairs and is usually suggestive of pastness. In contrast, (4. 2-17) and (4. 2-18) use imperfective forms in the main predicates.

The analysis of the counterfactual conditionals (4. 2-15)-(4. 2-26) seems to suggest that the presence of a structure formed with *bi-he* in a conditional construction—either in the protasis [(4. 2-16) and (4. 2-18)] or in the apodosis [(4. 2-19)-(4. 2-24)]—is a morphosyntactically *sufficient* condition for the counterfactual meaning. However, it is not a necessary condition, as seen in (4. 2-17), (4. 2-25) and (4. 2-26). This condition is a less strict version of the morphosyntax of the basic patterns of counterfactual conditionals, which all contain the structures formed with *bi-he* in the apodosis.

4.3 Constructions Expressing Temporal Meanings

A great number of constructions that contain conditional-converb structures in the subordinate clause receive a temporal interpretation instead of a conditional one. In particular, most such constructions seem to describe past states of affairs, while very few of them are used in a context related to the present or future. In the analysis that follows, the term "temporal constructions" is used to refer to this type of construction, unless otherwise specified.

4.3.1 Morphosyntax

Both the subordinate and the main clauses of these temporal constructions exhibit various forms of the predicate. Specifically, however, the subordinate clause can have either a simple predicate or a complex predicate. In the former case, the subordinate predicate consists of the conditional converb of a lexical verb, V-*ci*. In the examples below (using different main predicates), (4. 3-1) and (4. 3-2) describe past states of affairs, while (4. 3-3) describes a non-past state of affairs that takes place habitually.

(4.3-1) *beri* *dara-fi* *emgeri* *gabta-ci*, *majige*
bow draw.taut-PFV.CVB once shoot-COND a.little
amari-ha
fall.backwards-PFV.PTCP
As (I) drew the bow taut and shot (the arrow), (I) fell backwards a little.
(OJ2: 2)

(4.3-2) *tere* *hūntahan* *be* *gana-ci*, *dere* de
that/3SG mug ACC go.to.get-COND table DAT
gece-me *tokto-hobi*
freeze-IPFV.CVB fix-PFV.FIN
gece-me tokto-: to get stuck because of freezing, lit.: "to fix (by) freezing"
When (I) went to get that mug, (it) was frozen and had gotten stuck to the table. (AGA2: 84)

(4.3-3) *si* *damu* *honggon-i* *kalar* *se-re* *ici*
2SG just small.bell-GEN jingling say(AUX)-IPFV.PTCP direction
baihana-ci, *aifini* *šoforo-fi* *aliya-habi*
go.to.search-COND already seize-PFV.CVB wait-PFV.FIN
kalar se-: onomatopoeia imitating the sound of keys or small bells, to jingle
When you just go and search (for the hawk) in the direction of the small bell's jingling sound, (you'll see that the hawk) has seized (its prey) and has long been waiting (for you). (AGA4: 125)

When the subordinate predicate is complex, there are several possibilities. The first is the complex structure expressing desire or intention, consisting of the verb *se-* "to say" (as an auxiliary verb) and a preceding verb in the optative form V-*ki*.

(4.3-4) *bi* *okdo-me* *gene-ki* *se-ci*, *uksa*
1SG go.to.meet-IPFV.CVB go-OPT say(AUX)-COND suddenly
julergi *ergi* *de* *emu* *amba* *yohoron* *heture-hebi*
front side DAT one big canal block-PFV.FIN
okdo-me gene-: to go to meet
V-*ki se-*: complex structure expressing desire or intention
As I wanted to go to meet (the wild sheep), a big canal in front (of me) suddenly blocked (my way). (AGA1: 102)

The second possibility is a complex structure composed of the verb *bi-* "to exist/be" (as an auxiliary verb) in the form of the conditional converb *bi-ci* and a preceding perfective participle V-*hA*.

(4.3-5)

emu	*moro*	*šahūrun*	*muke*	*omi-ha*	*bi-ci*,
one	bowl	cold	water	drink-PVF. PTCP	be(AUX)-COND

ilihai	*andan-de*	*uthai*	*uju*	*nime-me*	*deribu-he*
immediate	instant-DAT	then	head	hurt-IPFV. CVB	begin-PFV. PTCP

ilihai andande: immediately, in an instant

When (I) had (just) drunk a bowl of cold water, (my) head began to hurt immediately. (OJ2: 22)

(4.3-6)

morin	*be*	*dabki-me*	*ta fa-ka*	*bi-ci*,
horse	ACC	whip-IPFV. CVB	go. up-PVF. PTCP	be(AUX)-COND

lo la	*ucara-ha*
unexpectedly	encounter-PFV. PTCP

As (I) whipped the horse and rode up (the slope), (I) ran unexpectedly into [it (the wild sheep)]. (AGA1: 103)

(4.3-7)

uncehen	*dahala-hai*	*amcana-ha*	*bi-ci*,
tail	follow-DUR. CVB	go. to. chase-PFV. PTCP	be(AUX)-COND

geli	*alin*	*be*	*daba-me*	*gene-hebi*
again	hill	ACC	pass-IPFV. CVB	go-PFV. FIN

As (I) went to chase (the gazelle), following its tail, (the gazelle) went past the hill. (OJ2: 2)

Additionally, a yet more complex structure is possible, combining the morphosyntactic features of the first two types of structures: it consists of the complex modal structure V-*ki se-*, as is seen in the first type, while the auxiliary takes the form of the perfective participle, *se-he*, which combines with the conditional converb *bi-ci*, as is seen in the second type:

(4.3-8)

sikse	*šolo*	*baha-fi*	*ji-ki*	*se-he*
yesterday	free. time	get-PFV. CVB	come-OPT	say(AUX)-PFV. PTCP

bi-ci,	*geli*	*aga-me*	*deribu-he*
be(AUX)-COND	again	rain-IPFV. CVB	begin-PFV. PTCP

V-*ki se-*: complex structure expressing desire or intention

Yesterday when (I), having some free time, wanted to come (to your house), it started to rain. (MFG: 43)

Concerning the form of the main predicate, the temporal constructions above contain either the perfective participle V-*hA* [(4. 3-1), (4. 3-5), (4. 3-6) and (4. 3-8)] or the perfective finite form V-*hAbi* [(4. 3-2), (4. 3-3), (4. 3-4) and (4. 3-7)]. Actually, as shown in the collected data, temporal constructions allow a greater variety of forms for the main predicate. In the following examples, one can also find the imperfective finite form V-*mbi* (4. 3-9), the negative imperfective participle V-*rakū* (4. 3-10), the progressive finite form V-*me bi* (4. 3-11), the mirative construction *dule... bi-he ni* (4. 3-12), existential structures containing the existential particle *bi* (4. 3-13) or the negative particle *akū* (4. 3-14), as well as a nominal predicate (4. 3-15).

(4. 3-9) *emu dabagan be daba-me gene-ci, emu*
one mountain ACC pass-IPFV. CVB go-COND one
boo-de emu hehe emu sarganjui arki unca-mbi
house-DAT one woman one girl wine sell-IPFV. FIN
As (he) went past a mountain, (he saw that) a woman and a girl were selling wine at a house. (SG: 251)

(4. 3-10) *hunio makta-fi waida-ci, muke eye-me*
bucket toss-PFV. CVB scoop-COND water flow-IPFV. CVB
tokto-rakū
fix-IPFV. PTCP. NEG
tokto-: to fix, here meaning "to stop"
As (she) tossed the bucket to scoop (water), the water wouldn't stop flowing (out of the bucket). (SG: 272)

(4. 3-11) *yafan be tuwana-me gene-ci, ilan uju-ngga*
garden ACC go. to. look-IPFV. CVB go-COND three headed
hutu yafan i dolo tubihe je-me bi
ghost garden GEN inside fruit eat-IPFV. CVB EXS. PTL
As/At the time (he) went to look at the garden, the three-headed ghost was eating fruit inside the garden. (SG: 406)

(4.3-12)

elhei	*waliya-me*	*tucibu-fi*	*tuwa-ci*,	*dule*	*jeren*
slowly	spit-IPFV.CVB	take.out-PFV.CVB	look-COND	in.fact	gazelle

yali	*i*	*dorgi*	*emu*	*sele-i*	*muhaliyan*	*bi-he*	*ni*
meat	GEN	inside	one	iron-GEN	bullet	be-PFV.PTCP	PTL

waliya-me tucibu-: to spit out, lit.: "to take out [by] spitting"

dule... bihe (ni): a mirative construction, meaning "I didn't know that... (but I have just realised it to my surprise)"

As (I) spat (it) out and took a look, (I found to my surprise that) it was an iron bullet in the gazelle's meat! (AGA2: 114)

(4.3-13)

emu	*bira*	*de*	*isina-ci*,	*sakda*	*mafa*	*mama*	*bi*
one	river	DAT	arrive-COND	old	grandpa	grandma	EXS.PTL

When [he] arrived at a river, [he saw that] there was an old man and an old woman. (SG: 237)

(4.3-14)

duka	*nei-ki*	*se-me*	*hūla-ci*,	*umai*
gate	open-OPT	say(AUX)-IPFV.CVB	call-COND	at.all

jabu-re	*niyalma*	*akū*
answer-IPFV.PTCP	person	NEG

When (I) called out, "Open the gate, please!" no one answered at all. (OJ1: 60)

(4.3-15)

ecimari	*cen-i*	*bithe*	*šejile-bu-ci*,	*emke*
this.morning	3PL(ce/cen)-GEN	book	recite-CAUS-COND	one

emken	*ci*	*eshun*
one	ABL	unfamiliar

When (I) made (them) recite the text this morning, (I found that) everyone was unfamiliar (with the text) [lit.: "one (was) more unfamiliar than (another) one"]. (OJ1: 51)

4.3.2 Interpretation

4.3.2.1 The Temporal Meaning Expressed

It is obvious from the constructions above that a variety of temporal relations is expressed by conditional-converb (V-*ci*) structures, which in a sense realise the semantic and syntactic functions exemplified by English conjunctions or phrases such as "*after*" "*while*", or "*at the time when*".

It has been mentioned that in the subordinate clause of these temporal constructions both the simple form of the conditional converb V-*ci* and the complex structure V-*hA bi-ci* can be used, where V is a lexical verb or an auxiliary verb. Between these two forms, however, no significant semantic difference is observed in that in both cases the state of affairs represented in the subordinate clause has (just) been realised. For instance, in (4. 3-1), the action of shooting an arrow has been completed; similarly, in (4. 3-6), the action of going upward has also been completed. However, the structure V-*hA bi-ci*, with the perfective participle in it, would presumably express a perfective aspectual meaning: the completeness of the action. Thus, the morphosyntactic difference between V-*ci* and V-*hA bi-ci* in the temporal constructions would be comparable to that between two temporal adverbials in English such as "after doing something" and "after having done something".

4. 3. 2. 2 The Temporal Meaning: Contrast with Conditionality

A question arises concerning how the temporal interpretation emerges. Before attempting to provide an answer to this question, it should be noted that the pastness of these constructions largely originates from the context. Although perfective verb forms (both participial, V-*hA*, and finite, V-*hAbi*), which are usually associated with completed acts (see Chapter 3), are used in the main clauses of some constructions, they cannot account for the past meaning, at least not directly. There are two reasons. First, the perfective verb forms employed as main predicates do not necessarily describe past states of affairs. This is clearly shown by (4. 3-3), which describes a non-past, habitual state of affairs. Second, other temporal constructions employ imperfective verb forms [(4. 3-9)-(4. 3-11)], or nominal structures (4. 3-15), which are common to factual conditionals, as discussed previously (Section 4. 1. 1. 1). Therefore, it seems that in main clauses, verb forms or predicate forms in general indicate the progress of the states of affairs rather than their temporal reference in relation to the moment of utterance.

Returning to the question, the temporal—as opposed to the

conditional—relation between two clauses of a construction emerges from the meanings of the component clauses. For instance, in (4. 3-2), the act represented in the subordinate clause, that is, (the speaker's) going to get the mug, given the context, by no means functions as the condition for the realisation of the state of affairs represented in the main clause, that is, (the mug's) being frozen and stuck to the table. It is obvious that the temporal relation is a reasonable interpretation in the context.

Furthermore, from the perspective of morphosyntax, the temporal constructions with main predicates similar to those of factual conditionals would otherwise yield the conditional interpretation; but the conditional relation is prevented for semantic reasons. On the other hand, it is obvious that the temporal constructions with perfective verb forms in the main clause distinguish themselves morphosyntactically from both factual and counterfactual conditionals that were analysed in Section 4. 1. Specifically, these constructions differ from factual conditionals in that the latter do not have perfective forms in the main clauses; and the temporal constructions differ from the basic patterns of counterfactual conditionals in that the latter contain complex structures using the perfective participle *bi-he* (as an auxiliary verb), while the former do not have such complex structures. One apparent counterexample to this claim is (4. 3-12), which, having the structure containing *bi-he* in the main clause, appears on the surface to be a counterfactual conditional. However, closer scrutiny reveals that the perfective participle *bi-he* is part of a mirative construction, *dule ... bi-he ni*. Thus, the structure of *bi-he* in (4. 3-12) should be distinguished from those structures without the mirative meaning. Apart from (4. 3-12) and similar cases, the constructions with perfective forms in the predicate are clearly distinguished from counterfactual conditionals.

It seems, therefore, that the conspicuous morphosyntactic distinction between the temporal constructions containing perfective forms in the main clauses [(4. 3-1)-(4. 3-8)] on the one hand, and conditional constructions proper on the other, can in a sense give rise to a distinct semantic status for the former, and by means of contrast it imposes a non-conditional interpretation—indeed a temporal one—on them. Nonetheless, it should be noted that the temporal constructions without perfective forms in either the subordinate or main clauses [(4. 3-9)-(4. 3-11), (4. 3-13)-(4. 3-15)] do not exhibit obvious morphosyntactic features that distinguish themselves from (factual) conditional constructions. They are only to be distinguished semantically.

4. 3. 2. 3 Conditional-converb Structures and Dative-Locative Participial Structures: Semantic Overlapping

Since conditional-converb structures—both simple and complex—used in the subordinate clause of a construction can express temporal relations in a past context between clauses, while the dative-locative participial structures, V-*hA*/*rA*-*de*, which are commonly used in temporal constructions, can in many cases express the conditional relation between clauses in a non-past context, one may wonder what connection possibly exists between these two mechanisms. In order to address this question, it is necessary, firstly, to examine the semantic composition of conditionality and temporality, respectively. The prototypical temporality represents the location in time of one state of affairs relative to another state of affairs. On the other hand, in a prototypical conditional relation, the realisation of one state of affair A serves as the condition or cause for the realisation of another state of affair B, and it is natural to assume that the time of state of affairs A is earlier or at least no later than the time of state of affairs B. Therefore, prototypical conditionality entails a causal relation as well as a temporal relation between states of affairs A and B, in that state of affairs A precedes state of affairs B both logically and temporally. Additionally, prototypical conditionality also implies—though it does not assert—that state of affairs A is not (yet) realised.

Secondly, though temporality and conditionality in Manchu are typically (and primarily) represented by dative-locative participial structures (V-*hA*/-*rA*-*de*) and by conditional-converb structures, respectively, the correspondence between the semantics and the morphosyntax is not strictly one-to-one, and the divergence enables alternative representations of a given meaning. Specifically, in a non-past context, (i) dative-locative participial structures (V-*hA*/-*rA-de*) represent the temporal relation required in conditionality; and (ii) the non-pastness of the context usually indicates that the states of affairs in question (of both clauses) are yet to take place. When the states of affairs are likely to be causally related, the conditional meaning can be yielded by such structures. It should be noted that, as stated in the discussion on non-prototypical conditional constructions (Section 4. 2. 1), the temporal meaning is compatible with the conditional meaning. On the other hand, in a past context, (i) conditional-converb structures maintain the temporal relation① of one state of affairs to the other; (ii) given the context, apparent causal relation usually does not exist between the states of affairs in question;② and (iii) in a past context, the state of affairs represented in the main clause is realised, according to the structure of the predicate—otherwise different structures (such as those containing the perfective participle *bi-he*) would be used to indicate the non-realisation of the state of affairs. ③ Therefore, the main clause is not a supposition but an assertion of the state of affairs, and consequently the state of affairs represented in the subordinate clause in a conditional-converb structure is not likely to express an unrealised state of affairs. Thus, while a temporal relation remains, the conditional meaning is not yielded, because it would not be compatible with the temporal meaning.

---

① Here it suffices to say that the temporal relation in general is maintained. It is argued in Section 4. 3. 2. 4 that the conditional-converb structures iconically reflect the temporal sequence; that is, the states of affairs represented by such structures precede the state of affairs of the main clause. However, such relations should be considered to belong to different domains. See Section 4. 3. 2. 4.

② Actually a causal relation can exist in some constructions such as (4. 3-5), where the act of drinking cold water (in the subordinate clause) does serve as a cause of the state of affairs of beginning to have a headache (in the main clause). However, the structure of the main predicate decides that this construction describes a factual state of affairs.

③ While a non-past context can usually indicate that the states of affairs involved are not realised, a past context cannot necessarily guarantee that the states of affairs involved have been realised, due to the existence of counterfactual states of affairs. This is the reason why the structure of the main predicate is considered in order to decide whether the state of affairs is realised or not: the analysis of (prototypical) counterfactual conditionals makes it possible to do so.

To summarise, dative-locative participial structures (V-*hA*/-*rA*-*de*), typically (and primarily) expressing temporality, and conditional-converb structures, typically (and primarily) expressing conditionality, can shift from their respective core semantic functions to expressing alternative meanings under certain lexical, morphosyntactic, or contextual circumstances. It should be pointed out, however, that the two types of structures undergo different processes: dative-locative participial structures obtain causality (from the whole construction and even the context) in expressing conditionality, while conditional-converb structures lose causality or hypotheticality—both of which are vital to typical conditionality—in expressing temporality.

4. 3. 2. 4 Temporal Constructions and Perception Verbs: The Temporal Meaning Revisited

Some of the temporal constructions containing perception verbs, such as *tuwa-* "to look",[①] *donji-* "to listen/hear", *amtala-* "to taste" are worthy of detailed analysis due to the particularity of the temporal meanings they express. Here are some examples [(4. 3-12) is also of such type].

(4. 3-16)	*uce*	*tuci-fi*	*tuwa-ci*,	*dule*	*ambarame*
	door	go. out-PFV. CVB	look-COND	in. fact	greatly
	labsa-me		*deribu-he*		
	snow. heavily-IPFV. CVB		begin-PFV. PTCP		

When (I) opened the door and looked (out), (I suddenly realised that) it had begun to snow heavily! (AGA2: 82)

(4. 3-17)	*fujin*	*gene-fi*	*tuwa-ci*,	*uyun*	*ursu*	*sele-i*	*hoton*
	lady	go-PFV. CVB	look-COND	nine	layer	iron-GEN	city

① Strictly speaking the verb *tuwa-* "to look" cannot qualify as a perception verb proper, since it denotes the act of observation rather than perception, while the visual perception is expressed by another verb, *sabu-* "to see". On the other hand, both the act of listening and the aural perception are expressed by the verb *donji-* "to listen/hear". Due to their syntactic similarity and their relationship to perception, verbs such as *tuwa-* and *donji-* are all considered as perception verbs here.

bi
EXS. PTL
When the lady went and looked, (she found that) there was a nine-layered iron city. (SG: 324)

(4. 3-18) *šan* *waliya-fi* *donji-ci*, *cib* *se-me*
ear throw-PFV. CVB listen-COND quiet say(AUX)-IPFV. CVB
heni *jilgan* *wei* *akū*
little sound tiny NEG
cib seme: *quitely*
wei akū: not a bit, none at all
When (I) pushed (lit.: "threw") my ear (against the window) to listen, (I heard) it was very quiet and there was no sound. (AGA1: 149)

(4. 3-19) *saifila-fi* *amtala-ci*, *šuwe* *ede-kebi*
use. a. spoon-PFV. CVB taste-COND completely go. bad-PFV. FIN
When (I) tasted (the food) using a spoon, (I found/realised that) it had gone completely bad. (AGA1: 97-98)

In these constructions, the states of affairs involved are located in a past context, and the states of affairs represented in the subordinate clauses—specifically acts of perception—have (just) been completed. However, the states of affairs represented in the main clauses do not necessarily follow the acts of perception temporally. For instance, in (4. 3-17) the state of affairs of the main clause, that is, the existence of a nine-layered city, has in fact been true for a period of time. Certainly, the beginning of the existence is located at some temporal point anterior to the act of perception (represented by *tuwa-* "to look"). In (4. 3-18) the state of affairs of the main clause, that is, there being no sound, may well have existed for a while before the act of perception *donji-* "to listen". On the other hand, it is clear that in each of these cases, the state of affairs of the main clause indicates the object of the realised perception. For instance, in (4. 3-16) the state of affairs of the main clause that it has begun to snow is the object of the realised perception represented by *tuwa-* "to look" of the subordinate clause. Also, in (4. 3-19) the state of affairs of the main clause that the going bad of the food is the object of the perception represented by *amtala-* "to taste" of the subordinate clause.

Furthermore, the main clause of such a construction can in a sense be regarded as falling within the semantic scope of an implied predicate that is part of a proposition that represents the realised state of affairs of perception. Such an implied predicate can be exemplified by the English verbs "see" and "hear", which serve to represent the realised states of affairs of perception of "looking" and "listening" respectively. In fact, such predicates are explicit in the following two temporal sentences.

(4. 3-20) *emu dobori lefu mederi baru tuwa-ci, emu amba*
one night bear sea toward look-COND one big
elden be sabu-mbi
light ACC see-IPFV. FIN
One night when the bear looked toward the sea, (he) saw a strong ray of light. (SG: 375)

(4. 3-21) *Urikan karun gene-fi yamji tuwa-ci, bata-i cooha*
PN sentry go-PFV. CVB evening look-COND enemy-GEN troops
Hunehe bira-i amargi de isinji-fi ing
PN river-GEN north DAT arrive-PFV. CVB camp
ili-fi, geren cooha buda ara-me
set. up-PFV. CVB all troops meal make-IPFV. CVB
dabu-ha tuwa-i elden abka-i usiha-i adali
light. up-PFV. PTCP fire-GEN light sky-GEN star-GEN like
sabu-mbi
see-IPFV. FIN
karun gene-: to go on sentry
ing ili-: to make camp
When Urikan went on sentry in the evening to reconnoitre (lit.: "to look"), (he could) see that the enemy had arrived at the north bank of the Hunehe River, and, as all the troops had made camp and were now preparing their meal, the light of the (camp) fire (was shining) like stars in the sky. (MYK2: 37)

In (5. 9-20) and (5. 9-21), the main predicate *sabu-* "to see" exactly represents the realised act of perception. A predicate of such type can reflect the intrinsic relation between the two clauses, both temporally and logically: the act of perception of the subordinate clause is anterior in time to the state of affairs represented by the predicate in question, and the latter is the object of the perception.

One can add implied predicates such as SEE or HEAR into the previous sentences[①] [(4. 3-16)-(4. 3-19)] without changing the meaning of the original construction more than revealing what is left unuttered and unspecified. Furthermore, as mentioned above, if the state of affairs represented by the implied predicate—implicit (as in the first few constructions) or explicit (in the last one)—is also considered in terms of temporal relation with the act (of perception) represented in the subordinate clause, the former is located posterior to the latter.

Such implied predicates can also be supplemented (semantically) to "embed" the main clause of some constructions such as (4. 3-9) and (4. 3-13) within their scope. In such constructions, the subordinate predicate is not a perception verb, and the state of affairs in the main clause does not appear to be posterior to the state of affairs of the subordinate clause. For instance, in (4. 3-9) the state of affairs of the main clause per se; that is, the woman and the girl's selling wine, is not posterior to the state of affairs of the subordinate clause, i. e. , going past the mountain. When the implied predicate, such as SEE, FIND or OBSERVE, is supplemented (semantically) to "embed" the original main clause within its scope, it becomes clear that the state of affairs represented by the implied predicate is posterior to the state of affairs in the subordinate clause.

Now it is argued that the conditional-converb structures represent the temporal anteriority of the state of affairs of the subordinate clause to the state of affairs of the main clause. It is important to note that, however, such temporal anteriority is represented in either of two different domains. Firstly, it can exist in the content domain, as shown by temporal

---

① In the cases where *tuwa-* "to look" occurs in the subordinate clause, the verb *sabu-* "to see" can be supplemented to "embed" the main clause within its scope, while in other cases, different perception verbs are also possible.

constructions in which the clause order (subordinate-main) iconically reflects the temporal sequence of the states of affairs involved [e.g., (4.3-1), (4.3-2), and (4.3-4)]. Secondly, the temporal anteriority can exist in the perceptual domain, where the main clause represents an act of perception that is related to the state of affairs of the subordinate clause. This case applies to the constructions discussed above that allow implied predicates in the main clause, where the act of (implied) perception is posterior to the state of affairs of the subordinate clause, be it an act of perception (*tuwa-* "to look", *donji-* "to listen", *amtala-* "to taste") or of other types (*isina-* "to arrive", *gene-* "to go"). In some cases the boundary between the two levels may not be very clear, allowing both interpretations. For instance, in (4.3-8) the temporal anteriority can be present in the content domain; that is, the desire to come is anterior to the beginning of the rain, while it can also exist in the perceptual domain; that is, the desire to come is anterior to the perception (such as awareness or sight) that it has started raining. Except for a few cases like this one, other temporal constructions tend to fall either into one category (temporal anteriority in the content domain) or into the other (temporal anteriority in the perceptual domain).

Therefore, it is reasonable to conclude that the conditional-converb structures V-*ci* (in all possible forms) reflect the temporal anteriority of the state of affairs of the subordinate clause in relation to the state of affairs of the main clause, either in a straightforward way (in the content domain) or metaphorically (in the perceptual domain). Thus, various temporal relations are unified in the morphosyntax of constructions containing the conditional converb V-*ci*.

4.4 Speech Act Conditionals

Some factual conditionals whose main clauses consist of imperative verb forms (rather than indicative verb forms) serve to perform the speech act of request. Here are some examples.

(4.4-1) *gosi-ci*, *min-de* *ala-me* *bu-reo*
have. mercy-COND 1SG(*bi*/*min*)-DAT tell-IPFV. CVB give-IMP
If (you) have mercy (on me), please tell me. (NSB: 25)

(4.4-2) *gosi-ci*, *min-i* *funde* *gisure-reo*
have. mercy-COND 1SG(*bi*/*min*)-GEN instead speak-IMP
min-i funde: instead of me, on my behalf
If (you) have mercy (on me), please speak on my behalf. (OJ1: 76)

(4.4-3) *muse-i* *fe* *gucule-he* *be* *gūni-ci*,
1PL. INCL-GEN old befriend-PFV. PTCP ACC consider-COND
min-i *ere* *baita* *be* *urunakū* *tere* *looye*
1SG(*bi*/*min*)-GEN this matter ACC surely that/3SG lord
de *ula-me* *gisure-reo*
DAT tell-IPFV. CVB speak-IMP
If (you) consider that we are old friends, please speak to that lord about this matter of mine. (MFG: 33)

(4.4-4) *han* *onco* *be* *gūni-ci*, *emu* *gisun* *be*
khan generosity ACC think-COND one word ACC
toktobu-fi *gene-re* *bi-he-o*
decide-PFV. CVB go-IPFV. PTCP be(AUX)-PFV. PTCP-Q
onco be gūni-: to be generous/kind, lit.: "to think of generosity"
gisun be toktobu-: to give a promise, lit.: "to decide on a word"
V-*rA bi-he-o*: a structure used to address someone superior to the speaker, which seems to have been replaced by the polite imperative V-*rAo* in the course of time, meaning "could/would you please (do something)"
Khan, if you are generous (to us), please give us a promise and then go (on your way). (MYK3: 46)

(4.4-5) *hata-me* *gūni-rakū* *o-ci*, *emu*
loath-IPFV. CVB think-IPFV. PTCP. NEG become(AUX)-COND one
gosi-re *gisun* *bu-reo*
have. mercy-IPFV. PTCP word give-IMP
hata-me gūni-: to consider as loathsome, to dislike
If (you) do not consider (him) as loathsome, please give (me your) kind words (about him). (OJ2: 70)

(4.4-6) *age* *si* *waliya-me* *gūni-rakū* *o-ci*,
sir 2SG abandon-IPFV. CVB think-IPFV. PTCP. NEG become(AUX)-COND

min-i *boo-de* *majige* *feliye-reo*
1SG(*bi/min*)-GEN house-DAT a. little walk-IMP
waliya-me gūni-: to despise, to have a low opinion of, lit.: "to think by dismissing"
feliye-: here meaning "to visit", "to drop by"
Sir, if you do not despise (me), please drop by at my house sometimes (lit.: "a little bit"). (MFG: 4)

Sentences (4.4-1)-(4.4-6) are quite uniform in terms of morphosyntax. First, the verb in the subordinate clause is either *gosi-* "to have mercy/to be kind" or *gūni-* "to consider", both of which reflect mental activities. The (unspecified) subject of the verbs is the second person, that is, the addressee of these utterances. Second, the predicate of the main clause takes the imperative form V-*rAo* [see (2) in Section 3.1.3.1] or a historically earlier form V-*rA bi-he-o*, which are used to express (polite) requests.

A conditional relation can be observed between the two clauses within each sentence. For instance, in (4.4-1), the addressee's having mercy serves as the condition for the intended act of the addressee's telling the speaker some information. However, on closer examination these constructions are different from ordinary conditionals with an imperative in the main clause such as the following.

(4.4-7) *age* *sin-de* *aika* *manju* *bithe* *bi-ci*, *emu*
sir 2SG(*si/sin*)-DAT if Manchu book be-COND one
udu *debtelin* *juwen* *bu-reo*
how. many volume loan give-IMP
emu udu: several, some
juwen bu-: to lend
Sir, if you have Manchu books, could you please lend (me) some volumes (of them)? (MFG: 41)

(4.4-8) *si* *unenggi* *sa-ra-ngge* *getuken* *o-ci*,
2SG really know-IPFV.PTCP-NMLZ clear be-COND
uthai *min-de* *ulhibu-me* *ala-rao*

then 1SG(*bi/min*)-DAT explain-IPFV. CVB tell-IMP

If you really know (it) clearly, then could (you) please tell me and explain it?

(MFG: 6)

In sentences (4.4-7) and (4.4-8), the subordinate clauses also serve to provide the conditions for the intended acts expressed by the main clauses. However, what differentiates (4.4-1)-(4.4-6) from (4.4-7) and (4.4-8) is that the "conditions" as shown in (4.4-1)-(4.4-6) are not authentic conditions. The reason is that, when the speaker utters a sentence like (4.4-1)-(4.4-6), he or she cannot really expect the addressee to negate the condition provided, such as the addressee's having mercy/being kind. In other words, the speaker already presupposes the condition to be true when she or he says this sentence: naturally, the addressee is expected to have mercy on the speaker, or to be kind, out of the socio-pragmatic consideration for maintaining a good interpersonal relationship or personal prestige.[①] Otherwise, negating this condition would invite the understanding that the addressee does not really care about the speaker, or the addressee's own prestige, which is inappropriate and undesirable. Thus, it seems that this condition itself suffices to justify the request. In this sense, this kind of condition is used by the speaker as a politeness strategy.

The utterances in (4.4-7) and (4.4-8), on the other hand, do not make such presupposition and consequently the conditions in (4.4-7) and (4.4-8) can be denied without (verbally) damaging the interpersonal relationship or the personal prestige. This is determined by the nature of the conditions: they do not concern the interpersonal relationship but only refer to matters irrelevant in this regard. For instance, in (4.4-7), the speaker is not sure whether the addressee has Manchu books or not, and the speaker's intention is to borrow such books in the circumstances that the addressee does have some. Similarly in (4.4-8), the speaker requests the addressee to explain some matter to him in the circumstances that the

① In (4.4-4) the addressee, a khan, is supposed to have the prestige of being generous.

addressee knows the matter clearly. In both (4. 4-7) and (4. 4-8) the addressee can reasonably negate this condition without damaging his relationship with the speaker. In fact, in their respective contexts, both (4. 4-7) and (4. 4-8) are indeed replied by the addressees' negation: sentence (4. 4-7) is followed by the utterance *min-de* [1SG(*bi*/*min*)-DAT] *bithe* [books] *akū* [NEG] "I have no books" (MFG: 42). Sentence (4. 4-8) is followed by the utterance *bi* [1SG] *yargiyan i* [really] *sarkū* [< *sarakū* know-IPFV. PTCP. NEG] *kai* [PTL] "I really don't know that!" (MFG: 6).

The analysis above is inspired by previous studies of similar phenomena in English. Van der Auwera (1986: 198-199) distinguishes two kinds of conditional sentences, "conditional speech acts" (Open the window, if I may ask you to) and "speech act (s) about a conditional" (If you inherit, will you invest?). Sweetser (1990) labels the former kind as "speech act conditionals", [①] in which the relation between clauses does not exist in the content domain but in the speech-act domain. Dancygier (1998: 89) notes that expressions such as "If I may ask" in the sentence "If I may ask, where were you last night?"—a "speech act conditional" according to Sweetser (1990)—are usually formulaic and idiomatic forms. Dancygier (1998: 91) argues that the expression "If I may ask" in the sentence above is used to "ensure the appropriateness of what is communicated in their main clause", and that the speaker of such a sentence believes what he or she says is appropriate but uses the condition to allow the addressee to disagree, since the speaker is uncertain about the addressee's opinion concerning whether the speech act is appropriate or not. Dancygier (1998) further points out that the speech act expressed by such a conditional is performed, and the performance is actually independent of the apparent condition (for instance, the condition that the speaker has the right to ask expressed by "If I may ask").

---

① In ensuing discussion I will adopt Sweetser's (1990) term "speech act conditionals" to refer to the conditionals such as (4. 4-1)-(4. 4-6), since the term "conditional speech acts" coined by Van der Auwera (1986) seems to focus on speech acts.

There are a variety of speech acts that may be expressed by the English conditionals, such as asking a question ("If I may ask, where were you last night?"); requests [such as the "conditional speech act" above given by Van der Auwera (1986)]; expressing an opinion ["If I can speak frankly, he doesn't have a chance" (Van der Auwera 1986: 199)]; or offering a favour ["I'll help you with the dishes, if it's all right with you" (Dancygier 1998: 89)]. In contrast, however, it seems that in Manchu the conditionals that adopt the "politeness strategy" are mainly used for asking favours from the addressee. One can observe this in (4.4-1)-(4.4-6). First, the verbs in the form of the conditional converb carry the connotation that the addressee is in a somewhat dignified position: the verb *gosi-* "to have mercy" and the complex verb phrases *hatame gūni-/waliyame gūni-* "to dislike/despise" all raise the position of the addressee in relation to the speaker. Second, from the verb forms used in the main clause, V-*rAo* or V-*rA bi-he-o*, one can also infer that the speaker is inferior to the addressee—a stance taken by the speaker at least at the moment of speech.

It seems reasonable to refer to Manchu conditionals such as (4.4-1)-(4.4-6) as "speech act conditionals" by analogy with the English examples. The category "speech act conditionals" in Manchu is thus defined: the condition stated in the subordinate clause serves as a politeness strategy on the part of the speaker to carry out a speech act, which is represented in the main clause. To clarify this definition it is necessary to state the distinguishing character of the politeness strategy (apart from "politeness") that the condition in the subordinate clause cannot be negated① without verbally damaging the personal relationship between the speaker and the addressee or the addressee's prestige. In the specific cases of (4.4-1)-(4.4-6), the politeness strategy has yet another imposing aspect: since the politeness condition in each example cannot be properly negated and is presupposed by the speaker to be true, it is as a consequence imposed on the addressee, who seems to be obligated to admit it. Failure to

① If the condition itself is expressed in a negative form, such as (4.4-6), it cannot be made affirmative via another negation.

admit this condition—and thus the request itself—would be interpreted as not showing kindness or goodwill towards the speaker. Thus, the politeness condition can be understood in this manner: "I (the speaker) assume that you are kind/merciful/considerate/generous... to me, and therefore it is reasonable that you, who are expected to behave accordingly, should accept my request".

The definition provided above automatically excludes such conditionals as (4.4-7) and (4.4-8), as previously discussed, but in principle still leaves open the possibility of other conditionals that do not necessarily express a request but rather a different kind of speech act—offering to help, asking for information, or giving remarks—in the main clause. Nevertheless, it just so happens that Manchu seems to be a language in which the so-defined speech act conditionals are mainly used for requests. On the other hand, various speech acts other than request may not be expressed by any conditional construction at all. Even if the speech acts (other than requests) are expressed by conditionals, these conditionals would turn out to be "ordinary" constructions in which the protasis is able to be negated, such as (4.4-7) and (4.4-8). This linguistic fact of Manchu is probably determined by its ways of expressing politeness.

4.5 Concessive Constructions

In general there are two types of concessive constructions: concessives (that is, concessives proper) and concessive conditionals. Both types of sentences consist of two clauses, and that the state of affairs represented in the second clause is contrary to what one expects given the state of affairs represented in the first clause. However, they are distinct from each other as to whether the state of affairs represented in the subordinate clause is entailed (that is, inferable as true) or not. Specifically, when the state of affairs of the first clause is entailed, the whole sentence is a "concessive (proper)", such as sentences containing the conjunction "although" in English (for example, "Although everyone played well, we lost the game"). When the state of affairs of the first clause is not entailed, the whole sentence is a "concessive conditional". [①] There are three types of concessive conditionals: [②] [(a) scalar concessive conditionals, such as the constructions introduced by "even if" in English (for example, "Even if I have to walk all the way, I will get there"); (b) alternative concessive conditionals, such as the constructions containing "whether... or..." in English (for example, "Whether it rains or not, we are playing football on Saturday", or "Whether she wins or whether she loses, this is her last tournament"); (c) universal concessive conditionals, such as the constructions introduced by "whatever/whoever/..." "no matter what/who..." in English (for example, "Whatever decision he made, I would support him").

Both concessives proper and all three types of concessive conditionals are found in Manchu. In particular, all of them can be realised by the constructions in which the subordinate clause has a conditional-converb (V-*ci*) structure. This section analyses these constructions. However, since there also exist alternative morphosyntactic patterns in Manchu that can function as concessives proper or concessive conditionals, the analysis here only describes one part of the whole range of possibilities, namely that which concerns the conditional converb.

4.5.1 Concessives Proper

The following are some Manchu examples of the concessives (proper) that contain conditional-converb structures in the subordinate clauses.

(4.5-1)	*cananggi*	*bu-mbi*	*se-ci*,	*bu-hekū*
	day.before.yesterday	give-IPFV.FIN	say-COND	give-PFV.PTCP.NEG

Though (he) said "(I'll) give (it to you)" the day before yesterday, (he) didn't give (it to me in the end). (MFG: 15)

① Xrakovskij (2012: 4) refers to what I call "concessives proper" here as "concessive causal constructions", as opposed to "concessive conditional constructions".

② The labels for these these types, i.e. "scalar", "alternative", and "universal", are borrowed from a questionnaire on concessive conditional clauses developed by Martin Haspelmath and Ekkehard König (available online at http://www.eva.mpg.de/lingua/tools-at-lingboard/pdf/ET_5_6_Haspelmath_concessive_conditional_clauses.pdf)

(4. 5-2) *age de emu baita yandu-ci, baibi angga juwa-ra*
sir DAT one matter request-COND merely mouth open-IPFV. PTCP
de manggaša-mbi
DAT be. hesitant-IPFV. FIN
angga juwa-: to open (one's) mouth, i. e. to utter
Sir, although (I have) something (for which) to request your favour, (I am) just hesitant (about whether I should) speak (my request). (OJ1: 85)

(4. 5-3) *bi ekše-me niyalma takūra-fi amca-bu-ci,*
1SG hurry-IPFV. CVB person send-PFV. CVB pursue-CAUS-COND
amcabu-hakū[①]
catch. up-PFV. PTCP. NEG
Although I hurriedly sent someone to run after (you), (the one I sent) didn't catch up (with you). (OJ1: 105)

(4. 5-4) *elhe be fonji-me jasi-ki se-ci,*
well-being ACC ask-IPFV. CVB send-OPT say(AUX)-COND
ildun i niyalma be baha-rakū
convenience GEN person ACC get-IPFV. PTCP. NEG
V-*ki se-*: complex structure expressing desire or intention
ildun i niyalma: a suitable person, lit.: "man of convenience"
Although (I) wanted to send (a letter) to ask (your) well-being, (I) couldn't find anyone availablc (to deliver it). (MFG: 27)

In terms of morphosyntax, one can see that the predicate in the subordinate clause of the concessives above is the conditional converb V-*ci*, where V is either a lexical verb [(4. 5-1)-(4. 5-3)] or an auxiliary verb (4. 5-4). The main predicate can be in an imperfective [(4. 5-2) and (4. 5-4)] or perfective form [(4. 5-1) and (4. 5-3)]. All of these predicate structures have been observed either in the basic patterns of conditional constructions (see Section 4. 1) or in the temporal constructions (see Section 4. 3). In terms of meaning, the states of affairs in the subordinate clauses are entailed, and can be located in the past [(4. 5-1), (4. 5-3) and (4. 5-4)] or in the present (4. 5-2).

Distinct from sentences (4. 5-1)-(4. 5-4), however, the more common

① In (4. 5-3) the verb forms *amca-bu-* and *amcabu-* are distinguished, as shown in the gloss.

patterns of Manchu concessives use the concessive converb V-*cibe* or the frame structure *udu*... V-*cibe* in the subordinate clauses. The following are some examples.

(4.5-5)	*niyalma-i*	*sukū*	*nere-cibe*,	*ulha*	*i*	*duha*	*kai*
	human-GEN	skin	cover-CONC	livestock	GEN	intestine	PTL

ulhai duha: cruel heart, lit.: "intestines of a domestic animal"
Although (he) is a human being (lit.: "covered with human skin"), (he has) a cruel heart (like a beast). (OJ2: 168)

(4.5-6)	*bi*	*udu*	*sain*	*ningge*	*etu-rakū*	*bi-cibe*,
	1SG	though	good	NMLZ	wear-IPFV.PTCP.NEG	be(AUX)-CONC
	gūnin	*dolo*	*elehun*			
	mind	inside	satisfied			

Although I don't wear good things (i. e. good clothes), (I am) satisfied inside (my) mind. (OJ1: 82)

4.5.2 Concessive Conditionals

As said above, concessive conditionals can be classified into three basic types, all of which can be found in Manchu, realised as constructions in which the subordinate clause contains a conditional-converb structure. The analysis in this subsection is arranged in the following order: (i) scalar concessive conditionals; (ii) alternative concessive conditionals; and finally, (iii) universal concessive conditionals.

4.5.2.1 Scalar Concessive Conditionals

One type of scalar concessive conditionals in Manchu is characterised by the morphosyntactic pattern "{(Subj1+) (*uthai*+) Pred1 [V-*ci*]} ↔ {(Subj2+) Pred2 [V-*kini*]}". The following are three examples (4.5-7)-(4.5-9). The verbs in the two clauses can either be the same [(4.5-7) and (4.5-9)] or different (4.5-8). When the main predicate is the optative of a verb that is different from that of the subordinate clause, it is usually the verb *o*- "to become/be", as in (4.5-8).

(4.5-7) *enenggi min-i baita be uthai tookabu-ci*,
today 1SG(*bi/min*)-GEN matter ACC even delay-COND
tookabu-kini! (*bi gene-re be naka-fi*, *age-i*
delay-OPT 1SG go-IPFV.PTCP ACC stop-PFV.CVB sir-GEN
boo-de darina-ki)
house-DAT go.to.drop.by-OPT
Even if (I should) delay my matter today, let me so delay it! [I'll quit going (where I planned to) and drop by at your house]. (MFG: 39)

(4.5-8) *ere ilan hūntahan nure de uthai sokto-me*
this three mug wine DAT even be.drunk-IPFV.CVB
buce-ci, *inu o-kini*! (*bi omi-ki*)
die-COND also become-OPT 1SG drink-OPT
Even if (I should) die drunk after drinking these three mugs of wine, so be it! [I'll drink (them anyway)]! (MFG: 47)

(4.5-9) *usha-ci hūi usha-kini dabala*
be.angry-COND any.how be.angry-OPT PTL
Even if (he) is angry (with me), let (him) be angry then (as he pleases)! (OJ1: 104)

However, although examples (4.5-7)-(4.5-9) all have a complete, subordinate-main clause structure [here excluding the parenthesised parts in (4.5-7) and (4.5-8), which constitute ensuing independent sentences], the main clauses do not contain new information. Rather, they only restate what is stated in the subordinate clauses. For instance, in the main clause of (4.5-7), the speaker does not say anything beyond supposing that he would delay his matter. On the other hand, if one considers the text following each of the constructions, one can better understand what state of affairs is relevant to the supposition made. For instance, in (4.5-7) the speaker will go to the addressee's house even if he delays his matter, and in (4.5-8) the speaker will drink with the addressee even if he will die drunk.

On the other hand, in Manchu there are some verb structures containing *uthai* "then" that can express the concessive meaning when used in the subordinate clauses. Such structures include *uthai*... V-*kini*, *uthai*... V-*hA se-me*, and *uthai*... V-*cibe*, as shown in the following examples. It should be noted that the sentences in which the structures in question occur are often complex, consisting of more than one clause.

(4.5-10) *aika* *tere* *gese* *gete-rakū* *juse* *banji-ha*
if that/3SG like wake-IPFV. PTCP. NEG children give. birth-PFV. PTCP
se-he-de, *in-i* *beye* *uthai* *yafan* *de*
say-PFV. PTCP-DAT 3SG(*i/in*)-GEN body even grave. yard DAT
te-kini, *hono* *ainahai* *emu* *afaha* *hoošan* *jiha*
live-OPT still not. necessarily one piece paper money
deiji-mbi-ni
burn-IPFV. FIN-PTL
geterakū juse: good-for-nothing children
hoošan jiha deiji-: to burn paper money offerings (to the deceased)
If, say, (one) raises good-for-nothing children like that, even if his body were buried in the graveyard (after his death), (his children) still (might) not necessarily burn even a piece of paper money (as offering for him). (OJ1: 107)

(4.5-11) *uthai* *baha-fi* *wesi-rakū* *yenderakū*
even get-PFV. CVB get. promoted-IPFV. PTCP prosper-IPFV. PTCP
o-kini, *beye* *bisi-re-de*, *niyalma* *mahala*
become(AUX)-OPT body be-IPFV. PTCP-DAT people hat
tuhe-me *kundule-me* *tuwa-mbi*
fall-IPFV. CVB respect-IPFV. CVB regard-IPFV. FIN
mahala tuhe-me: here meaning "taking off one's hat (to show respect)", lit.: "hat falling"
Even if (he) doesn't get promoted or get rich, as long as (he) is alive, people will regard (him) with respect. (AGA1: 118)

(4.5-12) *uthai* *muse-i* *kadala-ra* *niyalma*
even 1PL. INCL-GEN manage-IPFV. PTCP person
baicanji-ha *se-me*, *muse* *inu*
come. to. investigate-PFV. PTCP say(AUX)-IPFV. CVB 1PL. INCL also
mujilen *niyaman* *šoforo-bu-rakū* *o-mbi*
mind heart scratch-PASS-IPFV. PTCP. NEG become(AUX)-IPFV. FIN
kadalara niyalma: manager, administrator
niyaman šoforobu-: to be worried, lit.: "heart to be scratched"
Even if our manager comes to investigate us, we won't be worried at all.
(AGA3: 79)

(4. 5-13)

uthai	*ici*	*aca-rakū*	*o-cibe*,	*inu*
even	direction	suit-IPFV. PTCP. NEG	become(AUX)-CONC	also

nikede-me	*baitala-ci*	*aca-mbi*
make. do-IPFV. CVB	use-COND	suit(AUX)-IPFV. FIN

ici aca-: to suit, to conform

V-*ci aca-*: complex structure expressing obligation

Even if (it) doesn't suit (the needs), (we) still should make do with (it). (UH: 26)

The second type of scalar concessive conditionals share morphosyntax with the basic patterns of factual conditionals. The following are some examples.

(4. 5-14)

wesi-ki	*mukde-ki*	*se-ci*,	*ainahai*	*mute-re*
advance-OPT	go. up-OPT	say(AUX)-COND	how	be. able-IPFV. PTCP

wesi-/mukde-: here both meaning "to advance in rank", "to get promoted"

V-*ki se-*: complex structure expressing desire or intention

Even if (he) wants to get promoted, how can (he succeed)? (OJ1: 103)

(4. 5-15)

sin-i	*tacibu-re*	*sain*	*gisun*	*be*	*min-i*
2SG(*si/sın*)-GEN	teach-IPFV. PTCP	good	words	ACC	1SG(*bi/min*)-GEN

dolo	*buce-ci*	*inu*	*onggo-rakū*
inside	die-COND	still	forget-IPFV. PTCP. NEG

mini dolo: in my heart, lit.: "inside me"

Even if (I) die, (I) will not forget the kind words you teach me. (MYK7: 10)

(4. 5-16)

majige	*tathūnja-ci*,	*inu*	*haha*	*waka*
a. little	hesitate-COND	still	man	not

Even if (I) hesitate a little, (I will not) be (counted as) a real man! (OJ2: 140)

(4. 5-17)

buce-rakū	*o-ci*,	*sukū*	*inu*	*emu*	*jergi*
die-IPFV. PTCP. NEG	become(AUX)-COND	skin	still	one	layer

kobci-mbi
fall. off-IPFV. FIN

Even if (you) don't die, one layer of (your) skin will fall off. (AGA3: 35-36)

(4. 5-18)

yaya	*niyalma*	*belge-i*	*gese*	*erdemu*	*bi-ci*,	*beye*
any	person	grain. of. rice-GEN	like	talent	be-COND	self

de	*tusangga*
DAT	beneficial

(It will be) beneficial to anyone, even if (he or she) has a talent the size of a grain of rice. (MFG: 4)

In the sentences (4. 5-14)-(4. 5-18), the concessive meaning can arise from specific lexical items or from the context. For instance, the concessive meaning of (4. 5-14) is not obvious, but is inferred from the context. On the other hand, the adverb *inu* "also, still" in the main clauses of (4. 5-15)-(4. 5-17), the adverb of degree *majige* "a little" in the subordinate clause of (4. 5-16), and the phrase *belgei gese* "(as small) as a grain of rice" in the subordinate clause of (4. 5-18) all contribute to expressing the concessive meaning.

König (1986: 231) points out that, in general, concessive conditionals "relate a set of antecedent conditions to a consequent", and in the case of scalar concessive conditionals (that is, sentences introduced by *even if*), the set of antecedent conditionals is specified by "a focus marker" (that is, *even*). According to König (1986), the *even if* clause represents the least likely situation for bringing about the given consequent, and since the most unlikely situation can bring about this consequent, the other states of affairs can certainly bring it about also. A similar thought is expressed by Sweetser (1990: 136-137), who notes that even "is an explicitly scalar expression", and that *even if* "represents a relatively *extreme* possibility from among the possible conditions which can be expected to occur" to impede the consequent. These statements can shed light on how the Manchu expressions mentioned above, such as *majige* "a little" and *belgei gese* "(as small) as a grain of rice", contribute the concessive conditional meaning.

The concessive converb V-*cibe* seems to be a natural substitute for the conditional converb in the subordinate clause of a scalar concessive conditional. The following is an example, which nevertheless allows the interpretation as a concessive proper.

(4. 5-19) *udu* *tere* *ten* *de* *isina-me* *mute-rakū*
even that/3SG extreme DAT reach-IPFV. CVB be. able-IPFV. PTCP. NEG
bi-cibe, *inu* *urunakū* *hami-mbi* *dere*
be(AUX)-CONC still definitely be. close-IPFV. FIN PTL
Even if/Even though (we) can't reach his level (of excellence), (we) will definitely still be able to be close (enough). (OJ1: 20)

4. 5. 2. 2 Alternative Concessive Conditionals

The alternative concessive conditionals in Manchu juxtapose two conditional converbs in the subordinate clause. The following is an example:

(4. 5-20) *je-ci* *omi-ci* *amtan* *baha-rakū*
eat-COND drink-COND taste get-IPFV. PTCP. NEG
Whether (I) eat or whether (I) drink, (I) can't enjoy (any) taste (out of it) [lit. : "... I don't get (any) taste"]. (MFG: 30)

Sentences such as (4. 5-20) are rather few in number, but they are salient in morphosyntax, having two coordinate conditional converbs. There is also a similar type of construction in which two conditional converbs are juxtaposed in the first part of the sentence. However, the predicates of the main clauses, usually implicit, do not refer to entities in the outside world, but denote states of affairs represented by the subordinate clauses. The following sentence (4. 5-21) contains two such sentences [(4. 5-21a) and (4. 5-21b)], each of which is independent of the other. This example will also be analysed in Section 4. 7.

(4. 5-21a) *tuci-ci* *dosi-ci* *gemu* *waka*;
go. out-COND come. in-COND all not. right
(4. 5-21b) *te-ci* *ili-ci* *gemu* *mangga* *kai*
sit-COND stand-COND all difficult PTL
It is not appropriate either to go out or to come in; it is difficult whether one sits down or stands up. (OJ2: 124)

Despite sentences such as (4.5-20), the predominant pattern of alternative concessive sentences in Manchu juxtaposes the concessive converb (V-*ci*be) of two verbs (lexical or auxiliary)—instead of the conditional converb—in the subordinate clauses. In the following examples, sentence (4.5-22) comes from the same passage as (4.5-20), and demonstrates that the structures used respectively in the two sentences share the same syntactic function.

(4.5-22)

te-cibe	*ili-cibe*	*elhe*	*akū*
sit-CONC	stand-CONC	peace	NEG

Whether [I] sit down or whether [I] stand up, there is no peace [inside me]. (MFG: 29-30)

(4.5-23)

menggun	*o-cibe*,	*damtun*	*o-cibe*,	*min-de*
silver	become-CONC	pawn	become-CONC	1SG(*bi*/*min*)-DAT
majige	*aisila-rao*			
a. little	help-IMP			

Be it silver, or be it something that can be pawned, would you please help me a little [by giving me a loan]? (OJ1: 87)

(4.5-24)

uda-cibe	*uda-rakū*	*o-cibe*	*in-i*
buy-CONC	buy-IPFV. PTCP. NEG	become(AUX)-CONC	3SG(*i*/*in*)-GEN
cihai	*gama-kini*		
willingly	handle-OPT		

Whether [he] buys [it] or whether he doesn't buy [it], let him handle [it] according to his own will. (OJ2: 26)

4.5.2.3 Universal Concessive Conditionals

The universal concessive conditionals in Manchu contain interrogative words such as *ai* "what", *absi* "how" or *ya* "which" in the subordinate clause and in many cases in the main clause as well. Here are some examples.

(4.5-25)

muse-i	*ai*	*se-ci*,	*uthai*	*ai*	*gese gese*
1PL. INCL-GEN	what	say-COND	then	what	likewise
daha-me	*yabu-mbi*				

obey-IPFV. CVB act-IPFV. FIN

gese gese: likewise, accordingly

Whatever we say, (he) will act accordingly in obedience (to us) (lit.: "what we say, that he acts accordingly in obedience"). (OJ2: 110)

(4.5-26) *ai bi-ci, ai be tukiye-fi ulebu-mbi*

what be-COND what ACC hold. up-PFV. CVB feed-IPFV. FIN

tukiye-: to offer with both hands, to hold up

ulebu-: to feed, to treat someone to food

Whatever (food) (he) has, (he) will offer it with both hands and treat (his guests to it) [lit.: "what there is (at his house), that (he) will offer..."].

(AGA1: 141)

(4.5-27) *absi tuwa-ci, absi ubiyada*

how look-COND how disgusting

No matter how (you) look (at him), (you'll find him) so disgusting. (OJ2: 134)

(4.5-28) *te ci aika mim-be cooha-i dain de*

now ABL if 1SG(*bi/min*)-ACC troops-GEN battle DAT

absi gene-ø se-ci, bi absi daha-mbi

how go-IMP say-COND 1SG how obey-IPFV. FIN

cooha-i dain: battle, war

From now on no matter how (you) order me to join the army, I will definitely obey (your order) (lit.: "... in what manner you tell me to go to battles, I'll obey in that manner"). (AGA4: 41)

(4.5-29) *ya ba-be fonji-ci, i ya ba-be karu*

which aspect-ACC ask-COND 3SG which aspect-ACC reply

giyangna-mbi

explain-IPFV. FIN

No matter which aspect (I) ask (him) about, he will explain (it) in reply.

(AGA1: 58)

(4.5-30) *yaya we mim-be baihanji-ci, boo-de akū*

any who 1SG(*bi/min*)-ACC come. to. visit-COND home-DAT NEG

se-me jabu-ø

say-IPFV. CVB reply-IMP

No matter who comes to visit me, reply (to them) that (I'm) not at home.

(OJ1: 105)

(4.5-31)

si	*ai*	*jaka*	*gaji-ø*	*se-ci*,	*bi*	*sin-i*
2SG	what	thing	bring-IMP	say-COND	1SG	2SG(*si/sin*)-GEN
gūnin	*de*	*aca-bu-me*		*uda-fi*		*hūlaša-ki*
mind	DAT	fit-CAUS-IPFV. CVB		buy-PFV. CVB		trade-OPT

gūnin de acabu-me: by making (something) fit (one's) mind, according to (one's) intention

Whatever you want (me) to bring, I will buy (it) as you wish and exchange (it with you for what I want from you) [lit.: "what you tell me to bring, that (I will) buy according to your intention and exchange (it)"]. (OJ2: 148)

The co-occurrence of interrogative words with the conditional converb in the subordinate clause and the usual repetition of the same interrogative words in the main clause can well explain how the universal concessive conditionals relate to ordinary conditional constructions. Example (4.5-26) is used for illustration. First, let a sentence be constructed as (4.5-26) except that the interrogative word *ai* "what" in both clauses of (4.5-26) are replaced by X, which stands for an unidentified nominal structure.

(4.5-32) X *bi-ci*, X *be tukiyefi ulebumbi*

"If (he) has X, (he) will offer X with both hands and treat (his guests to X)"

One can see that (4.5-32) qualifies as a factual conditional in terms of morphosyntax and meaning. Then let S be the set of entities $\{x_1, x_2, \ldots, x_N\}$, which, in the speaker's mind, X can refer to. Thus, exhausting all the possible choices of X (within S), one can have a series of conditionals as (4.5-32), only with different lexical content for X, as shown by Formula (A):

(A) x_1 *bi-ci*, x_1 *be tukiyefi ulebumbi*;

x_2 *bi-ci*, x_2 *be tukiyefi ulebumbi*;

...

x_N *bi-ci*, x_N *be tukiyefi ulebumbi*.

Then, the series of conditionals one obtains can be further represented by Formula (B).

(B) $\forall X \in S$: he has X → he offers X with both hands and treats his guests to X

This formula can be translated into natural language as "whatever (food) he has, he will offer it with both hands and treat his guests to it". Manchu has no lexical items that conveniently correspond to words such as "whatever" or "whoever", but relies on complex structures to express similar meanings. Specifically, by directly putting the interrogative word *ai* "what" in the positions of X in the conditional (4. 5-32) and transforming this construction into (4. 5-26), Manchu expresses the meaning of formula (4. 5-34), which contains a universal quantifier. In terms of syntax, formula (4. 5-34) embodies both the interrogative word *ai* "what" (through the universal quantifier, the symbol X and the recurring positions of X) and the conditional relationship (through the inter-clausal connection).

It should be mentioned that the formulaic analysis above is inspired by König's (1986) approach to scalar concessive conditionals. For instance, to analyse "Even if you drink a little, your boss will fire you", König (1986: 244) uses a series of ordinary conditionals which differ from each other (and also differ from the concessive conditional) in terms of scale, such as "If you drink only a drop of alcohol, your boss will fire you", "If you drink a glass of alcohol, your boss will fire you", ① and so forth.

The constructions that do not have recurring interrogative words [(4. 5-30) and (4. 5-31)] need some clarification here. In (4. 5-30), only the subordinate clause contains the interrogative word, but functionally it is the same as sentences (4. 5-25)-(4. 5-29). The structure *yaya we* (literally, "every who") in the subordinate clause of (4. 5-30) seems to perform the same function as "whoever" does in English, thus making it unnecessary to repeat the interrogative word "we who" in the main clause. As for (4. 5-31), where the interrogative word *ai* "what" also occurs only in the subordinate clause, the phrase *sini gūnin de acabume* "according to

① The underlinings are added by the author.

your intention" in the main clause has the same semantic content with the interrogative word in the main clause.

In Manchu, the expression of universal concessive meaning via interrogative words combined with the conditional converb exhibits the interrelation between the universal concessive meaning and the conditional meaning. This is all the more evident in (4.5-28), in which the conditional connector *aika* "if" also occurs in the subordinate clause, in addition to the interrogative word *ai* "what". This construction clearly combines the characteristic of a basic type of factual conditional and a universal concessive conditional.

It is worth mentioning that a number of universal concessive sentences in Manchu do not use the conditional converb in the subordinate clause, but instead use the concessive converb (V-*cibe*) or the structure V-*hA se-me*. The interrogative words also occur, but only in the subordinate clause. The following are three examples.

(4.5-33)

absi	*gisure-cibe*	*gisun*	*banjina-rakū-ngge*	*akū*
how	speak-CONC	words	produce-IPFV. PTCP. NEG-NMLZ	NEG

gisun banjina-: to (manage to) utter words

No matter how (one) speaks, there will be no (such) situation that (one) cannot utter words (fluently). (OJ1: 4)

(4.5-34)

ai	*hacin*	*i*	*taci-ha*	*se-me*	*inu*	*ere*	*hūman*	*dabala*
what	kind	GEN	learn-PFV. PTCP	say(AUX)-IPFV. CVB	still	this	capability	only

No matter what kind of (method I use to) learn (Manchu), (my) capability (will) only (be like) this. (OJ1: 24)

(4.5-35)

yaya	*ba-de*	*isinji-cibe*,	*derengge*	*etenggi*	*sukdun*	*inu*	*gaibuša-rakū*
whichever	place-DAT	arrive-CONC	honourable	powerful	air	also	lose-IPFV. PTCP. NEG

Wherever (he) goes, (he will) not lose (his) manners as an honourable and powerful man. (AGA1: 119)

4.6 Parallel Constructions

This section analyses several types of constructions that use the conditional converb in the subordinate clauses. They all share the same morphosyntax as the basic factual conditionals, but do not necessarily express the conditional meaning (though in a few cases they do). What the constructions to be analysed also have in common is the parallel relation between the two clauses within the whole sentence. It should be noted that since the syntactic status of the two clauses is not equal, their parallelism mostly concerns the semantic content. In the following analysis the constructions are divided into four groups according to the inter-clausal semantic relation: (i) contrastive conditionals; (ii) comparison conditionals; (iii) disjunction conditionals; and (iv) degree conditionals.

4.6.1 Contrastive Conditionals

Sentences containing the conditional converb in the subordinate clause can express contrast between the two component clauses. Here are examples.

(4.6-1)	*si*	*adasun*	*be*	*ufi-ci*,	*bi*	*uthai*	*jurgan*	*goci-mbi*
	2SG	lapel	ACC	sew-COND	1SG	then	line	draw-IPFV.FIN

jurgan goci-: to mark the lines (on cloth)

While you sew the lapel, I'll mark the lines (of the clothes) (lit.: "if you sew the lapel, then I'll mark the lines"). (OJ2: 52)

(4.6-2)	*ere*	*ogo*	*be*	*jafa-ci*,	*tere*	*monggon*	*haya-mbi*
	this	hole	ACC	hold-COND	that/3SG	collar	trim-IPFV.FIN

ogo: a particular hole in a helmet

While this (person) holds the hole of the helmet, that (person) trims the collar (of the coat). (OJ2: 54)

(4.6-3)	*julergi*	*alin*	*de*	*emu*	*dobori*	*dedu-ci*,	*amargi*	*alin*
	south	mountain	DAT	one	night	stay-COND	north	mountain

de	*emu*	*dobori*	*dedu-ø*
DAT	one	night	stay-IMP

While (you should) stay one night in the south mountain, stay one night in the north mountain (as well)! (MYK5: 6)

(4.6-4)

emu	*jui*	*tuba-de*	*bisi-re*	*jušen*	*irgen*	*adun*
one	son	that. place-DAT	be-IPFV. PTCP	serf	people	herd
ulha	*be*	*tuwa-me*	*gene-ci*,	*emu*	*jui*	*uba-de*
livestock	ACC	look-IPFV. CVB	go-COND	one	son	this. place-DAT
bisi-re	*ama*	*be*	*tuwa-me*	*bi-kini*		
be-IPFV. PTCP	father	ACC	look-IPFV. CVB	be-OPT		

Let one son take care of the serfs, people, herd and livestock, which are staying in that place, and let the other son take care of the father, who is staying in this place. (MYK6: 23)

(4.6-5)

erin	*forgon*	*oyonggo*	*se-ci*,	*faššа-ra-ngge*
time	season	important	say-COND	exert. effort-IPFV. PTCP-NMLZ
inu	*oyonggo*			
also	important			

erin forgon: the right moment, opportunity

If (one) says opportunities are important, (one should likewise say that) exerting effort is also important. (MFG: 25)

(4.6-6)

ji-he	*cooha*	*geren*	*se-ci*,	*muse-i*	*cooha*
come-PFV. PTCP	troops	many	say-COND	1PL. INCL-GEN	troops
inu	*geren*				
also	many				

If (you) say the troops that have come are many, (I would likewise say that) our troops are also many. (MYK2: 41)

The contrast of clauses describes two states of affairs, which are realised by either different agents [(4.6-1), (4.6-2) and (4.6-4)] or the same agent (4.6-3). It may imply that the two states of affairs involved are taking place or are expected to take place simultaneously, as shown in (4.6-1), (4.6-2) and (4.6-4). For instance in (4.6-1), one's sewing the lapel is simultaneous with the other's marking the lines. In (4.6-4), one son's taking care of the serfs and the herd, and so on, is expected to take place at the same time as the other son's taking care of their father. In

(4. 6-3) two similar—and related—states of affairs are mentioned, though they do not take place at the same time: it expresses the command by the speaker that the troops should stay in different places on different nights.

Furthermore, the contrast can exist between two views or statements, as shown in (4. 6-5) and (4. 6-6). In (4. 6-5), one view is that opportunities are important and the other view is that exerting effort is also important. An implied predicate *se-* "to say" is omitted in the main clauses of (4. 6-5) and (4. 6-6), which can correspond to the same predicate in the subordinate clauses.

The function of the conditional converb in sentences (4. 6-1)-(4. 6-6) needs explanation here. Judging by the meaning of the sentences as a whole, the relation between the two clauses is contrast. Yet, the prototypically conditional relation does not seem to be expressed. Nevertheless, closer examination reveals that conditionality is demonstrated in the following domains other than the content domain: the perceptual domain, the speech-act domain or the epistemic domain. Specifically, in (4. 6-1)-(4. 6-3), where one can perceive (see or hear) the two states of affairs described, it is reasonable to assume that the perception of one event enables or causes the perception of the other event, since both of them take place simultaneously. Here the conditional relation is presented in the perceptual domain. In (4. 6-3) and (4. 6-4), which express the speakers' commands, the issuing of one command enables or causes the issuing of the other, since in each sentence the two commands are inseparable from each other. In these two sentences, the conditional relation is present in the speech-act domain. In (4. 6-5) and (4. 6-6), each of which expresses two views, the acceptance of one view necessarily enables or causes the acceptance of the other view, since the two views are based on the same principle (that is, the importance of matters, and the number of troops, respectively). Thus the conditional relation is present implicitly in the epistemic domain, functioning between acts of reasoning.

4. 6. 2 Comparison Conditionals

Some sentences containing the conditional converb can express comparison between states of affairs represented in the component clauses. The states of affairs being compared are similar but differ in a certain aspect in terms of degree. Here are some examples.

(4. 6-7) *age* *si* *sim-be* *banji-re* *de* *mangga*
sir 2SG 2SG(*si*/*sin*)-ACC live-IPFV. PTCP DAT difficult
se-ci, *min-i* *ere* *beye-re* *omiholo-ro*
say-COND 1SG(*bi*/*min*)-GEN this freeze-IPFV. PTCP starve-IPFV. PTCP
gosihon *i* *ba-be* *we-de* *alana-ra*
bitterness GEN situation-ACC who-DAT go. to. tell-IPFV. PTCP
Sir, if you think that it is difficult for YOU to make a living, (then) who should I go to tell about MY bitter suffering from cold and hunger? (MFG: 31)

(4. 6-8) *si* *sim-be* *ali-me* *mute-rakū* *se-ci*,
2SG 2SG(*si*/*sin*)-ACC take-IPFV. CVB be. able-IPFV. PTCP. NEG say-COND
i *sin-ci* *geli* *ali-me* *mute-rakū* *kai*
3SG 2SG(*si*/*sin*)-ABL still take-IPFV. CVB be. able-IPFV. PTCP. NEG PTL
If you say you cannot take (the responsibility), (then you should know that) he, even more (so) than you, cannot take (the responsibility, either).
(MFG: 25)

(4. 6-9) *si* *ere* *se-de* *uthai* *uttu* *oibo-ko*
2SG this age-DAT already so become. decrepit-PFV. PTCP
o-ci, *se* *baru* *o-ho* *manggi* *adarame*
become(AUX)-COND age toward become-PFV. PTCP after how
boo *boigon* *be* *jafa-me* *baita* *be* *icihiya-ci*
house family ACC hold-IPFV. CVB matter ACC manage-COND
o-mbi
become(AUX)-IPFV. FIN
se baru o-: to become aged, to get old
boo boigon: household
V-*ci o-*: complex structure expressing possibility/permission
If you are already so decrepit at this age, how could you manage your household and handle matters after you get (really) old? (MFG: 59)

(4. 6-10) *ere* *gese* *fijire-me* *goi-ha* *be*,
this like scrape. along. ground-IPFV. CVB hit. mark-PFV. PTCP ACC

si *aika* *dabu-ci*, *tere* *ca-fi* *jorin*
2SG if take. into. account-COND that/3SG miss-PFV. CVB target
goi-ha-ngge *be*, *aika* *colgoroko* *mangga*
hit. mark-PFV. PTCP-NMLZ ACC whether outstanding expert
se-me *kundule-ci* *aca-mbi-o*
say(AUX)-IPFV. CVB respect-COND suit(AUX)-IPFV. FIN-Q
fijire-me goi-: (of arrows) to scrape long the ground and hit the mark
ca-fi jorin goi-: (of arrows) to hit the mark by missing (a little)
V-*ci aca-*: complex structure expressing obligation
If you think that scraping along the ground and hitting the mark like this can be taken into account (as satisfactory), should (you also) respect those as outstanding experts, whose arrows miss the target (by a few inches) like that? (AGA1: 83-84)

(4. 6-11) *si* *untuhun* *beye* *ji-me* *šada-ci*, *wehe*
2SG empty body come-IPFV. CVB feel. tired-COND stone
jerguwen *juwe-fi* *hecen* *saha-ra* *niyalma*
material carry-PFV. CVB city build-IPFV. PTCP people
šada-rakū-n
feel. tired-IPFV. PTCP. NEG-Q
untuhun beye: empty-handed, lit.: "empty body"
While you, coming (here) empty-handed, feel tired, do those people not feel tired who, carrying stone materials, are building a city? (MYK6: 42)

As shown above, in (4. 6-7) the comparison concerns the hardship of living; in (4. 6-8) the comparison concerns the inability to take responsibility; in (4. 6-9) the comparison is about decrepitude; in (4. 6-10) the comparison is about skillfulness in archery; and (4. 6-11) concerns tiredness. Such comparison can serve to draw the addressee's attention to the latter state of affairs [(4. 6-9) and (4. 6-11)], or express the speaker's doubt about the state of affairs represented in the subordinate clause, which is usually admitted as true by the addressee in the previous context [(4. 6-7), (4. 6-8) and (4. 6-10)].[①]

① In its context, the addressee of (4. 6-7) has complained about hardships in his life; the speaker of (4. 6-8) implies in the context that the addressee has previously admitted that he (the addressee) cannot take responsibility; and the speaker of (4. 6-10) implies that the addressee has expressed his (the addressee's) opinion of good archery.

The conditional relation exists between the states of affairs described by the constructions, but not always in the content domain as it appears. It is necessary to analyse the constructions separately. First, in (4. 6-9) the speaker's observation that the addressee is decrepit at this age serves as a condition for the speaker's reasonable concern that in years to come the addressee may become unable to manage his household. In (4. 6-12), the speaker's (temporarily) accepting that the addressee is feeling tired serves as a condition for his logical reasoning that city-builders are also feeling tired, since they are labouring greatly while the addressee has not done any physical work. Similar are the cases of (4. 6-8) and (4. 6-11). In all these cases, the conditional relation concerns an inference from one state of affairs to another.

In (4. 6-7), the addressee's claim that he finds it difficult for himself to make a living is *not* a condition for the speaker's *telling* someone about his own suffering. Rather, according to the speaker, the addressee's claim would automatically justify the speaker's claim that he is suffering more in his life (thus, telling someone else or not is not the point). Since it is not the speaker but the addressee of this sentence who first brought up the topic of difficulty of life, the addressee, who actually suffers less than the speaker, is not justified to claim that life is difficult for him. In (4. 6-10), the addressee's view that the archery of someone whose arrows scrape along the ground and hit the mark is considered as satisfactory would automatically justify the view that those archers whose arrows miss the mark by only a few inches—who obviously outperform the former—should be respected as experts. Since in fact common sense dictates that the archery of the latter level cannot be considered as outstanding, it naturally follows that it is absurd to consider the archery of the former level as satisfactory. Here the reasoning method of *reductio ad absurdum* is used.

However, although in (4. 6-10) the conditional relation concerns the epistemic activity of inference, it is located in the content domain, not the epistemic domain. The reason is that each clause of this sentence explicitly describes an event of evaluation (*dabu-* "to take into account" in the subordinate clause; *kundule-* "to respect" in the main clause), and one event can logically lead to the other.

Declerck and Reed (2001: 331), in explaining English sentences similar to the comparison conditionals analysed here, argue that such sentences "create a transition from one (genuine) topic to another by finding or forcing, some feature common to old and new information". This explanation undoubtedly sheds some light on the function of such sentences. However, this statement somewhat fails to capture how the function is realised. In fact, from the analysis of the sentences above one can see that the conditional relation necessarily exists between the two states of affairs described in a sentence. This relation is distinctive in that it concerns the epistemic activity of inference from one point of view to another. The first point of view in the sentence may be temporarily accepted as true by the speaker, but can usually be refuted by the consequent reasoning of *reductio ad absurdum*.① It should be noted that while such a conditional relation can be present in the epistemic domain, it can also remain in the content domain in cases in which the construction itself consists of two events of evaluation (4. 6-10).

4.6.3 Disjunction Conditionals

Some conditionals can be used as disjunctive constructions, approximately corresponding to "either... or" in English. Here are some examples.

(4. 6-12) *balai*	*fiyente-me*		*gisun*	*eye-bu-rakū*	
unreasonably	spread. rumours-IPFV. CVB		words	flow-CAUS-IPFV. PTCP. NEG	
o-ci,	*uthai*	*niyalma*	*de*	*gebu*	*ara-mbi*
become(AUX)-COND	then	people	DAT	name	make-IPFV. FIN

fiyente-me gisun eyebu-: to spread rumours, lit.: "spreading rumours, make (them) flow"

gebu ara-: to call (someone) names

---

① However, in (4. 6-9) and (4. 6-11), which aim to draw the addressee's attention to the second part of the constructions, the presumptions made in the first part of the constructions are retained.

(He) either spreads rumours or calls people all kinds of names [lit. : "if (he) does not spread rumours, (he) will then call people names"]. (AGA4: 75)

(4.6-13) *ere* *be* *bai-rakū* *o-ci*, *tere* *be*
this ACC request-IPFV. PTCP. NEG become(AUX)-COND that/3SG ACC
nanda-mbi
demand-IPFV. FIN

(He) either requests this (man) or demands that (man) (to satisfy his wish) [lit. : "if (he) doesn't request this (man), (he) will demand that (man)"]. (OJ1: 94)

(4.6-14) *ere* *be* *nungne-rakū* *o-ci*, *tere* *be*
this ACC annoy-IPFV. PTCP. NEG become(AUX)-COND that/3SG ACC
neci-mbi
offend-IPFV. FIN

(He) either annoys this (man) or offends that (man) [lit. : "if (he) doesn't annoy this (man), (he) will offend that (man)]". (AGA3: 42-43)

(4.6-15) *ere* *be* *sure-bu-rakū* *o-ci*, *tere* *uthai*
this ACC yell-CAUS-IPFV. PTCP. NEG become(AUX)-COND that/3SG then
habšanji-mbi
come. to. accuse-IPFV. FIN

Either (he) makes this (man) yell, or that (man) will come to accuse (him of causing troubles) [lit. : "if (he) does not make this (man) yell, that (man) will come to accuse (him of causing troubles)"]. (AGA4: 78)

(4.6-16) *niyalma* *goro* *bodo-rakū* *o-ci*, *urunakū*
people far plan-IPFV. PTCP. NEG be(AUX)-COND definitely
hanci *jobolon* *bi*
near trouble EXS. PTL

goro bodo-: to plan about the future, lit. : "to plan far (into the future)"

hanci jobolon: current troubles, lit: "troubles nearby"

People either plan for the future or are concerned about current troubles (lit. : "if people don't plan for the future, (they) definitely have troubles at present").

(OJ2: 106)

One common characteristic of the disjunctive conditionals (4.6-12)-(4.6-16) is that the subordinate predicates take the negative form, consisting of the negative imperfective participle V-*rakū* and the conditional converb *o-ci*, while the main predicates take the affirmative form, either the imperfective finite form V-*mbi* or the existential particle *bi*.

The disjunctive conditionals describe two complementary states of affairs in the two clauses which nonetheless share the same topic and even the same subject.① For instance, (4.6-12)-(4.6-15) describe how a particular man behaves in an annoying manner, and (4.6-13)-(4.6-15) mention two victims of his mischief [*ere* "this (man)", *tere* "that (man)"]. It should be noted that the states of affairs described are used only to exemplify the speaker's view concerning the current topic, while the states of affairs themselves are usually generic in nature rather than specific. Therefore, the demonstratives such as *ere* "this (man)" and *tere* "that (man)" in (4.6-12), (4.6-13) and (4.6-15) do not necessarily refer to specific individuals in the speaker's mind, nor do the states of affairs refer to exactly what the speaker has witnessed: the fact known to the speaker may be much more complicated. It is possible that in (4.6-12)-(4.6-15) the speakers use the two events as examples because they are typical of what this particular person does, and thus general information is delivered by the speaker to the addressee about the person's behaviour. In the case of (4.6-16), it seems that planning for the future and worrying about the present are regarded as two typical aspects of the topic involved—what people think of their lives.

Despite the implicit information suggested by these sentences (that is, there is in fact much more to be said of the topic than what is represented in the constructions), it is important to concentrate on their explicit content in order to interpret the use of conditionals in juxtaposing two states of affairs concerning the same topic. The two states of affairs in a construction present a situation with two "choices", so that that if one does not hold, the other automatically does. This involves syllogism: the major premise is that one of the two states of affairs (and probably only one state of affairs) holds, the minor premise is that one of the states of affairs does not hold, and the conclusion is that the other state of affairs necessarily holds. Between the two states of affairs per se there may not be a

① In (4.6-12)-(4.6-14), the subordinate clause and main clause share the same subject, which is implicit in all cases. In (4.6-15), the main clause has a different subject from that of the subordinate clause, but both clauses share the same topic—this particular man's mischief.

conditional relation; rather, the conditional relation demonstrates itself in the mental leap required for inferring the affirmation of one state of affairs from the negation of the other state of affairs. Therefore, the conditional relation is presented in the epistemic domain.

From the analysis of the three types of conditionals, one can see a common pattern as to how the conditional relation—the prototypical meaning of the conditional converb—is realised: it concerns the act of perception or reasoning. Therefore, the conditional relation is usually—though not in every case—present in the perceptual domain or the epistemic domain.

4.6.4 Degree Conditionals

A small number of conditional sentences employ the adverb *ele* "more" together with the conditional converb in the subordinate clause, while the adverb *ele* (or in the form *elei*, which is not distinguishable in meaning from *ele*) is repeated in the main clause. Such constructions express the same meaning as the English comparative construction "the more..., the more...". Here are some examples.

(4.6-17) *ele* *juhe* *muke* *omi-ci*, *ele* *kangka-mbi*
more ice water drink-COND more be. thirsty-IPFV. FIN
The more iced water (I) drink, the thirstier (I) become. (OJ2: 152)

(4.6-18) *si* *ele* *tafula-ci*, *ele* *cilcin* *mada-mbi*
2SG more advise-COND more lump swell-IPFV. FIN
cilcin mada-: to be angry, lit.: "a lump to swell"
The more you (try to) appease (his anger), the angrier (he) becomes. (AGA4: 29)

(4.6-19) *gidaša-ra* *hūsun* *elei* *amba* *o-ci*,
oppress-IPFV. PTCP force more big become-COND
isele-re *hūsun* *elei* *amba* *o-mbi*
resist-IPFV. PTCP force more big become-IPFV. FIN
The greater the oppression (becomes), the stronger the resistance (will become). (IMN: 334)

On the surface the comparative meaning in the examples is not conditional. Sweetser (1996: 324-325), however, correlates the English construction "the Xer..., the Xer..." ("Xer" stands for the comparative of adjectives) to conditional constructions, arguing that they share a semantic structure. For instance, "The colder it gets, the happier we'll be" entails a conditional relation "If it gets colder, we'll be happier". Moreover, the degree of change of the two states of affairs seems to be proportionate to each other. The Manchu examples can also be analysed in a similar way. It can be inferred from the sentences that the states of affairs of the subordinate clause cause or enable the states of affairs of the main clause: in (4.6-17), the drinking of more iced water causes the stronger feeling of thirst, while in (4.6-19), greater oppression causes stronger resistance. In this sense, sentences (4.6-17)-(4.6-19) behave in much the same way as factual conditionals in Manchu, except for the presence of the adverb of degree *ele* "more" in both clauses. Furthermore, the causal relation between the two states of affairs can sometimes seem counter-intuitive: in (4.6-17) it is expected that drinking iced water would quench thirst, which is contrary to what is expressed by the sentence in question. Nevertheless, this unusual causal relation is exactly what the speaker intends to express in the context.

4.7 Evaluative Conditionals

In some sentences that share the basic morphosyntactic patterns of conditionals, the subject of the main clause, usually implicit, refers to the state of affairs represented by the subordinate clause. The main predicate can be regarded as an evaluation of the state of affairs represented by the subordinate clause. Semantically, these sentences consist of an overall single subject-predicate structure.

Just like ordinary conditionals, the predicates of the subordinate clauses can be either simple or complex. The following are some examples in which the subordinate clauses have simple predicates, which consist of the conditional converb of lexical verbs.

(4.7-1) *jurgan giyan be gai-me yabu-ci, beye-i teisu*
righteous principle ACC take-IPFV.CVB act-COND self-GEN responsibility
It is (one's) own responsibility to act in accordance with righteous principles [lit.: "if (one) acts in accordance with righteous principles, (it is one's) own responsibility"]. (AGA1: 117)

(4.7-2) *yaya ulin jaka-i mangga suilacun be sa-ci, oyonggo*
any wealth thing-GEN difficult hardship ACC know-COND important
mangga suilacun: difficulty and hardship
It is important (for one) to know the difficulty of (obtaining) any wealth [lit.: "if (one) knows the difficulty of (obtaining) any wealth, (it is) important"]. (AGA2: 8)

(4.7-3) *tuba-de sebderile-me te-ci, icangga*
that.place-DAT rest.in.a.shade-IPFV.CVB sit-COND comfortable
It is comfortable (for us) to sit there resting in the shade [lit.: "if (we) sit there, resting in the shade, (it'll be) comfortable"]. (MFG: 45)

(4.7-4) *emu tukiyesi simne-me dosi-ci, udu sali-mbi*
one provincial.graduate take.exams-IPFV.CVB enter-COND how.much be.worth-IPFV.FIN
simne-me dosi-: to take the examination and be admitted, to pass the examination
How much does it cost (one) to take an exam to become a provincial graduate? [lit.: "If (one) takes an exam to become a provincial graduate, how much does (it) cost (one)?"] (AGA3: 77)

There are some cases in which the subordinate clause consists of two juxtaposed converbs. The following example (4.7-5), which is also shown in the analysis of alternative concessive conditionals in Section 4.5.2.2 (4.5-20), consists of two independent sentences of the same type [(4.7-5a) and (4.7-5b)]. In both sentences, the subordinate clause consists of two coordinate clauses, each represented by a conditional converb (with its own implicit subject).

(4.7-5)(a) *tuci-ci* *dosi-ci* *gemu* *waka*;
go.out-COND come.in-COND all inappropriate
(b) *te-ci* *ili-ci* *gemu* *mangga* *kai*
sit-COND stand-COND all difficult PTL
It is inappropriate either to go out or to come in; it is difficult either to sit down or to stand up [lit.: "if (one) goes out, or if (one) comes in, (these are) both inappropriate; if (one) sits down, or if (one) stands up, (these are) both difficult"]. (OJ2: 124)

While the subordinate clauses in (4.7-1)-(4.7-5) have simple predicates, complex predicates can also be used, consisting of the conditional converb of an auxiliary verb and a certain form of a lexical verb as required by the auxiliary verb. The following are some examples. In the subordinate clause of (4.7-6) the predicate contains the conditional converb of the auxiliary *o-*, *o-ci*, forming a complex structure with the imperfective participle of a lexical verb V-*rA* (4.7-6). In (4.7-7b), the predicate of the subordinate clause contains *o-ci*, which in turn forms a complex structure with the negative imperfective participle, V-*rakū*. In (4.7-7a), the predicate of the subordinate clause contains the conditional converb of the auxiliary verb *se-*, *se-ci*, which forms a complex structure, V-*ki se-ci*, However, in (4.7-8) and (4.7-9) the predicates of the subordinate clauses are formed using the auxiliary bi- with converbs of lexical verbs.

(4.7-6) *sain* *ningge* *be* *alhūda-me* *yabu-re*, *ehe-ngge*
good NMLZ ACC imitate-IPFV.CVB act-IPFV.PTCP bad-NMLZ
be *targacun* *obu-re* *o-ci*, *beye* *gūnin*
ACC taboo make-IPFV.PTCP become(AUX)-COND body mind
de *ambula* *tusangga*
DAT greatly beneficial
targacun obu-: to beware of (something bad), lit.: "to make a taboo"

It is greatly beneficial to (one's) body and mind to act in imitation of what is good and to beware of what is bad [lit. : "if (one) acts in imitation of what is good and bewares of what is bad, (it is) greatly beneficial to (one's) body and mind"]. (OJ1: 79)

(4.7-7)(a) *bi* *gene-ki* *se-ci*, *inu* *min-i* *ciha*;
1SG go-OPT say(AUX)-COND also 1SG(*bi/min*)-GEN desire

(b) *gene-rakū* *o-ci*, *inu* *min-i ciha*
go-IPFV.PTCP.NEG be(AUX)-COND also 1SG(*bi/min*)-GEN desire

V-*ki se-*: complex structure expressing desire or intention

If I want to go (it is up to) my desire; if I do not go, (it is) also (up to my) desire. (MFG: 5)

(4.7-8) *damu* *ishunde* *mujilen* *de* *tebu-me* *bi-ci*,
only mutually heart DAT put-IPFV.CVB be(AUX)-COND
teni *gucu-i* *doro*
only.then friend-GEN way

gucu-i doro: the way of (being true) friends

Only if/when (people) put each other in (their) hearts (can it be) the way of (being true) friends. (MFG: 7)

(4.7-9) *boo-de* *noro-hoi* *bi-ci*, *absi* *ališacuka*
home-DAT stay-DUR be(AUX)-COND how boring

How boring it is to stay at home (all the time)! [lit: "if (one) stays at home (all the time), how boring (it will be)!"] (OJ2: 88)

In a few cases, the main clause can have an explicit subject expressed by a demonstrative, *tere* "that", which does not have a designatum in the outside world but refers to the state of affairs represented by the subordinate clause. The following is an example.

(4.7-10) *daruhai* *age-i* *tacibu-re* *be* *donji-ci*, *tere* *yala*
often sir-GEN teach-IPFV.PTCP ACC listen-COND that really
min-i *kesi* *o-ho*
1SG(*bi/min*)-GEN favour become-PFV.PTCP

If (I) can often hear your counsel, that will really be a favour for me.

(MFG: 26)

As stated at the beginning of this section, the main predicate of (4.7-1)-(4.7-10) serves to express an evaluation of the state of affairs represented by subordinate clause: the main predicate states something about the state of affairs (of the subordinate clause). It will be shown later that the same function of expressing evaluations is also realised in some examples that share the same morphosyntax as counterfactual conditionals [see (4.7-11)-(4.7-13)].

As shown in Section 4.1, ordinary conditionals typically have two subject-predicate structures (in terms of semantics), one in each clause. The semantic structure of a conditional can be represented by the formula "{Subj1+Pred1} ↔ {Subj2+Pred2}". Both "Subj1" and "Subj2" refer to entities in the outside world. However, when the main subject (Subj2) refers to the state of affairs represented by the subordinate clause ({Subj1 + Pred1}), the whole sentence semantically has a single subject-predicate structure. In particular, when the main subject does not have an explicit phonetic form, the formula becomes "Subj2{Subj1 + Pred1} ↔ Pred2", with only one overall subject-predicate structure. In a sense, the examples of this section are reduced or degenerate conditionals. It should be noted that this analysis only concerns semantics, while in terms of morphosyntax, the examples are not distinct from the basic patterns of factual conditionals. The lack of explicit subjects in the main clauses of (4.7-1)-(4.7-9) is also frequent elsewhere in Manchu.

Apart from the constructions (4.7-1)-(4.7-9), which share the morphosyntax of factual conditionals, some sentences which are morphosyntactically identical with counterfactual conditionals can also be considered to be evaluative conditionals. The states of affairs in question are counterfactual. The following are some examples.

(4.7-11)	*han*	*ahūn-de*	*emu*	*hebe*	*o-fi*,	*muse*	*de*
	khan	elder.brother-DAT	one	plan	become-PFV.CVB	1PL.INCL	DAT
	kimungge	*Daiming*	*gurun*	*be*	*daila-ki*	*se-me*	
	hostile	Daiming	empire	ACC	make.war	say(AUX)-IPFV.CVB	
	unggi-he		*bi-ci*,		*sain*	*bi-he*	*kai*

send-PFV. PTCP be(AUX)-COND good be-PFV. PTCP PTL

emu hebe o-: to collaborate, to be on the same side, lit.: "to be of one plan"

It would have been good if (you) had collaborated with my elder brother the khan, and had sent (a message) saying that (you would like to) wage war against the Daiming Empire, which is hostile to us (both). (MYK6: 26-27)

(4.7-12) *ine mene* *gama-ha* *bi-ci*, *sain* *bi-he*

willingly take-PFV. PTCP be(AUX)-COND good be-PFV. PTCP

ine mene: willingly, as one wishes

If (you) had taken that away as you wished, it would have been good. (OJ2: 150)

(4.7-13) *bi* *aika* *edun* *i* *cashūn* *bi-he* *bi-ci*,

1SG if wind GEN backward be-PFV. PTCP be(AUX)-COND

hono *yebe* *bi-he*

still good be-PFV. PTCP

edun i cashūn: with the back toward the wind

If I had been (walking) with my back toward the wind, (it) would have been good. (OJ2: 10)

In (4.7-11)-(4.7-13), the subordinate clauses contain the complex structure V-*hA bi-ci*, where V stands for a lexical verb [including the verb *bi-* "to exist/be", in the form *bi-he*, in the subordinate clause of (4.7-13)]. The main predicates invariably consist of a nominal (*sain* "good") and the perfective participle of the verb *bi-* "to exist/be" i.e., *bi-he*. The function of expressing evaluation is transparent.

Like the factual examples (4.7-1)-(4.7-10), the counterfactual evaluative conditionals also consist of an overall single subject-predicate structure in terms of semantics (but not morphosyntax). Thus, sentences (4.7-11)-(4.7-12) can be regarded as (semantically) reduced or degenerate counterfactual conditionals.

4.8 Conditionals and Topic Constructions

Numerous studies have addressed the important questions of how to define subject and topic, and how to distinguish the two concepts from each other in languages of different grammatical systems. (e. g. Li and Thompson 1976; Chafe 1976) In his well-known paper, Keenan (1976) proposes a detailed method that can be applied to nouns or nominal structures in order to determine whether or not they are subjects. In Altaic languages (Turkic, Mongolic and Tungusic languages), which are not topic-prominent, nominals used to encode the subject can denote an agent, an experiencer, or some other semantic role, while at the same time functioning as the topic. ① When semantic and pragmatic structures do not coincide, Altaic languages normally use certain markers to indicate the topic. In this respect, Manchu (and probably Classical Mongolian as well) occupies a special status among Altaic languages, since it has developed—in addition to simple topic markers—a series of special syntactic structures to mark the topic. (Gorelova 2004: 61; Gorelova and Orlovskaja 2010) This section analyses some sentences in Manchu that formally appear to be factual conditionals but are actually topic constructions. In such a sentence a conditional converb (V-*ci*) and a preceding component form a left-dislocated structure that functions as the topic. The conditional converb can be that of the copular verb *o-* "to become/be", the quotative verb *se-* "to say", or of any lexical verb. The following analysis is arranged in accordance with the choice of conditional converb.

The first type of topic construction makes use of the conditional converb of the verb *o-* "to become/be", *o-ci*, which is placed after a nominal [(4. 8-1)-(4. 8-5)], or after a nominalised structure (4. 8-6). The topicalised nominal structures can consist of only a single noun [(4. 8-1), (4. 8-4) and (4. 8-5)] or of a noun modified by a clause [(4. 8-2) and (4. 8-3)]. Here are some examples.

(4. 8-1)	*booha*	*o-ci*,	*amtan*	*suwaliyata*,	*guwejihe*
	delicacies	TOP(<become-COND)	taste	miscellaneous	stomach

① It should be noted that in contrast to Altaic languages, the Altaic-like (or quasi-Altaic) languages, Korean and Japanese, are subject- and topic-prominent (Li and Thompson 1976: 460), and possess distinct markers for both the subject and the topic.

kokira-bu-mbi
harm-PASS-IPFV. FIN
Speaking of delicacies, (their) tastes are miscellaneous, (and because of this) one's stomach will be harmed. (AGA2: 111)

(4.8-2) *Manju bithe hūla-ra niyalma o-ci,*
Manchu book read-IPFV. PTCP people TOP (< become-COND)
urunakū hergen tome gemu getukele-me sa-ci
definitely word every all make. clear-IPFV. CVB know-COND
aca-mbi
suit(AUX)-IPFV. FIN
V-*ci aca-*: complex structure expressing obligation
Concerning the people who read Manchu books, (they) should make clear (the meaning of) each and every word (of the books). (MFG: 3)

(4.8-3) *im-be sa-rkū urse o-ci,*
3SG(*i/in*)-ACC know-IPFV. PTCP. NEG people TOP (< become-COND)
tere be durun ara-mbi se-mbi
that/3SG ACC form make-IPFV. FIN say-IPFV. FIN
sa-rkū < *sa-ra* [know-IPFV. PTCP] + akū [NEG]
durun ara-: to be pretentious, to put on airs
As for those people who do not know him (well), (they) will say that he is pretentious. (lit.: "... say him to be pretentious") (MFG: 56)

(4.8-4) *tubihe o-ci, ure-re hanci-kan banji-me*
fruit TOP (< become-COND) ripen-IPFV. PTCP rather. near grow-IPFV. CVB
gai-fi teni sain
take-PFV. CVB only. then good
ure-re hancikan: when nearly ripe, lit.: "rather near ripening"
As for fruits, (it is) good to take (and eat them) only when (the fruits) grow until they are nearly ripe. (AGA2: 119)

(4.8-5)(a) *dulga o-ci, ji-he elcin be wa-ki*
half TOP (< become-COND) come-PFV. PTCP messenger ACC kill-OPT
se-mbi;
say-IPFV. FIN
(b) *dulga o-ci, oforo šan be faita-fi*
half TOP (< become-COND) nose ear ACC cut-PFV. CVB
unggi-ki se-mbi
send-OPT say-IPFV. FIN

As for half (of them), (they) say, "(let's) kill the messenger"; As for (the other) half (of them), (they) say, "(let's) cut off (the messenger's) nose and ears and send (him back)!" (MYK6: 19)

(4. 8-6)

tere	*taci-re*	*de*	*bulcakū-ngge*	*o-ci*,
that/3SG	learn-IPFV. PTCP	DAT	lazy-NMLZ	TOP (< become-COND)
damu	*sefu-i*	*šorgi-re*	*be*	*tuwa-mbi*
only	teacher-GEN	urge-IPFV. PTCP	ACC	look-IPFV. FIN

As for those lazy at learning, (they) only depend on the teacher's urging (them) [lit: "... only look to the teacher's urging (them)"]. (AGA1: 62)

In (4. 8-1)-(4. 8-6) except (4. 8-1), the subject is omitted, which is common in Manchu. The nominal or nominalised structures marked by the conditional converb *o-ci*, which serve as the topics, refer to the same entities as the (omitted) subjects [(4. 8-2), (4. 8-3), (4. 8-5) and (4. 8-6)] as well as the object [of the verb *gai-* "to get" in (4. 8-4)] of the ensuing clauses. For instance, in (4. 8-2), the topicalised nominal structure *manju bithe hūla-ra niyalma* "people reading Manchu books" refers to exactly the same entity as does the omitted subject of the following clause. In (4. 8-4) the nominal *tubihe* "fruits" has two roles. First, it is logically the omitted subject of the verb structure *ure-re hancikan banji-me* "growing till almost ripe"; second, it is also the omitted object of the verb *gai-(fi)* "taking", which has its implicit subject, "people (in general)".

In (4. 8-1), where no subject or object is omitted in the clauses following the conditional converb *o-ci*, the nominal *booha* "delicacies" is a topic proper, bearing relevance to the following clauses without logically being the subject or object of either of them: the subject of the first clause *amtan* "taste" is relevant to *booha* "delicacies", and the second clause *guwejihe kokirabumbi* "the stomach will be harmed" is causally linked to the first clause and therefore also relevant to *booha*.

It should also be noted that (4. 8-5) consists of two sentences [(4. 8-5a) and (4. 8-5b)], each of them an independent topic construction. They are juxtaposed for contrast.

The second type of construction uses the conditional converb of the quotative verb *se-* "to say", *se-ci*. It can follow a nominal or pronominal structure [(4. 8-7)-(4. 8-9)] in the same way as the conditional converb *o-ci*, while it can also take a complement clause whose predicate has a finite verb form (4. 8-10). The following are some examples.

(4. 8-7)

inenggi	*se-ci*,	*moo-i*	*abdaha*	*ci*	*hono*	*fulu*	*kai*
day	TOP (< say-COND)	tree-GEN	leaf	ABL	still	many	PTL

"Speaking of (our) days (in the future), (they are) indeed more numerous than the leaves of a tree". (MFG: 21)

(4. 8-8)

nure	*se-ci*,	*horon-i*	*okto*	*geli*	*waka*,
wine	TOP (< say-COND)	poison-GEN	drug	even	NEG
oktolo-me	*wa-ra*	*de*	*gele-mbi*	*semeo*	
poison-IPFV. CVB	kill-IPFV. PTCP	DAT	fear-IPFV. FIN	PTL	

horon i okto: poisonous drug

oktolo-me wa-: to poison to death

Speaking of wine, (it is) not even poison; (do you) fear (that it will) poison (you) to death? (MFG: 47)

(4. 8-9)

(a)	*bi*	*se-ci*,	*Manju*	*gurun*;
	1SG	TOP (< say-COND)	Manchu	people
(b)	*suwe*	*se-ci*,	*Hūlun*	*gurun*
	2PL	TOP (< say-COND)	Hulun	people

As for me, (I am of) the Manchu people; as for you, (you are of) the Hulun people. (MYK2: 26)

(4. 8-10)

(a)	*buda*	*je-mbi*	*se-ci*,	*bi*	*yargiyan i*	*sin-de*	
	meal	eat-IPFV. FIN	TOP (< say-COND)	1SG	really	2SG(*si*/*sin*)-DAT	
	isi-rakū;						
	reach-IPFV. PTCP. NEG						
(b)	*nure*	*omi-ki*	*se-ci*,	*si*	*min-ci*	*cingkai*	
	wine	drink-OPT	TOP (< say-COND)	2SG	1SG(*bi*/*min*)-ABL	completely	
	eberi						
	weak						

Speaking of eating, I really am no match for you (lit.: "I cannot reach your level"); (but) speaking of drinking, you are absolutely too weak (a match) for me (lit: "If we say 'let's drink', you are much worse than I am").

(MFG: 52)

In (4. 8-7), the nominal *inenggi* "day(s)", highlighted by the converb *se-ci*, is referentially the real subject of the following clause. Similarly in (4. 8-8), the nominal *nure* "wine" is the real subject of the first clause/ predicative structure (i. e. not being poison), and the subject of the embedded verb structure *oktolo-me wa-ra* "killing by poisoning" of the second clause. Example (4. 8-9) consists of two topic constructions, just as (4. 8-5), functioning as contrastive topics. However, it differs from (4. 8-5) in that the topic marker is *se-ci* instead of *o-ci*, and that the topicalised components are pronouns [*bi* "I", and *suwe* "you (pl.)"].

Example (4. 8-10) also consists of two topic sentences, which together show a contrast. However, the topicalised information in each construction is a state of affairs, represented by a finite verb structure instead of a nominal one (which represents only a state, rather than an action). Specifically, in the first clause, the state of affairs represented by *buda jembi* "eat (meals)" is topicalised, while in the second clause, it is the state of affairs represented by *nure omi-ki* "drink wine". In each of the clauses, the subject and the predicate are related to the topicalised state of affairs. For instance, in the first clause, the speaker's considering himself not as good as the addressee is relevant to the topic of eating meals. Thus, the conditional converb *se-ci* in (4. 8-10) serves to set the background for the information of the ensuing clause. This function lies exactly at the core of conditionality in that the realisation of one state of affairs can be understood as the background for the realisation of the other state of affairs. Nevertheless, conditionality mostly denotes a causal relation, which is lacking in topicality.

It should be noted that the nominalised participles of the quotative verb *se-* "to say", just like its conditional converb, can also serve as a topic marker. The following are two examples where the form *se-re-ngge* serves as a topic marker, which takes as its complement a nominal structure (4. 8-11) or a finite verb form (4. 8-12). Functionally, they are identical to (4. 8-7)-(4. 8-10).

(4. 8-11) *tere* *age* *se-re-ngge*, *muse-i* *fe*
that young. man TOP (< say-IPFV. PTCP-NMLZ) 1PL. INCL-GEN old
adaki *kai*
neighbour PTL
Speaking of that man, (he is actually) our old neighbour. (OJ1: 29)

(4. 8-12) *gabta-mbi* *se-re-ngge*, *muse-i*
shoot. arrow-IPFV. FIN TOP (< say-IPFV. PTCP-NMLZ) 1PL. INCL-GEN
Manju-sa-i *oyonggo* *baita*
Manchu-PL-GEN important matter
Speaking of archery [lit.: "saying that (one) shoots arrows"], (it is) an important matter for us Manchus. (OJ1: 39)

Returning to the conditional converb *o-ci*, it seems that apart from nominals and nominalised structures, case structures (that is, nominal or pronominals governed by postposed case markers) can also be topicalised, especially the dative-locative (governed by *de*) and the accusative (governed by *be*) structures. Here are some examples.

(4. 8-13)(a) *alban* *de* *o-ci*, *emu julehen i* *yabu-mbi*;
duty DAT TOP (< become-COND) whole-heartedly act-IPFV. FIN
(b) *boo* *de* *o-ci*, *emu suihen i* *banji-mbi*
home DAT TOP (< become-COND) clear-mindedly live-IPFV. FIN
emu julehen/suihen i: both meaning basically the same, "with (one's) whole heart/a clear mind"
When (he is) on duty, (he) acts whole-heartedly; when (he is) at home, (he) lives a life with a clear mind. (OJ1: 50)

(4. 8-14) *te* *min-de* *o-ci*, *min-i* *jalin* *de*
now 1SG(*bi/min*)-DAT TOP (< become-COND) 1SG(*bi/min*)-GEN sake DAT
gūwa *be* *geli* *gabta-rakūbi-o*
other ACC also shoot-IPFV. NEG. FIN-Q
Now as for me, would I not shoot (arrows) at other people for my (own) sake?
(MYK2: 2)

(4. 8-15) *ler ler* *se-re* *bithe-i* *niyalma* *be*
amiable say(AUX)-IPFV. PTCP book-GEN people ACC
o-ci, *durun* *tuwakū* *obu-me* *alhūda-ra*

TOP (< become-COND) model example make-IPFV. CVB imitate-IPFV. PTCP

giyan

reason

ler ler sere: amiable

bithei niyalma: the literati, lit.: "people of books"

V-*rA giyan*: structure expressing obligation/necessity

As for the amiable literati, (people) should make them (good) examples (for others) to follow. (UH: 31)

(4. 8-16) *hoo hoo* *sere* *cooha-i* *niyalma* *be*

brave say(AUX)-IPFV. PTCP army-GEN people ACC

o-ci, *kalka* *hecen* *obu-me* *nikendu-re* *giyan*

TOP (< become-COND) shield city. wall make-IPFV. CVB depend-IPFV. PTCP reason

hoo hoo sere: brave

cooha-i niyalma: warrior(s), lit.: "man/people) of the army"

kalka hecen: shield and wall

As for brave warriors, (people) should make them the shield and wall (on which) to depend (to protect the city). (UH: 32)

(4. 8-17) *aika* *cen-i* *gese* *asihata* *be* *o-ci*,

if 3PL(ce/cen)-GEN like youngster ACC TOP (< become-COND)

min-i *yasa-i* *hošo-de* *inu* *dabu-rakū*

1SG(*bi*/*min*)-GEN eye-GEN corner-DAT even take. into. account-IPFV. PTCP. NEG

kai

PTL

Speaking of young people like them, I wouldn't take them seriously (at all) [lit.: "... take (them) into account (by glancing at them) from the corner of my eye"]. (OJ1: 82)

The same as (4. 8-5), (4. 8-9) and (4. 8-10), example (4. 8-13) also consists of two topic constructions, each of which sets the domain of the topic for the state of affairs of the following clause. Apart from the gloss of (4. 8-13), it seems that the verb *o-* in the two constructions can also be interpreted as a verb meaning "to become/be", which has an implicit subject "he". In this case the translation provided is literally understood as expressing a temporal relation: the time when he is working and the time when he is staying at home. Still, the temporal relation can also set the background for a state of affairs, and the temporal subordinate clause can serve as a topic.

Example (4.8-14) topicalises the dative-locative structure *min-de* "to me", while the following clause reveals information concerning the speaker (myself). However, in contrast with (4.8-13), the conditional converb *o-ci* in (4.8-14) serves as a topic marker, and *min-de o-ci* cannot be interpreted as a structure expressing a temporal (or conditional) relation. The reason is that no subject referring to an entity in the outside world can be properly identified for *o-ci* in the structure *min-de o-ci*. Rather, this "subject" could only be identified as one referring to a discourse or textual entity such as "the state of affairs in question" or "the current conversational topic", in which the structure *min-de o-ci* could be understood as "if/when the state of affairs in question is to/about me". Then one would find that, despite its form as a temporal or conditional structure, this understanding would also lead to the same function (topicalisation) as the phrase "as for me" in the English translation.

When the conditional converb *o-ci* follows an accusative case structure, as in (4.8-15)-(4.8-17), its role as a topicaliser becomes all the more salient. The reasons are that, first, the accusative case structure in question is obviously the real argument of the lexical verb in the following clause, and that without the converb *o-ci* it fits perfectly in the clause. Second, the conditional converb *o-ci* performs no other function than drawing the addressee's attention to the accusative case structure. In this respect, (4.8-15) is similar to (4.8-14) in that there cannot be a subject referring to an outside-world entity for the converb *o-ci*, but perhaps only a subject which refers to a discourse or textual entity. Yet, even if one assumes that such a subject of *o-ci* exists, one still has to account for the presence of the accusative marker *be*, which indicates the existence of a verb requiring the accusative case—a verb denoting an action, or at any rate "what to do" with the entity denoted by the nominal structure governed by the accusative case. Such a verb is missing in the structure since it is present only in the following clause, for instance, *obu-* "to make" and *alhūda-* "to imitate" in (4.8-15).

The attempt to identify the abstract subject may shed some light on the cognitive process involved in the adoption of the conditional converb *o-*

ci as a topic marker; that is, how conditionality is related to topicalisation here. Example (4. 8-17) is particularly revealing in this respect, which makes use of the conditional connector *aika* "if" together with the conditional converb *o-ci* in topicalising the accusative case structure. By itself (4. 8-17) is not a conditional construction, but the conditional connector *aika* seems to represent the mental activity of supposition. It is then reasonable to analyse it in a domain of representation different from the content domain—indeed in the speech-act domain. The function of the framed structure *aika ... be o-ci* becomes clear: the supposition that the current conversational topic concerns what to do with the young people [therefore indicated by *asihata* in (4. 8-17) in the accusative case] leads to the speech act of offering the comment that one (the speaker) does not take those young people seriously. The supposition, which is expressed via linguistic forms, naturally highlights, or topicalises, the accusative case structure. In a similar way, this analysis also applies to (4. 8-15) and (4. 8-16), though they do not contain the conditional connector *aika*.

Following this line of thought, the mechanism involved in the previously analysed topic constructions (4. 8-1)-(4. 8-10), which contain the conditional converbs *o-ci* or *se-ci* but no dative-locative or accusative case structures, can also be explained. First, in the case of topic constructions containing the converb *o-ci*, an abstract, discourse subject denoting "the current conversational topic" can be reasonably identified, just as in the analysis of (4. 8-14). For instance, in (4. 8-1), *booha o-ci* can be interpreted in a verbose way as "if the current conversational topic concerns dishes", while the following clause can be interpreted as the speaker's speech act: "I offer the following comment that... ". Thus the conditional relation is established in the speech-act domain, but not in the content domain of the construction. Second, in the case of topic constructions containing the converb *se-ci*, it suffices to consider the original meaning (to say) and the common function of the quotative verb *se-*, in which case a subject (referring to a human being) can be identified for it. For instance, in (4. 8-7), *nure se-ci* can be interpreted as "if I/we speak of wine", and the following clause, just as in (4. 8-1), can be considered as a performance of a speech act: "I offer the following comment that...".

Some of the dative-locative case structures topicalised by *o-ci* have become fixed or nearly fixed expressions in Manchu, serving as text connectors. Their function is comparable to the English expressions "for one thing..., for another..." or "on the one hand..., on the other..." The following are two examples.

(4.8-18) *emu-de o-ci, min-de ungga jalan-i*

one-DAT TOP (< become-COND) 1SG(*bi/min*)-DAT senior generation-GEN

niyalma bi, ere age be sabu-re unde;

people EXS.PTL this young.man ACC see-IPFV.PTCP not.yet

jai-de o-ci, ji-he taitai-sa,

second-DAT TOP (< become-COND) come-PFV.PTCP madame-PL

min-i mentuhun sarganjui be inu majige tuwa-ki

1SG(*bi/min*)-GEN foolish daughter ACC also a.little look-OPT

min-i mentuhun sarganjui: a humble way of referring to one's own daughter, lit.: "my foolish daughter"

For one thing, there are people of the elder generation (in my family), (who) haven't met this young man yet; for another thing, Mesdames, (you) who have come (to my house), please take a look at my daughter as well. (OJ2: 70)

(4.8-19) *suwe emu ergi-de o-ci, menggun be*

2PL one side-DAT TOP (< become-COND) money ACC

baitala-ki se-re jalin, emu ergi-de

use-OPT say(AUX)-IPFV.PTCP sake one side-DAT

o-ci, madagan be baha-ki se-re

TOP (< become-COND) interest ACC get-OPT say(AUX)-IPFV.PTCP

turgun sui akū men-i akdula-ra niyalma

reason guilt NEG 1PL.EXCL(*be/men*)-GEN warrant-IPFV.PTCP people

be ušabu-fi aina-mbi

ACC implicate-PFV.CVB do.what-IPFV.FIN

V-*ki se-*: complex structure expressing intention/desire

sui akū: innocent, lit.: "no guilt"

akdula-ra niyalma: warrantor(s)

V-*fi aina-*: why do something, what is the point of doing something

Why do you, for the sake of using money on one hand, and in order to earn interest on the other, implicate us, (who are) the innocent warrantors? (MFG: 58)

Apart from the conditional converb of the auxiliary verbs, topic constructions can also employ the conditional converbs of ordinary lexical verbs, as in the following examples. Except for (4. 8-23), examples (4. 8-20)-(4. 8-23) each of them consists of two parallel, semantically related topic sentences.

(4. 8-20)(a) *kangna-ci*, *eihen* *ja*;
ride-COND donkey easy
(b) *bungna-ci*, *aha* *ja*
bully-COND slave easy
A donkey is easy to ride on; a slave is easy to bully (lit. : "As for riding, a donkey is easy; as for bullying, a slave is easy"). (Proverb) (OJ2: 38)

(4. 8-21)(a) *yabu-ci*, durun;
walk-COND model
(b) *ašša-ci*, *kemun*
move-COND standard
When (he) walks, (he can be seen as) a model; when (he) moves, (he can be regarded as) the standard. (OJ1: 50)

(4. 8-22)(a) *je-ci*, *jete-re-ngge* *akū*;
eat-COND eat-IPFV. PTCP-NMLZ NEG
(b) *etu-ci*, *etu-re-ngge* *akū*
wear-COND wear-IPFV. PTCP-NMLZ NEG
As for eating, there is nothing to eat; as for clothing, there is nothing to wear. (OJ1: 64)

(4. 8-23) *aika* *jobo-ci*, *saman* *gege* *fulu* *jobo-ho*
if toil-COND shaman lady much toil-PFV. PTCP
If (anyone) has toiled, (it is) the shaman (who) has toiled. (NSB: 88)

In all the four examples above, the lexical verb in the form of a conditional converb serves to set the domain of topic for the state of affairs in the following clause, but does not display any real conditional or temporal relation. For instance, in (4. 8-20), the conditional converb *kangna-ci* [ride-COND] sets the domain of the topic for the statement *eihen* [donkey] *ja* [easy]. Furthermore, there is a semantic relation between the converb and the nominal *eihen* [donkey], the latter being the former's patient (thematically). Similarly in (4.8-21), the person being described, though only implied, is the one who performs the act denoted by the conditional converb *yabu-ci* [walk-COND]. The two sentences in example (4.8-22) first set the domain of the topic with the conditional converb of a lexical verb [*je-ci* in (4.8-22a), *etu-ci* in (4.8-22b)] and then repeats the same lexical verb in the nominalised structures (*jete-re-ngge* in [4.8-22a] and *etu-re-ngge* in [4.8-22b]), which in turn serves as the subject of the clause. Finally, in (4.8-23), the conditional converb *jobo-ci* [toil-COND] determines the topic concerning who has toiled, and the following clause is a comment on the toil of a relevant person. Similarly (4.8-17), the topic structure of (4.8-23) has the conditional connector *aika* "if", which can be regarded as an indicator of the mental activity of supposition involved.

With all the examples analysed, the following is a general remark on previous studies concerning the relation between conditionals and topic constructions. Haiman (1978) argues that conditionals are actually topics, since conditionals share the characteristic of topics, that is, the givenness of information. This view of identifying conditionals with topics has been criticised by other scholars. Sweetser (1990) points out that a conditional usually has a hypothetical nature and therefore its protasis is not presupposed to be true. In this sense, the protasis of a conditional is not given information. As Sweetser (1990: 126) argues, the protasis "is given only relative to the apodosis". Moreover, according to Sweetser, the protasis serves as a sufficient condition for the fulfilment of the apodosis. Similarly, Gorelova (2006) points out that the causal relation exists within conditionals but not in topic constructions. Gorelova also stresses a difference between conditionals and topics: topic is a pragmatic relation, and conditional is semantic. Thus, conditionals are conceptually distinct from topics.

Nonetheless, conditionals and topics are somehow interrelated. Traugott (1985) notes that diachronically topic markers are among the forms in which conditional markers may originate. On the other hand,

Gorelova (2006) explores the use of existential verbs[①] and verbs of speech as topic markers in Altaic languages (including Manchu), in particular the cases where these verbs occur as conditional converbs. Gorelova (2006) states that existential verb structures introduce indefinite nominals, through which the nominals become given in context and can serve as topics. However, Gorelova (2006) does not elaborate further on the mechanism involved in topicalisation concerning how the givenness of conditionality leads to the givenness of topicality. This is where the present study makes its contribution. The analysis of this section adopts the cognitive perspective in explaining how the core meanings of the verbs *o-* and *se-* cooperate with the conditional converb in topicalising other structures: operating in the speech-act domain, the converb *o-ci/se-ci* connects the supposition about the current conversational topic and the speech-act of offering a relevant topic through conditionality.

4.9 Constructions Containing Perception Verbs or Cognition Verbs

In a number of conditional-like constructions in Manchu, the verbs in the subordinate clauses that occur as the conditional converb denote acts of perception, or of obtaining or processing information. On the other hand, the main clauses specify the content of perception, the information obtained, or the result of the processed information. As a whole, these constructions function to indicate the source of information—evidentiality, an important concept that has been extensively studied cross-linguistically (Chafe and Nichols 1986; De Haan 1999, 2001, 2006; Palmer 2001; Aikhenvald 2003, 2004), or the mental activities involved in processing information.

In terms of the interclausal relation within these constructions, it seems that conditionality does not exist directly between the two states of

① Gorelova (2006: 149) terms the verbs *bi-* "to exist/be" and *o-* "to become/be" both as "existential verbs".

affairs involved. In some cases, the conditional relation can be found in a domain other than the content domain. In other cases, the temporal relation can be established. Constructions of the last type can be regarded as a special subtype of temporal construction.

4.9.1 Evidential Strategies in Manchu

In Manchu, evidentiality does not constitute a grammatical category as such, but is expressed through lexical and syntactic means. Specifically, it is expressed by structures formed using perception verbs such as *tuwa-* "to look",① *donji-* "to listen/hear" and *amtala-* "to taste", when their subjects designate the speaker of the sentence. Relevant to this study are cases in which the perception verbs occur as the conditional converb (V-*ci*) in the subordinate clause. The following are some examples in which the verb *tuwa-* "to look" is used.

(4.9-1)	*min-i*	*beye*	*nimeku*	*arbun*	*be*	*tuwa-ci*	*ujen*
	1SG(*bi/min*)-GEN	self	illness	situation	ACC	look-COND	serious

The situation of my illness appears to be serious [lit.: "Looking at the situation of (my) illness myself, (I find it) serious"]. (NSB: 7)

(4.9-2)	*sim-be*	*tuwa-ci,*	*arki*	*nure*	*de*	*haji*
	2SG(*si/sin*)-ACC	look-COND	liquor	wine	DAT	dear

You seem to be fond of liquor and wine [lit.: "Looking at you, (I find that you are) fond of liquor and wine"]. (OJ2: 184)

(4.9-3)	*im-be*	*tuwa-ci,*	*gebsere-fi*	*giranggi*	*teile*
	3SG(*i/in*)-ACC	look-COND	emaciate-PFV.CVB	bone	only
	funce-hebi				
	remain-PFV.FIN				

Looking at him, (one could see/I saw that he) was emaciated, (and) only bones remained (of him). (OJ2: 132)

---

① As already pointed out in Section 4.3.2.4, the verb *tuwa-* "to look" is considered as a perception verb in a rather general sense. It seems that the verb denoting visual perception, *sabu-* "to see", does not occur in the form of the conditional converb in the same syntactic position as the conditional converb of *tuwa-*.

(4. 9-4) *ere-be* *tuwa-ci*, *jalan i* *baita* *teksin* *akū* *mujangga*
this-ACC look-COND world GEN affairs equal NEG true
Looking at this, (one can see that) the affairs of the world are really not the same (as each other). (OJ2: 74)

(4. 9-5) *te* *bi* *tuwa-ci*, *suwen-i* *ere* *cooha* *de* *afa-ha*
now 1SG look-COND 2PL(suwe/suwen)-GEN this troops DAT fight-PFV. PTCP
se-me *tusa* *akū*, *urunakū* *buce-mbi*
say(AUX)-IPFV. CVB benefit NEG certainly die-IPFV. FIN
V-*hA se-me*: the concessive structure meaning "even if someone does something"
Now it appears to me (lit.: "as I look") that even if (my troops) fight against your troops, there will be no benefit (for me), —(I) will certainly die.
(MYK7: 11)

In (4. 9-1)-(4. 9-4), the perception verb *tuwa-* "to look" takes a direct object—nominal (4. 9-1) or pronominal [(4. 9-2)-(4. 9-4)] in the accusative case—which represents the perceived entity, while the main clause of each construction expresses the speaker's (referentially also the perceiver's) evaluation of this perceived entity [(4. 9-1)-(4. 9-3)] or the speaker's inference or conclusion [(4. 9-4) and (4. 9-5)]. In (4. 9-5) the verb *tuwa-* "to look" does not have an explicit direct object, but the existence of the perceived entity can be inferred from the context, which is the status quo of the warfare. While the perception verb *tuwa-* "to look" would be expected to indicate that the information is obtained via visual perception, it usually represents it in a metaphorical way. Specifically, visual perception is literally represented in (4. 9-1)-(4. 9-3), whereas in (4. 9-4) and (4. 9-5), the verb *tuwa-* "to look" actually refers to the mental activity of knowing, which is metaphorically the visual perception of one's mind's eye.

In some cases the perception verb *tuwa-* "to look" takes a complement clause, instead of a simple nominal or pronominal as its object, as shown by (4. 9-6) and (4. 9-7).

(4.9-6) *gucu-se* *gemu* *sim-be* *leole-he* *be* *tuwa-ci*,
friend-PL all 2SG(*si/sin*)-ACC discuss-PFV.PTCP ACC look-COND
sin-de *inu* *majige* *bi-fi* *dere*
2SG(*si/sin*)-DAT also a.little be-PFV.CVB PTL
Looking at (the fact) that all your friends have been talking about you, (I suppose that) probably there is something (true in what they say) about you.
(OJ2: 6)

(4.9-7) *in-i* *tere* *baita-be* *getukele-me* *yargiyala-rakū*,
3SG(*i/in*)-GEN that affair-ACC clarify-IPFV.CVB verify-IPFV.PTCP.NEG
kalu mulu *tuttu* *yabu-re* *be* *tuwa-ci*,
careless that.way behave-IPFV.PTCP ACC look-COND
aimaka *emu* *pulu pala* *muwa* *niyalma-i* *gese*
seemingly one disorderly imprudent person-GEN like
kalu mulu: careless
pulu pala: disorderly
aimaka... *i gese*: a similative structure meaning "seemingly like..."
Looking at (the fact) that he does not clarify or verify that matter, (and) behaves carelessly that way, (I think that he looks) like an unorganised, imprudent person. (AGA4: 92)

The perception verb *donji-* "to listen/hear" occurs as the conditional converb *donji-ci* to indicate that the information is gained via hearsay, as shown by (4.9-8)-(4.9-11) below. Particularly, in (4.9-8), (4.9-9) and (4.9-11), the quotative verb *se-* "to say" is also used in combination with *donji-*, a usage described in the Qing Dynasty grammars (e.g., UH: 68). Moreover, (4.9-10) specifies the source of information as *niyalma-i ala-ra* "people's saying". Also, the time of the hearsay is not restricted to the time of utterance (the present), and past time reference is also permissible: (4.9-11) specifies the time of hearsay as *sikse* "yesterday".

(4.9-8) *donji-ci*, *si* *te* *Manju* *bithe* *taci-mbi* *se-mbi*
hear-COND 2SG now Manchu book learn-IPFV.FIN say-IPFV.FIN
[I] hear [people] say that you read Manchu books. (OJ1: 17)

(4. 9-9) *te* *donji-ci*, *mujakū* *hūwaša-fi* *hafan* *o-ho*
now hear-COND truly grow. up-PFV. CVB official become-PFV. PTCP
se-re
say-IPFV. PTCP
Now (I) hear (people) say that (he) has truly grown up and become an official. (OJ1: 29)

(4. 9-10) *niyalma-i* *ala-ra* *be* *donji-ci*, *tere* *niyalma*,
people-GEN tell-IPFV. PTCP ACC hear-COND that man
fuhali *enduri* *adali* *banji-habi*
really god like grow-PFV. FIN
(I) hear people say that that man is grown (in such way that he looks) like a god. (OJ2: 28)

(4. 9-11) *sikse* *donji-ci*, *muse-i* *hebeše-he* *songkoi*
yesterday hear-COND 1PL. INCL-GEN discuss-PFV. PTCP according
yabu-bu-ha *se-mbi*
handle-PASS. PFV. PTCP say-IPFV. FIN
Yesterday (I) heard that (the matter) was handled according to (the result of) our discussion. (AGA3: 6)

The sense of taste as the source of information is indicated by the perception verb *amtala-* "to taste" in (4. 9-12).

(4. 9-12) *bi* *amtala-ci* *majige* *nitan*
1SG taste-COND a. little insipid
To me, the dish tastes a little insipid [lit.: "As I taste (the dish), (I feel that its taste is) a little insipid"]. (LQD: 52)

There are also sentences which indicate that the information is obtained via investigation. The following examples (4. 9-13) and (4. 9-14) contain the conditional converb of *baica-* "to investigate". This type of sentence was used frequently in memorials submitted by ministers to the Manchu emperors, and became a fixed style.

(4.9-13)

baica-ci,	*hūda-i*	*urse*	*udu*	*bele*	*be*	*uda-fi*
investigate-COND	business-GEN	people	although	grain	ACC	buy-PFV. CVB
asara-cibe	*bele*	*kemuni*	*hecen*	*de*	*bi-mbi*	
store-CONC. CVB	grain	still	city	DAT	be-IPFV. FIN	

hūda-i urse: business people, merchants

(Upon review we find that) even though merchants buy and accumulate grain, still there is grain in the city. (Li 2010: 193)①

(4.9-14)

baica-ci,	*Kašigar*	*i*	*karun*	*te-re*	*Mergen*	*ere*
investigate-COND	Kashgar	GEN	sentry	sit-IPFV. PTCP	PN	this
aniya nadan	*biya-de*	*isibu-me*	*ilan*	*aniya*	*jalu-kabi*	
year seven	month-DAT	reach-IPFV. CVB	three	year	fulfil-PFV. FIN	

(Upon review we find that) Mergen, who is stationed at the sentry post of Kashgar, has completed his three-year term in the seventh month of the year. (Li 2010: 193)

Unlike the verbs *tuwa-* "to look", *donji-* "to listen/hear", and *amtala-* "to taste", the verb *baica-* "to investigate" does not indicate perception as such, but represents the intentional act of obtaining information. On the other hand, however, it serves, as do the perception verbs, to indicate the source of information [that is, investigation, or review, as shown in the translations of (4.9-13) and (4.9-14)]. Additionally, in terms of morphosyntax, the examples (4.9-13) and (4.9-14) are similar to (4.9-1)-(4.9-12) in that the subordinate clauses end in the conditional converb. Therefore, sentences like (4.9-13) and (4.9-14) can also be considered as instances of evidentiality.

In Section 4.3, which discusses the temporal meaning expressed by conditional-converb structures, the cases of perception verbs are also examined (Section 4.3.2.4). However, those sentences do not necessarily exhibit evidential meanings. When the subject of the perception verb does not designate the speaker of the sentence, the perception verb does not by any means represent the speaker's source of information. For instance, though in (4.9-15) and (4.9-16) below, the verbs *tuwa-* "to look" and

---

① The translations of (4.9-13) and (4.9-14) are quoted from Li (2010: 193).

donji- "to listen" are used respectively, the speaker of (4. 9-15) describes the visual perception of the lady in question, while the speaker of (4. 9-16) describes what Nishan Saman (she) heard. Neither sentence indicates the speaker's source of information.

(4. 9-15)

fujin	*gene-fi*	*tuwa-ci*,	*uyun*	*ursu*	*sele-i*	*hoton*
lady	go-PFV. CVB	look-COND	nine	layer	iron-GEN	city
bi						
EXS. PTL						

When the lady went and looked, (she found that) there was a nine-layered iron city. (SG: 324)

(4. 9-16)

donji-ci,	*dolo*	*hutu*	*songgo-ro*	*jilgan*	*ambula*	*bi*
listen-COND	inside	ghost	cry-IPFV. PTCP	sound	many	EXS. PTL

As (she) listened, (she heard) there were many crying sounds of the ghosts. (NSB: 75)

On the other hand, when the perceiver and the speaker are one and the same entity, the sentence is able to express an evidential meaning. The following are some examples, among which (4. 9-20) and (4. 9-21) are also discussed in Section 4. 3. 2. 4 [sentences (4. 3-18) and (4. 3-19), respectively].

(4. 9-17)

sangga	*deri*	*dosi*	*tuwa-ci*,	*ere*	*tede*	*darabu-mbi*,
hole	ABL	inward	look-COND	this	that. DAT	invite. to. drink-IPFV
tere	*ede*	*bederebu-mbi*				
that/3SG	this. DAT	return-IPFV. FIN				

When (I) looked inside through the hole (of the window), (I saw that) they were inviting each other to drink [lit.: "this (man) was inviting that (man) to drink, and that (man) was returning (a toast)"]. (OJ1: 77)

(4. 9-18)

šehun	*bigan*	*de*	*isina-fi*	*tuwa-ci*,	*niyengniyeri*
barren	wilderness	DAT	arrive-PFV. CVB	look-COND	spring
arbun	*absi*	*buyecuke*			
appearance	how	lovely			

When (I) arrived at the wilderness and had a look, (I saw) what a lovely spring (it was)! (OJ2: 90)

(4.9-19)

sek seme	*gete-fi*	*donji-ci,*	*cin*	*i*	*boo-de*
suddenly	wake-PFV. CVB	listen-COND	main	GEN	house-DAT

niyalma	*ji-fi*	*den*	*jilgan*	*i*	*gisun*	*gisure-mbi*
man	come-PFV. CVB	loud	voice	GEN	word	speak-IPFV. FIN

sek seme: suddenly

cin i boo: main room, i. e. living room

den jilgan i: in a loud voice

Waking up suddenly, (I) heard [lit.: "when (I) listened, (I heard)"] a man come into the living room speaking in a loud voice. (OJ2: 156)

(4.9-20)

šan	*waliya-fi*	*donji-ci,*	*cib se-me*	*heni*	*jilgan*	*wei*
ear	throw-PFV. CVB	listen-COND	quiet	little	sound	tiny

akū
NEG

cib seme: quietly

wei akū: none at all

When (I) pushed (lit.: "threw") my ear (against the window) to eavesdrop, (I heard) it was very quiet and there was no sound at all. (AGA1: 149)

(4.9-21)

saifila-fi	*amtala-ci,*	*šuwe*	*ede-kebi*
use. spoon-PFV. CVB	taste-COND	completely	go. bad-PFV. FIN

When (I) tasted (the food) using a spoon, (I found that it) had gone completely bad. (AGA1: 97-98)

It should be noted that the perception verb *tuwa-* "to look" in (4.9-17) and (4.9-18) describes concrete acts of visual perception in its literal sense. Also, the perception verb *donji-* "to listen/hear" in (4.9-19) and (4.9-20) describes concrete acts of auditory perception, distinct from its usage in (4.9-8)-(4.9-11), which describe hearsays, and thus can be seen as acts of auditory perception in a metaphorical sense.

In general, the perception verbs in (4.9-17)-(4.9-21) represent specific intentional acts of perception that form part of a temporal sequence with other actions: the acts of arriving and looking in (4.9-18), the acts of waking up and listening in (4.9-19), and so forth. This characteristic distinguishes them from (4. 9-1)-(4. 9-14), in which the acts of perception are represented in a general way in the sense that no specific intentional act of perceiving is described. Here different types of syntactic behaviours are observed among the examples. Specifically, the uses of perception verbs in (4. 9-17)-(4. 9-21) are the most literal and the verb structures all take objects. In these sentences the temporal meaning is primary and the evidential meaning is secondary. On the other hand, the perception verbs in (4. 9-8)-(4. 9-14) are left-dislocated and take no explicit object or complement, behaving as grammatical markers. The evidential meaning in these sentences is (almost) exclusive. Between the two types are sentences such as (4. 9-1)-(4. 9-4), (4. 9-6) and (4. 9-7), in which the perception verbs take explicit objects or complements. In these sentences no temporal meaning is expressed and evidentiality is expressed exclusively.

It is demonstrated that the perception verbs *tuwa-* "to look" and *donji-* "to listen/hear" are both capable of encoding more than one type of evidentiality. This phenomenon is by no means unheard of in various other languages, in which the verbs denoting visual and auditory perceptions are also shown to be polysemous in indicating evidentiality. (Witt 2009; Chafe and Nichols 1986; and Aikhenvald 2003, 2004) In Manchu, the syntactic behaviour of perception verbs (as shown above) and the type of evidentiality seem to be interrelated. In (4. 9-17)-(4. 9-21), where the two verbs represent specific acts of perception in temporal sequences with other acts, the types of evidentiality are visual (for *tuwa-*) and auditory (for *donji-*) respectively. In (4. 9-1)-(4. 9-7), the verb *tuwa-* "to look" indicates visual perception in a more or less abstract way. Similarly, in (4. 9-8)-(4. 9-11), the verb *donji-* "to listen/hear" indicates hearsay, which, as the source of information, can be regarded as an abstract form of auditory perception.

From the perspective of semantics and syntax, the relation between the structure formed by a conditional converb V-*ci* and the rest of the sentence still remains to be explained. It can be stated from the outset that there is no direct conditional or temporal relation characterised by the conditional converb, within each construction. However, in light of the analysis in Section 4. 3. 2. 4, one is still able to elucidate what the conditional converb contributes in a construction as a whole, if a proper implied predicate (as part of a proposition) that involves an act of perception is considered in the main clause. Thus, the conditional converb relates two states of affairs, both concerning acts of perception, which can be examined in terms of conditionality or temporality. Meanwhile, the domains in which such a relation is presented should also be identified. The following will examine each of the verbs in question including the perception verbs, as well as the verb *baica-* "to investigate".

First, concerning the perception verb *tuwa-* "to look", in (4. 9-1) the speaker's looking at the state of his own illness leads to his conclusion that he is seriously ill. In (4. 9-18), the speaker's intentional act of looking leads to the result of his seeing the lovely scene of spring, and his intentional act and his perception are in a temporal sequence, since they are concrete, realised states of affairs (in the past). Second, concerning the perception verb *donji-* "to listen/hear", in (4. 9-8) the speaker's listening (to other people's words) leads to his knowing or hearing (the news) that the addressee reads Manchu books. The same can be stated of constructions (4. 9-9)-(4. 9-11). In (4. 9-19), the speaker's intentional act of listening leads to his hearing someone speak loudly, and his intentional act and his perception are temporally related. The same applies to (4. 9-20). Third, since the verb *amtala-* "to taste" is not polysemous with *tuwa-* and *donji-* when indicating evidentiality, it is plain to see that in both (4. 9-12) and (4. 9-21), the speaker's trying the food leads to his discovering the taste. In (4. 9-21), the states of affairs, set in the past, are temporally interrelated. Finally, concerning the verb *baica-* "to investigate", in (4. 9-13) the speaker's investigation leads to his discovering the situation in the city.

In each case analysed above, the latter could be reasonably inferred and represented by an implied proposition (in the main clause), whose predicate is a perception or cognition verb (SEE, HEAR, TASTE, KNOW, CONCLUDE, and so forth). Such a verb shares the same subject with the perception verb in the form of V-*ci*. This can be shown by the translations of some of the constructions. For instance, the translation of

(4. 9-17), "when (I) looked inside through the hole (of the window), (I saw that) they were inviting each other to drink" has an implied proposition in which the predicate is SEE, which embeds the main clause within its scope. Bringing out these implied propositions also helps identify the domains in which the semantic relations are presented. Specifically, the constructions that have SEE, HEAR, or TASTE① as the implied predicate represent the semantic relation (that is, causation or temporal sequence, characterised by the conditional converb) in the perceptual domain. On the other hand, the constructions that have KNOW or CONCLUDE as their implied predicate represent the semantic relation in the epistemic domain.

It should be noted that the perception verbs do not necessarily determine that the predicates of the implied propositions should also be perception verbs. Therefore, the presence of perception verbs in the constructions does not mean that the semantic relation is necessarily presented in the perceptual domain. For instance, both (4. 9-2) and (4. 9-3) have an implied predicate, CONCLUDE (or INFER), and thus involve the epistemic domain rather than the perceptual domain, despite the presence of *tuwa-* "to look".

4. 9. 2 Constructions Containing Cognition verbs

Apart from perception verbs such as *tuwa-* "to look" and *donji-* "to listen/hear", and verbs indicating the obtaining of information such as *baica-* "to investigate", cognition verbs such as *gūni-* "to think" and *bodo-* "to consider" can also occur as the conditional converb and introduce a clause. Such verbs may take accusative case structures as their own objects (4. 9-27), but this is not obligatory. The following are some examples.

---

① It seems that in (4. 9-12) and (4. 9-21), which involve the gustatory perception, the implied predicate TASTE cannot be added into the main clause of the English translation, due to the grammatical properties of the English verb "taste". This is why alternative expressions are used in translation, such as "(I feel that its taste is) a little weak" and "(I found that) it had gone completely bad". Conceptually, however, the implied predicate TASTE can still make sense in expressing the involved perception, in the same way as the other perception verbs SEE and HEAR.

(4.9-22) *gūni-ci*, *geli* *suihu-me* *omi-ha*
think-COND again be. rowdy drink-PFV. PTCP
suihu-me omi-: to be drunk and be rowdy
(I) think that (he) is drunk and being rowdy again. (OJ1: 99)

(4.9-23) *bi* *gūni-ci*, *onco* *tondo* *mujilen* *ci* *dele* *akū*
1SG think-COND broad righteous mind ABL top NEG
I think (that) there is nothing greater than a broad and righteous mind.
(MYK4: 17)

(4.9-24) *bodo-ci*, *sin-i* *feliye-re* *ba* *umesi*
consider-COND 2SG(*si*/*sin*)-GEN frequent-IPFV. PTCP place very
tongga *kai*
few PTL
I think that there are indeed very few places that you frequent. (OJ1: 35)

(4.9-25) *fe* *be* *bodo-ci*, *sin-i* *emgi* *yabu-ha*
old ACC consider-COND 2SG(*si*/*sin*)-GEN together go-PFV. PTCP
gucu-se *gemu* *amban* *o-ho*
friend-PL all high. official become-PFV. PTCP
sini emgi yabu-: to work with you, lit.: "to go (to the workplace) with you"
Thinking of the old days, (one can see that) those friends who used to work with you have all become high officials. (OJ1: 56)

The verb *gūni-* "to think" can also co-occur with a preceding perception verb, *tuwa-* "to look", which indicates the information based on which the inference is drawn.

(4.9-26) *tetele* *umai* *mejige* *akū* *be* *tuwa-ci*, *gūni-ci*
up. till. now at. all news NEG ACC look-COND think-COND
aifini *hū* *i* *da* *i* *amala* *makta-fi*
already back. of. neck GEN base GEN behind throw-PFV. CVB
onggo-hobi
forget-PFV. FIN
hū i da: the base of the back of the neck
hū i da i amala maktafi onggo-: to forget completely (lit.: "to forget by throwing behind one's neck")

Seeing that up until now there is no message (from him) at all, (I) think that (he) has completely forgotten (what I told him to do). (OJ2: 182)

By means of the conditional converb of cognition verbs, each of the constructions (4.9-22)-(4.9-25) functions mainly to present the speaker's opinion explicitly—in the sense that the speaker says I think before his or her statement, which contrasts with an ordinary statement without such an expression.

In (4.9-22)-(4.9-25), just as in the constructions containing perception verbs previously analysed, the semantic relation characterised by the conditional converb is not presented directly within the construction. It is not difficult, however, to discover that this semantic relation is presented in the epistemic domain. For instance, in (4.9-1), the speaker's thinking leads to his conclusion that his guests are hungry. The case of (4.9-28) is slightly more complex, since it involves a perception verb as well. Yet, the semantic relation is also in the epistemic domain: the speaker's looking at the situation leads to his thinking, which in turn leads to his conclusion that the person he mentions has forgotten what is supposed to do.

4.9.3 Summary

The constructions analysed in this section involve perception or cognition verbs in the form of the conditional converb, and indicate the source of information, and/or the obtaining or processing of information. All of these constructions share a uniform morphosyntax, which can be represented by Formula (c).

(c) (Speaker-Subject+) (Object/Complement+) Perc. /Cog. V-*ci*, Statement

A few characteristics of this formula should be clarified. First, "Speaker-Subject" means that the subject of the verb V refers to the speaker of the whole sentence; that is, the subject should be either implicitly or explicitly the first person singular pronoun "I" (or a first person plural pronoun "we"). Second, "Object/Complement", which is not obligatory, represents a state of affairs that is perceived, searched or considered. Third, "Statement" refers either to what the speaker perceives or to the inference or conclusion that she or he makes.

For each construction, an implied proposition can be inferred, of which the predicate embeds the main clause (statement) within its scope, in order to shed light on how the semantic relation characterised by the conditional converb is presented. This is the same method applied in Section 4. 3. 2. 4 when analysing temporal constructions with perception verbs. The type of this implied predicate—whether concerning perception or epistemic activity—determines the domain in which the semantic relation is presented: perceptual or epistemic. The implied predicate can be of a type different from that of V in the subordinate clause of (4. 9-27), especially in a construction containing the verb *tuwa-* "to look" in which the main clause is a conclusion or an inference [see (4. 9-2), (4. 9-4) and (4. 9-5) for instance]. In this case the implied predicate would be CONCLUDE or INFER, and the semantic relation would be presented in the epistemic domain, not the perceptual domain.

When the verb V in (4. 9-27) does not take an object, that is, when V occurs alone as a conditional converb or together with the first person singular pronoun (*bi* "I"), the whole construction is rendered as one consisting of a matrix clause and an embedded clause, sentence "I see/hear/think that something happens" in English. The similarity is brought about by the order of V and the statement, which is mirrored in English, as well as in many other European languages. However, such syntactic similarity is only superficial. There are two reasons. First, the conditional converb V-*ci* is syntactically dependent on the clause following it, while in English the preceding clause (I see/hear/think/...) is syntactically (but not semantically) independent. Second, not all the Manchu verbs (of perception or cognition) previously analysed can take the clause following them as their authentic complement.

As for the second reason, one can examine whether it is possible to put this clause in front of the verb, via inserting, if necessary, the accusative marker *be*, or the imperfective converb of the quotative verb *se-*, *se-me*, which usually serves as a complementiser similar to that in English. Admittedly, the verbs *donji-* "to listen/hear" and *gūni-* "to think" can take preceding complements, which would be expected to be the default syntactic type for an SOV language such as Manchu. The following are two examples, showing the two verbs taking preceding complements respectively.

(4.9-28) *Yehe-i* *cooha* *be* *enenggi* *ji-mbi*, *cimari*
Yehe-GEN army ACC today come-IPFV.FIN tomorrow
ji-mbi *se-me* *donji-ha*
come-IPFV.FIN say(AUX)-IPFV.CVB hear-PFV.PTCP
(I) have heard (people say) that Yehe's army will come today, or (that) they'll come tomorrow. (MYK2: 37)

(4.9-29) *ere* *amba* *gurun* *i* *Daiming* *han* *be* *abka-i*
this great empire GEN Ming khan ACC heaven-GEN
emu *šajin* *i* *banji-mbi* *dere* *se-me* *gūni-ha*
one law GEN live-IPFV.FIN PTL say(AUX) think-PFV.PTCP
bi-he
be(AUX)-PFV.PTCP
(I) used to think that the lord of the Great Ming Empire would certainly live in accordance with the law of heaven. (MYK5: 43)

The complements governed by *se-me* in (4.9-28) and (4.9-29) represent the content of hearsay and of thinking respectively, just as in (4.9-8) and (4.9-22). Therefore they can be expected to follow the conditional converb of their respective governing verbs in constructions such as (4.9-27), as postposed complements. In contrast, other verbs analysed previously, such as *tuwa-* "to look", *amtala-* "to taste", and *baica-* "to investigate", cannot take complement clauses in the same way as *donji-* and *gūni-*. Therefore, in constructions containing the verbs *tuwa-*, or *amtala-*, which have the morphosyntax represented by (4.9-27), the "statement" clauses cannot be regarded as postposed complements of these verbs.

Constructions such as (*bi*) *tuwa-ci*/*donji-ci*/*gūni-ci*/... are syntactically different from the English constructions "I see/hear/think that...", and they occur quite frequently in Manchu. Their frequent usage distinguishes the verbs *tuwa-*, *donji-*, and *gūni-*, from other verbs. In addition, they should be distinguished from the temporal constructions containing the same verbs, which primarily express temporal sequence.

Finally, it should be pointed out that perception or cognition verbs can also occur in structures other than the conditional converb, while realising the same functions as their conditional converb in the constructions analysed in previous subsections. These structures include V-*hA-de* [V-PFV. PTCP-DAT] and V-*hA* [V-PFV. PTCP] *ba-de* [place-DAT]. The former usually expresses a temporal relation, and sometimes expresses a conditional relation (see Section 4. 2. 1). The following are some examples.

(4. 9-30)

ere	*be*	*tuwa-ha*	*de*,	*ubaliyambu-re*	*be*
this	ACC	look-PFV. PTCP	DAT	translate-IPFV. PTCP	ACC
taci-re	*onggolo*,	*neneme*	*Manju*	*gisun*	*taci-re*
learn-IPFV. PTCP	before	firstly	Manchu	language	learn-IPFV. PTCP
be	*oyonggo*	*o-bu-re*	*be*	*sa-ci*	*aca-mbi*
ACC	important	make-IPFV. PTCP	ACC	know-COND	suit(AUX)-IPFV. FIN

V-*rA be oyonggo obu-*: to make it a priority to do something, lit.: "to make doing something important"

V-*ci aca-*: complex structure expressing obligation/responsibility

Looking at this, (I think that one) should know (the reason for) making it a priority to learn the Manchu language first before learning to translate. (OJ1: 3)

(4. 9-31)

donji-ha	*ba-de*,	*emu*	*gucu*	*se*	*asihan*	*bime*,	*geli*
hear-PFV. PTCP	place-DAT	one	friend	age	young	and	also
beleni	*sefu*	*bi*,	*bithe*	*de*	*asuru*	*kice-rakū*	
available	teacher	EXS. PTL	book	DAT	very	be. diligent-IPFV. PTCP. NEG	

I hear that a friend, who is young and has a teacher available, isn't very diligent in learning (lit.: "in books"). (Stary 1983: 442)

(4.9-32) *ere-be* *gūni-ha-de*, *ai* *hacin* *i* *baili* *jafa-ki*
this-ACC think-PFV. PTCP-DAT what kind GEN kindness hold-OPT
se-he *se-me*, *tumen* *de* *emgeri*
say(AUX)-PFV. PTCP say(AUX)-IPFV. CVB ten. thousand DAT once
tehere-bu-me *mute-mbi-o*
equal-CAUS-IPFV. CVB be. able-IPFV. FIN-Q
baili jafa-: to repay kindness
V-*ki se-*: complex structure expressing desire or intention
ai hacin i ... V-*hA se-me*: no matter how (one) does something
Thinking (about) this, (then consider:) how can (one) possibly repay the kindness (of one's parents), no matter how (one) wants to do so, by making (one's effort) equal to even (so little as) a ten-thousandth (of the kindness)?
(AGA1: 34-35)

4.10 Other Types of Constructions

This section analyses two types of conditionals that do not neatly fall into the categories previously analysed: inferential conditionals and performative speech-act conditionals.

4.10.1 Inferential Conditionals

In some conditional sentences, the state of affairs of the subordinate clause does not serve as a condition for the state of affairs of the main clause, but it is possible to make an inference of the state of affairs of the main clause based on that of the subordinate clause. In these sentences, the subordinate clause usually describes a concrete, particular state of affairs, while the main clause describes a more abstract one, a conclusion drawn from the former state of affairs. Here are some examples.

(4.10-1) *manjura-rakū* *o-ci*, *uthai* *da* *sekiyen* *be*
speak. Manchu-IPFV. PTCP. NEG become(AUX)-COND then root source ACC
onggo-ho *kai*
forget-PFV. PTCP PTL
da sekiyen: origin, true identity

If (one) does not speak Manchu, (it will mean that one) has forgotten (his) true (Manchu) identity. (AGA1: 17)

(4.10-2) *juwe* *ajige* *deo* *be* *gosi-rakū*
two little younger. brother ACC love-IPFV. PTCP. NEG
o-ci, *han* *ama* *be* *onggo-ho* *dere*
become(AUX)-COND khan father ACC forget-PFV. PTCP PTL
If (we) do not love (our) two little younger brothers, (it will mean that we) have forgotten (our) father the khan. (MYK8: 44)

(4.10-3) *damu* *majige* *angga* *isi-ci*, *uthai* *mim-be*
only a. little mouth reach-COND then 1SG(*bi/min*)-ACC
gosi-ha
favour-PFV. PTCP
angga isi-: a respectful way of saying "to taste"
If only (you could) so much as taste (it) a little, (I would consider it as a sign that you have) shown me favour. (OJ1: 79)

In (4.10-1), what the speaker means is not that the behaviour of not speaking Manchu leads to one's having forgotten his or her Manchu identity. Rather, the speaker wants to point out that the behaviour of not speaking the language is characteristic of someone who has forgotten his or her ethnic identity. Thus, if a Manchu person does not speak his/her native language, one can infer that this person has forgotten his or her identity. Similarly in (4.10-2), if the speaker does not love his younger brothers, one can infer that the speaker has forgotten his father. Likewise in (4.10-3), if the addressee would like to taste the food offered by the speaker, the speaker will infer that the addressee does so to show his favour. Just as mentioned above, in each sentence the first state of affairs—a behaviour—is concrete, and is only a sign, or a piece of evidence of the second state of affairs, which is an abstract state of mind.

Similar conditional sentences in English, such as "If Ann is wearing a wedding ring, she and Bob finally got married" (Dancygier 1998: 86), have long been studied (Sweetser 1990; Dancygier 1998). Sweetser (1990: 117) labels them as "epistemic conditionals", arguing the relation between the two clauses is one at the epistemic level, where "the knowledge causes the conclusion". Thus, in light of previous studies, it is arguable that in conditional sentences (4.10-1) to (4.10-3), the conditional relation, which is presented between premises and conclusions, is in the epistemic domain (or, at the epistemic level).

4.10.2 Performative Speech-act Conditionals

Section 4.4 analyses speech-act conditionals in which the conditional relation holds true, but the condition itself (concerning personal feelings of the addressee) is used as a politeness strategy. In the so-called "performative speech-act conditionals" analysed here, no politeness strategy is involved, and the verbs in the main clauses are performative verbs (as defined by Austin 1962), that is, verbs that perform the speech acts they denote when they are simply uttered (for example, the verb "promise" in "I promise that I will do my duty", where the speaker makes a promise by uttering the verb). Additionally, in these conditionals, the state of affairs represented in the subordinate clause specifies the content of the speech act represented in the main clause. In the following examples, (4.10-4) expresses a speech act of oath-taking, while (4.10-5) expresses a speech act of making a bet.

(4.10-4)	*enenggi*	*fiyaratala*	*tanta-rakū*	*o-ci*,	*bi*
	today	very. much	beat-IPFV. PTCP. NEG	become(AUX)-COND	1SG
	uthai	*gashū-kini*			
	then	take. oath-OPT			

fiyaratala tanta-: to beat someone very badly

If (I) do not beat (him) very badly, let me take an oath. (OJ2: 38)

(4.10-5)	*lahin*	*fasilan*	*tuci-rakū*	*o-ci*,	*muse*
	troublesome	discord	come. out-IPFV. PTCP. NEG	become(AUX)-COND	1PL. INCL
	aika	*mekte-kini*			
	if	bet-OPT			

lahin fasilan: troubles, problems

If troubles don't happen (because of him), let's make a bet. (AGA4: 101)

As stated above, the verb *gashū-* "to take an oath" in (4.10-4) is a performative verb, as is the verb *mekte-* "to bet" in (4. 10-5), since the speaker makes an oath when he utters *gashū-kini* "let me take an oath!" and the speaker plays his part in making a bet when he utters *mekte-kini* "let's make a bet". ①

The conditional relation presented in (4. 10-4) and (4. 10-5) is unusual. Specifically, in (4. 10-4) the speaker's not beating someone badly does not lead to his taking an oath. In (4. 10-5) the troubles' not happening does not lead to the speaker's making a bet with the addressee. Both cases need explanation. Since speech acts are involved, it is reasonable to examine the content of these speech acts, regardless of the conditional morphosyntax. In (4. 10-4), what the speaker wishes to express can be paraphrased as "I swear that I will beat him very badly today, and if I do not beat him very badly today, may Heaven punish me for breaking my oath". What the speaker of (4. 10-5) wishes to say is "Let's make a bet: I believe that troubles will happen. If troubles do not happen as I expect, may I lose the bet and you win it". The content of these speech acts is actually specified in the subordinate clause, although in the form of negation ("if I don't beat him very badly today" "if troubles don't happen").

In light of the explanation, it can be shown that the speech acts expressed by (4. 10-4) and (4. 10-5) are performed, and not made conditional on the state of affairs represented in the subordinate clause. In (4. 10-4) and (4. 10-5), the conditional relation is in fact between the non-realisation of the speaker's prediction (the non-realisation is expressed via a negative form in the subordinate clause) and what the speaker views as an undesirable consequence.

On the other hand, the conditional sentences themselves seem to put the conditional relation between the non-realisation of the speaker's prediction and the speech act expressed by the main clause. Pragmatic considerations may help explain this. Usually, people do not feel the need to take an oath or make a bet when they express their opinions. However,

---

① It does not matter much whether the addressee is willing to take part in this bet, since the most important thing about (4. 10-5) is that the speaker shows that he will not hesitate to make this bet.

when their statements sound unbelievable to their addressees, or when they want to show their determination to carry out something, they may need to take an oath (or make a bet) to guarantee the truth of their words. Thus, if one regards the non-realisation of the speaker's prediction as the addressee's potential disbelief, one can also consider the conditional relation in sentences such as (4. 10-4) and (4. 10-5) as present between the addressee's disbelief (regarding the speaker's prediction) and the speaker's performance of the speech act of taking an oath or making a bet. In such cases, the conditional relation is present in the speech act domain.

This may appear to contradict the previous analysis, which states that the conditional relation is present between the non-realisation of the speaker's prediction and the undesirable consequence facing the speaker. Nevertheless, the inconsistency disappears when one considers how taking an oath or making a bet serves to dispel the addressee's disbelief regarding the speaker's prediction. That is, when one takes an oath or makes a bet and one's words prove to be untrue, one will be punished for breaking an oath—either by a deity or by other people—or be made to pay for losing a bet. Therefore, the addressee's potential disbelief serves as a condition for the speaker to take an oath or to make a bet, which guarantees the truth of the speaker's words through guaranteeing a certain undesirable consequence for the speaker if he or she is proved to be wrong.

Chapter 5 Discussion

Based on the analysis in Chapter 4, this chapter addresses two important issues of the present study: first, identifying prototypes for conditional constructions in Manchu; second, relating all the other constructions to the prototypes by investigating the shared aspects of semantics. These two issues are discussed in Section 5.1 and Section 5.2 respectively.

5.1 The Prototypes of Conditional Constructions

Some work is done in Section 4.1 in exploring the basic patterns of both factual and counterfactual conditionals, which serves as a foundation for the search for the prototypes. The conditional relation is evident between the clauses of the basic patterns of conditionals. However, from the analysis in other sections, one can see that the semantic relation within a construction cannot always be determined merely by means of morphosyntax, since the meanings of specific lexical items and the context also play important roles. Yet, this is not tantamount to denying the existence of "good" examples—the prototypes—of conditional constructions. The present section aims to define the prototypes in terms of morphosyntax and identify them in actual use of language.

It should be stated from the outset that the morphosyntactic criteria to be used are not obligatory for a construction to express the (factual or counterfactual) conditional meaning. The reason is that in order to express the conditional meaning, one can choose from a variety of means, including semantic, morphosyntactic and pragmatic strategies (Section 4. 2 analyses factual conditionals that would otherwise be temporal sentences and counterfactual conditionals that would otherwise be interpreted as factual conditionals). Rather, the constructions that meet the criteria are those least dependent on context or other factors and the most likely to give rise to the conditional interpretation. The present study takes into consideration the Qing Dynasty Manchu grammars and the frequency of usage among the data collected. It is assumed that the grammatical structures of which the usage came to be recorded in the Qing Dynasty Manchu grammars were considered by the authors to be significant and in a sense prototypical. The usage of structures in the data can either corroborate the statements of the Qing Dynasty grammars or supplement them.

The discussion of prototypes is given below according to the type of conditionals: factual conditionals and counterfactual conditionals. The dichotomy is made on account of the morphosyntactic distinctiveness of the two types of constructions. As stated in Section 4. 1, though Manchu also has hypothetical conditionals, they do not have a distinctive morphosyntax as factual or counterfactual conditionals do. Rather, they are morphosyntactically indistinguishable from factual conditionals, and the hypothetical meaning is inferred from the context. Therefore, prototypes cannot be found for hypothetical conditionals in terms of morphosyntax.

It is seen from the analysis in Chapter 4 that, when *aika* or *aikabade* is combined with a conditional-converb structure in a subordinate clause, the conditional meaning is expressed. On the other hand, one can also see that, without the presence of *aika/aikabade*, constructions containing conditional-converb structures serve to realise a variety of functions apart from expressing conditionality, even when morphosyntactically they do not differ from the basic group of factual conditionals. Here are some examples:[①] (5.1-1) expresses the temporal meaning, (5.1-2) expresses the concessive meaning, (5.1-3) constitutes a disjunctive construction, and (5.1-4) is a topic construction.

(5.1-1) *tere* *usin-i* *haha* *ekše-me* *gene-fi* *gai-ci*,
that field-GEN man hurry-IPFV.CVB go-PFV.CVB get-COND
aisin *be* *sabu-rakū*
gold ACC see-IPFV.PTCP.NEG
usin i haha: peasant, lit.: "man of field"
When the peasant went hurriedly to get (the gold), (he) did not see the gold.
(OJ2: 82)

(5.1-2) *age* *de* *emu* *baita* *yandu-ci*, *baibi* *angga*
sir DAT one matter request-COND merely mouth
juwa-ra *de* *manggaša-mbi*
open-IPFV.PTCP DAT be.hesitant-IPFV.FIN
angga juwa-: to open (one's) mouth, to speak up
Sir, (I have) something (for which) to request your favour, but (I am) just hesitant (about whether) to say (it). (OJ1: 85)

(5.1-3) *balai* *fiyente-me* *gisun* *eye-bu-rakū*
unreasonably spread.rumours words flow-CAUS-IPFV.PTCP.NEG
o-ci, *uthai* *niyalma* *de* *gebu* *ara-mbi*
become(AUX)-COND then people DAT name make-IPFV.FIN
fiyente-me gisun eyebu-: to spread rumours, lit.: "spreading rumours, make (them) flow"
gebu ara-: to call (someone) names
(He) either spreads rumours or calls people all kinds of names [lit.: "if (he) does not spread rumours, (he) will then call people names"]. (AGA4: 75)

(5.1-4) *tere* *taci-re* *de* *bulcakū-ngge* *o-ci*,
that learn-IPFV.PTCP DAT lazy-NMLZ TOP (< become-COND)
damu *sefu-i* *šorgi-re* *be* *tuwa-mbi*
only teacher-GEN urge-IPFV.PTCP ACC look-IPFV.FIN
Speaking of those lazy at learning, (they) only depend on the teacher's urging (them) [lit: "...only look to the teacher's urging (them)"]. (AGA1: 62)

---

① Sentences (5.1-2)-(5.1-4) are also analysed in different sections of Chapter 4: sentence (5.1-2) is presented as (4.5-2); (5.1-3) as (4.6-12); and (5.1-4) as (4.8-6).

It can then be concluded that from the perspective of morphosyntax, it is the framed structure consisting of both the connector *aika*/*aikabade* and the conditional converb V-*ci* in the subordinate clause of a sentence that gives rise to the conditional interpretation. This makes a sentence containing the framed structure *aika*/*aikabade*... V-*ci* a candidate for prototypical (factual) conditional constructions. However, apart from the conditional converb, the connector *aika*/*aikabade* can also combine with dative-locative participial structures (especially V-*hA*-*de*) in expressing the conditional meaning. The participle can be that of a lexical verb [(5. 1-5)-(5. 1-7)], or of an auxiliary verb such as *o*-, which forms a complex structure with a lexical verb (5. 1-8). The following are some examples:[①]

(5. 1-5)	*aikabade*	*muse-i*	*alban-i*	*niyalma*	*gai-bu-ha*
	if	1PL. INCL-GEN	labour-GEN	people	take-PASS-PFV. PTCP
	de,	*aina-mbi*			
	DAT	do. what-IPFV. FIN			

alban i niyalma: labourers

What (will we) do if our labourers are taken (by the enemy)? (MYK5: 17)

(5. 1-6)	*si*	*aikabade*	*daila-ha*	*de*,	*bi*	*sim-be*
	2SG	if	wage. war-PFV. PTCP	DAT	1SG	2SG(*si*/*sin*)-ACC
	tookabu-mbi					
	destroy-IPFV. FIN					

If you wage war (against me), I will destroy you. (MYK6: 25)

(5. 1-7)	*yali*	*booha*	*be*	*aika*	*udu*	*erin*	*nurhūme*
	meat	dish	ACC	if	several	meal	successively
	dubi-he			*de*,	*oforo-i*	*hanci*	*fime-ci*
	get. used. to-PFV. PTCP			DAT	nose-GEN	near	put-COND
	ojo-rakū						
	become(AUX)-IPFV. PTCP. NEG						

V-*ci o*-: complex structure expressing possibility or permission

If (one) gets used to having meat dishes for several meals in a row, (he) cannot (bear to) put (meat) near (his) nose. (AGA2: 122)

---

① Sentences (5. 1-22) and (5. 1-24) are analysed in Section 4. 2, as (4. 2-4) and (4. 2-5) respectively.

(5.1-8)	*bi*	*aika*	*sin-de*	*emu*	*baita*	*fonji-me*
	1SG	if	2SG(*si*/*sin*)-DAT	one	thing	ask-IPFV.CVB
	o-ho-de,			*si*	*uthai*	*sa-rkū*
	become(AUX)-PFV.PTCP-DAT			2SG	then	know-IPFV.PTCP.NEG
	se-re					
	say-IPFV.PTCP					

sarkū < *sa-rakū* < *sa-ra* [know-IPFV.PTCP] + akū [NEG]

If I ask you about something, then you will say you don't know. (MFG: 6)

The framed structure *aika*/*aikabade*... V-*hA-de* exemplified by (5.1-5)-(5.1-8) can serve to express the conditional meaning unambiguously. It is noteworthy that the structure *aika*/*aikabade*... (V-*me*) *o-ho-de* was already recorded in the Qing Dynasty grammars (UH: 50; AMH: 16-17), in parallel with the structure *aika*/*aikabade*... V-*ci*. Nevertheless, all else being equal, sentences containing the structure *aika*/*aikabade*... V-*ci* would be more appropriate as the prototypes of factual conditional constructions than those containing the structure *aika*/*aikabade* ... V-*hA-de*. There are several reasons: (1) both structures can equally express conditionality; (2) the conditional converb V-*ci* is morphologically simpler than the dative-locative participle V-*hA-de*; (3) and conditional constructions making use of V-*ci* are predominant.

Thus, the prototypes of factual conditional constructions can be defined and identified in terms of a set of morphosyntactic criteria, stated as follows. A prototypical factual conditional consists of two clauses, the first being a subordinate clause and the second a main clause. The subordinate clause contains the connector *aika*/*aikabade*, with the conditional converb V-*ci* of a lexical verb serving as the subordinate predicate if the clause is affirmative, or with the structure V-*rakū* [V-IPFV.PTCP.NEG] *o-ci* [become(AUX)-COND] if the clause is negative. The main clause contains the imperfective finite form (V-*mbi*) of a lexical verb as the main predicate if the clause is affirmative, or the negative imperfective participle (V-*rakū*) of a lexical verb if the clause is negative. The presence of a subject is not obligatory in either clause, since Manchu is a pro-drop language. Table 5. 1 shows all these patterns of construction, which are exemplified by (5. 1-9)-(5. 1-12). ①

Table 5. 1 Syntactic Patterns of Prototypes of Factual Conditional Constructions

Subordinate Clause (Protasis)	Main Clause (Apodosis)	Example
{*aika*/*aikabade*+(Subj1+) Pred1[V-*ci*]}	{(Subj2+) Pred2 [V-*mbi*]}	(5. 1-9)
{*aika*/*aikabade*+(Subj1+) Pred1 [V-*ci*]}	{(Subj2+) Pred2 [V-*rakū*]}	(5. 1-10)
{*aika*/*aikabade*+(Subj1+) Pred1 [V-*rakū o-ci*]}	{(Subj2+) Pred2 [V-*mbi*]}	(5. 1-11)
{*aika*/*aikabade*+(Subj1+) Pred1 [V-*rakū o-ci*]}	{(Subj2+) Pred2 [V-*rakū*]}	(5. 1-12)

(5. 1-9) *aikabade in-i baru emu gūnin mujilen-i baita*
if 3SG(i/in)-GEN toward one thought mind-GEN matter
be hebdene-ci, damu oilori deleri se-me
ACC go. to. discuss-COND only superficial say(AUX)-IPFV. CVB
jabu-mbi
reply-IPFV. FIN
oilori deleri se-me: superficially, perfunctorily
If (you) go to discuss something (that is) on your mind, (he) will only reply to you perfunctorily. (MFG: 7)

(5. 1-10) *muse aika kunggur se-me gene-ci, tere*
1PL. INCL if in. droves say(AUX)-IPFV. CVB go-COND that/3SG
boo-i niyalma urunakū niyalma geren se-me
house-GEN people definitely people many say-IPFV. CVB
eime-me dedu-bu-rakū
dislike-IPFV. CVB spend. night-CAUS-IPFV. PTCP. NEG
kunggur se-me: in droves, in large numbers
dedu-bu: to accommodate, lit.: "to make (people) spend the night"
If we go there in droves, people of that house will definitely dislike (us) because (our) people are too many, and (they) will not accommodate (us).
(LQD: 105)

---

① Sentences (5. 1-9) and (5. 1-11) are analysed in Section 4. 1, as (4. 1-17) and (4. 1-18) respectively.

(5.1-11) *age* *si* *enenggi* *aikabade* *min-i* *boo-de*
sir 2SG today if 1SG(*bi*/*min*)-GEN house-DAT
dosi-rakū *o-ci*, *bi* *yargiyan i* *sim-be*
enter-IPFV.PTCP.NEG become(AUX)-COND 1SG really 2SG(*si*/*sin*)-ACC
usha-mbi
be.angry-IPFV.FIN
yargiyan i: really < yargiyan "real" + i [GEN/INS]
Sir, if you don't come into my house today, I will be really angry with you.
(MFG: 49)

(5.1-12) *aika* *suntan* *be* *telebu-me* *mute-rakū*
if net.bag ACC stretch.taut be.able-IPFV.PTCP.NEG
o-ci, *taka* *sim-be* *erge-mbu-rakū*
become(AUX)-COND temporarily 2SG(*si*/*sin*)-ACC rest-CAUS-IPFV.PTCP.NEG
If you cannot stretch taut that net bag, (I) will not let you rest for the moment. (AGA4: 132)

In the analysis of counterfactual conditionals (Sections 4.1.2 and 4.2.2), it was shown that the presence of a structure containing the perfective participle *bi-he* in either clause of a conditional construction suffices to produce the counterfactual meaning. The rather rare exceptions to this, it seems, are those in which the structure containing *bi-he* (in the main clause of a conditional-like sentence) forms a mirative construction with sentential particles, as shown in (5.1-13) and (5.1-14). ①

(5.1-13) *elhei* *waliya-me* *tucibu-fi* *tuwa-ci*, *dule* *jeren* *yali*
slowly spit-IPFV.CVB take.out-PFV.CVB look-COND in.fact gazelle meat
i *dorgi* *emu* *sele-i* *muhaliyan* *bi-he* *ni*
GEN inside one iron-GEN bullet be-PFV.PTCP PTL
waliya-me tucibu-: to spit out
dule...bihe (ni): a mirative construction
As (I) spat (it) out and took a look, (I realised to my surprise that) it was an iron bullet in the gazelle's meat! (AGA2: 114)

---

① Sentence (5.1-13) is presented in Section 4.3 (4.3-12) and sentence (5.1-14) is presented in Section 3.2.2.3 (3.2-27).

(5.1-14)	*dengjan*	*dabu-fi*	*tuwa-ci*,	*umesi*	*yobo*,	*dule*	*emu*
	lamp	light-PFV.CVB	look-COND	very	funny	in.fact	one
	butu	*hūlha*	*jortai*	*hutu*	*ara-me*	*niyalma*	*be*
	sneaky	thief	intentionally	ghost	pretend-IPFV.CVB	people	ACC
	gele-bu-mbihe	*ni*					
	fear-CAUS-PST.IPFV	PTL					

As (I) lit the lamp up to take a look, (I suddenly realised to my surprise that) very funnily, (it was) in fact a sneaky thief, (who was) intentionally pretending to be a ghost to frighten people! (OJ2: 68)

Sentences such as (5.1-13) and (5.1-14) are distinguishable by means of morphosyntax: the sentential particles *dule* "in fact" and *ni* (interrogative/mirative particle), which combine with structures containing *bi-he*, help to rule out such sentences when prototypes of counterfactual conditionals are being considered.

It seems that the conditional connector *aika/aikabade* is not obligatory in order to identify the prototypes of counterfactual conditionals, since the structures containing *bi-he* guarantee (with only a few identifiable exceptions, as stated above) the counterfactual meaning in a conditional sentence. Therefore, the morphosyntactic criteria for identifying the prototypes of counterfactual conditionals centre round structures containing *bi-he*. It should be noted that, although the presence of structures containing *bi-he* in either the subordinate or the main clause is sufficient for the counterfactual meaning, a prototype of counterfactual conditional would be expected to contain such a structure in the main clause. This is in accordance with the majority of examples of counterfactual conditionals: they either have an affirmative main clause ending in the structure V-*me bi-he*/V-*mbihe*, or a negative main clause ending in the structure V-*rakū bi-he*. In addition, it is indicated in the Qing Dynasty Manchu grammars that the perfective participle *bi-he* is used in the main clause of counterfactual conditionals. (UH: 30-31; AMH: 15-16) Thus the main clause of prototypical counterfactual conditionals can be defined as containing the structure V-*me bi-he*/V-*mbihe* (affirmative) or V-*rakū bi-he* (negative).

The morphosyntactic criteria for the subordinate clause of prototypical counterfactual conditionals need further discussion. First, for most examples of counterfactual conditionals, the affirmative subordinate clause contains the complex structure V-*hA* [V-PFV. PTCP] *bi-ci* [be(AUX)-COND].① Therefore, it is appropriate to consider this structure as prototypical for the affirmative subordinate clause. Second, concerning the negative subordinate clause, there seems to exist more than one morphosyntactic pattern that can be considered as the prototype, since they co-exist in Manchu and none of them seems to be predominant. One such pattern is the complex structure V-*rakū* [V-IPFV. PTCP. NEG] *bi-he* [be (AUX)-PFV. PTCP] *bi-ci* [be(AUX)-COND], which is used (together with the complex structure V-*hA bi-ci*) as an illustration for counterfactual conditionals (5. 1-17). A similar pattern is one that replaces V-*rAkū* with V-*hakū* [V-PFV. PTCP. NEG] in the complex structure, thus producing V-*hakū bi-he bi-ci* (5. 1-19). In contrast, the participle *bi-he* is removed in the other pattern, which contains the complex structure V-*hAkū bi-ci* or V-*rakū bi-ci* [(5. 1-20) and (5. 1-21), respectively]. Morphologically, the complex structure V-*hAkū bi-ci* (< V-*hA akū bici*) can be regarded as the negative counterpart of the structure V-*hA bi-ci*, which is used in the affirmative subordinate clause; therefore, V-*hAkū bi-ci* may also qualify as a prototypical structure in the negative subordinate of a counterfactual conditional. Table 5. 1. 2 shows the morphosyntax of the prototypes (as defined above) of counterfactual conditionals, exemplified by (5. 1-15)-(5. 1-21). All the examples of counterfactual conditionals are also analysed in Section 4. 1. 2.

---

① When V in the structure is an auxiliary verb, it can further build complex structures with preceding lexical verbs. For instance, the auxiliary verb bi- can build a structure as V-*mbihe* (V-*me bi-he*), in which V is a lexical verb. Together they form the complex structure V-*mbihe bi-ci* (< V-*me bi-he bi-ci*).

Table 5.2 Syntactic Patterns of Prototypes of Counterfactual Conditional Constructions

Subordinate Clause (Protasis)	Main Clause (Apodosis)	Example
{(Subj1+) (*aika/aikabade*+) Pred1 [V-*hA bi-ci*]}	{(Subj2+) Pred2 [V-*mbihe*/V-*me bi-he*]}	(5.1-15)
{(Subj1+) (*aika/aikabade*+) Pred1 [V-*hA bi-ci*]}	{(Subj2+) Pred2 [V-*rakū bi-he*]}	(5.1-16)
{(Subj1+) (*aika/aikabade*+) Pred1 [V-*rakū bi-he bi-ci*]}	{Subj2+ Pred2 [V-*mbihe*/V-*me bi-he*]}	(5.1-17)
{(Subj1+) (*aika/aikabade*+) Pred1 [V-*rakū bi-he bi-ci*]}	{Subj2+Pred2 [V-*rakū bi-he*]}	(5.1-18)
{(Subj1+) (*aika/aikabade*+) Pred1 [V-*hakū bi-he bi-ci*]}	{Subj2+Pred2 [V-*rakū bi-he*]}	(5.1-19)
{(Subj1+) (*aika/aikabade*+) Pred1 [V-*hAkū bi-ci*]}	{Subj2+Pred2 [V-*mbihe*/V-*me bi-he*]}	(5.1-20)
{(Subj1+) (*aika/aikabade*+) Pred1 [V-*rakū bi-ci*]}	{Subj2+Pred2 [V-*rakū bi-he*]}	(5.1-21)

(5.1-15) *donji-ha* *bi-ci*, *inu* *tuwanji-mbihe*
hear-PFV. PTCP be(AUX)-COND also come. to. see-PST. IPFV
If (I) had heard (about your news), (I) would also have come to see (you). (OJ1: 89)

(5.1-16) *weri* *i* *jombu-ha* *be* *majige* *gai-ha*
other. people GEN advise-PFV. PTCP ACC a. little take-PFV. PTCP
bi-ci, *inu* *e-de* *tuhene-rakū*
be(AUX)-COND also this-DAT fall-IPFV. PTCP. NEG
bi-he
be(AUX)-PFV. PTCP
If (you) had taken even a little advice from other people, (you) would not have fallen into this (trap). (AGA3: 35)

(5.1-17) *Nomina* *Naikada* *alana-rakū* *bi-he*
PN PN go. to. tell-IPFV. PTCP. NEG be(AUX)-PFV. PTCP
bi-ci, *Nikan Wailan* *be* *baha-mbihe*
be(AUX)-COND P. N. ACC get-PST. IPFV
If Nomina and Naikada had not gone to inform (him), (we) would have caught Nikan Wailan. (MYK1: 36)

(5.1-18) *bi* *jakan* *giyalame giyalame* *sin-de*
1SG just.now intermittently 2SG(*si/sin*)-DAT
jombu-rakū *bi-he* *bi-ci*,
remind-IPFV.PTCP.NEG be(AUX)-PFV.PTCP be(AUX)-COND
si *kemuni* *wacihiyame* *šejile-me* *mute-rakū*
2SG still completely recite-IPFV.CVB be.able-IPFV.PTCP.NEG
bi-he
be(AUX)-PFV.PTCP
If I had not reminded you from time to time, you would still have been unable to recite (it) completely. (AGA1: 54)

(5.1-19) *taci-hakū* *bi-he* *bi-ci*, *inu*
learn-PFV.PTCP.NEG be(AUX)-PFV.PTCP be(AUX)-COND also
ulhi-me *mute-rakū* *bi-he*
understand-IPFV.CVB be.able-IPFV.PTCP.NEG be(AUX)-PFV.PTCP
If (I) had not learnt it, (I) would not have been able to understand it. (UH: 30)

(5.1-20) *min-i* *jui* *be* *dahūme* *aitu-hakū*
1SG(*bi/min*)-GEN child ACC again save-PFV.PTCP.NEG
bi-ci, *fulehe* *lakca-me* *bi-he*
be(AUX)-COND root be.severed-IPFV.CVB be(AUX)-PFV.PTCP
dahūme aitu-: to revive, lit.: "to save (one to let one live) again"
If you had not revived my child, the root (of my family) would have been severed. (NSB: 87)

(5.1-21) *bi* *moo-i* *funghūwang* *ara-rakū*
1SG wood-GEN phoenix make-IPFV.PTCP.NEG
bi-ci, *fujin* *be* *boo* *leose* *ci* *tucibu-ci*
be(AUX)-COND lady ACC house building ABL rescue-COND
ojo-rakū *bi-he*
become(AUX)-IPFV.PTCP.NEG be(AUX)-PFV.PTCP
V-*ci ojo-rakū*: "may not do sth" "cannot do sth", the negation of the structure V-*ci o-*, expressing permission or possibility
If I had not made the wooden phoenix, (we) could not have rescued the lady from the building. (SG: 245-246)

With all the prototypes of factual conditionals (see Table 5.1) and counterfactual conditionals (see Table 5.2) identified in terms of morphosyntax, only a final step would still be needed to examine the relation between the subordinate clause and the main clause within each construction in order to ensure that the conditional meaning is expressed. In fact, it turns out that all of the constructions identified as prototypes above express the conditional meaning (either factual or counterfactual). In addition, each of the two clauses of any conditional describes a state of affairs, and the conditional relation is present in the content domain, involving two propositions. Therefore, these sentences in question qualify as true prototypes of conditionals.

5.2 Prototypical Conditionals and Their Relations to Other Non-conditional Constructions

As demonstrated in Chapter 4, each of the various types of constructions shares certain characteristics with the prototypical conditionals. On the one hand, the non-prototypical conditionals that use dative-locative participial structures V-*hA-de* (see Section 4.2.1) share with the prototypes the conditional meaning. On the other hand, all the other types of constructions contain conditional-converb structures in the first half of the sentence. However, when all the constructions are considered together, they do not necessarily have common characteristics. Rather, with the prototypes in the centre, they constitute a semantic-morphosyntactic network, which can be seen as the definition of "conditional constructions" in the most general sense. The present section will review (and summarise) the relations between the prototypical conditionals and the non-prototypical constructions and the relations between the non-prototypical constructions.

It should be noted that the categories of constructions in Chapter 4 are not always mutually exclusive, since the constructions are not classified along one and the same axis. Rather, the categorisation aims to highlight a certain particularity in terms of semantics and function. For instance the speech-act conditionals analysed in Section 4.3 are identical with some of the basic patterns of conditionals analysed in Section 4.1, but the former are distinctive in terms of pragmatic environment. Also, some of the constructions analysed in Section 4.9—those involving perception verbs and set in the past—can also be assigned to the category of temporal constructions in Section 4.3. In this case constructions of these two categories have an overlap, but neither subsumes the other.

Before re-examining all the constructions analysed in the previous chapter, it is useful to restate what constitutes prototypical conditionality. The present study takes the speaker of a sentence and the context into consideration. It holds that prototypical conditionality involves two states of affairs A and B, such that in the context the speaker of the sentence considers both states of affairs as unrealised and that A causes or enables B (in the sense that A is an insufficient but necessary state of affairs in a set of unnecessary but sufficient states of affairs that leads to the realisation of B; see Section 2.1.3.1). As stated in Section 2.3, the reality status of conditionality in natural language is not always absolute and its interpretation is largely dependent on context. Categories such as "factual" "hypothetical" and "counterfactual" are conceptually distinct from each other, but they can by no means cover the whole range of reality statuses of linguistic conditionality. Still, prototypical semantics can be defined for these categories, especially for "factual" and "counterfactual" conditionals. Specifically, in a prototypically factual conditional relation, both A and B are in the non-past temporal plane, and the speaker considers them to be unrealised but realisable (and therefore B as well). In a prototypically counterfactual conditional relation, A and B can either be in the past temporal plane or in the present, and the speaker considers A and B both unrealised and unrealisable in the temporal plane concerned.

One can see that prototypical conditionality generally includes the following properties: (i) suppositiveness; (ii) causality or enablement; and (iii) temporal sequence. The present study assumes that all constructions using conditional-converb (V-*ci*) structures embody at least one of these aspects, conditioned by other factors such as pragmatics and context. This assumption is held regardless of the meanings expressed by the constructions, which may not appear to be related to any of these properties. This leads to another assumption of the present study, that is, the aspects of meaning in question can be presented in any of several domains: the content domain, the speech-act domain, the epistemic domain and the perceptual domain.

The following summary of the constructions examines the properties in which the meaning conveyed by each category of construction is related to prototypical conditionality, and the domain in which the conditional converb V-*ci* functions.

5.2.1 Temporal and Conditional Relations

It is known from the analysis in Section 4.2 (on non-prototypical conditionals) and in Section 4.3 (on temporal constructions) that conditional-converb structures and dative-locative participial structures have a functional overlap, both of which can express either the temporal meaning or the conditional meaning. However, they differ in their mechanism when they express the same meaning. First, their basic functions are different. As pointed out by the Qing Dynasty grammars of Manchu, the basic function of the conditional-converb structure is to express the conditional relation IF. (UH: 17; AMH: 13) The basic function of the dative locative participial structure, on the other hand, is to express the temporal relation "when" (AMH: 1). Second, when the dative-locative participial structure expresses the conditional meaning, the constructions can still allow the temporal interpretation (5.2-1), whereas the temporal constructions containing the conditional-converb structure are incompatible with the conditional interpretation (5.2-2). The following two examples, illustrating this contrast, were taken from Section 4.2 (4.2-3) and Section 4.3 (4.3-2), respectively.

(5.2-1)	*si*	*tuttu*	*te-he-de*,	*bi*	*absi*	*te-mbi*
	2SG	like.that	sit-PFV.PTCP-DAT	1SG	how	sit-IPFV.FIN

If/When you sit down like that, how will I sit? (OJ1: 25)

(5.2-2)	*tere*	*hūntahan*	*be*	*gana-ci*,	*dere*	*de*	*gece-me*
	that	mug	ACC	go.to.get-COND	table	DAT	freeze-IPFV.CVB

tokto-hobi
fix-PFV. FIN
gece-me tokto-: to get stuck because of freezing, lit.: "fix (by) freezing"
When (I) went to get that mug, (it) was frozen and got stuck to the table.
(AGA2: 84)

Sentence (5. 2-1) is in a non-past context and the states of affairs described cannot be inferred as true. The dative-locative participial structure does not exclude the temporal interpretation because temporal relations are not limited to any specific temporal context. In contrast, (5. 2-2) is in a past context, and the states of affairs described in this sentence, along with others, are in a temporal sequence, all of which can be inferred as true. This is incompatible with conditionality, which concerns suppositions rather than factual states of affairs.

To sum up, dative-locative participial structures, which usually express the temporal relation, can obtain a causal interpretation and express the conditional relation, when the given context concerns the present or the future. On the other hand, conditional-converb structures, which usually express the conditional relation, can lose their suppositive nature and confine themselves to expressing the temporal relation, when the given context concerns the past.

Finally, a brief remark is needed concerning the counterfactual conditionals analysed in Section 4. 2. 2. In terms of their morphosyntax, they are less complex than the prototypes of counterfactual conditionals (see Section 4. 1. 2 and Section 5. 1) in different ways and to various degrees. Specifically, some share with the prototypes the patterns of subordinate clauses, some share the patterns of main clauses, while others appear to be factual conditionals. This fact demonstrates that in expressing counterfactual conditionality, Manchu can resort to morphosyntax or context.

5.2.2 Conditionals Involving Speech Acts

Two different types of conditionals involving speech acts are analysed in Chapter 4. The first type is termed "speech-act conditionals" (Section

4.4), and the second type "performative (speech-act) conditionals" (Section 4.10).

Speech-act conditionals morphosyntactically belong to one of the basic patterns of conditional constructions (analysed in Section 4.1) whose main clause does not serve as a statement but a request or command. The conditional relation is presented between one state of affairs and a (non-declarative) speech act. However, the speech-act conditionals stand out in the choice of the verb in the subordinate predicate. Specifically, the choice of this verb is limited to one of the few that describe personal feelings about other people, namely, emotive verbs, such as *gosi-* "to love/favour" (see [5.2-3]). More importantly, the state of affairs described in the subordinate clause cannot be denied by the addressee on pragmatic grounds—denying them would be pragmatically infelicitous and would potentially damage the personal relationship between the speaker and the addressee, or cause the addressee dishonour. This is different from an ordinary conditional that does not concern personal feelings, in which the state of affairs in the subordinate clause can be denied [see (5.2-4)].

Thus, when the speaker utters a speech-act conditional (characterised by a non-deniable subordinate clause), he or she only appears to make a supposition about the state of affairs (concerning the addressee's personal feelings), while in fact presupposing it, and in a sense imposing it on the addressee as well. Therefore, the subordinate clause of such a conditional only serves as a politeness strategy for the speaker to utter his or her request, which is expressed in the main clause. The following sentences are taken from Section 4.4 [(4.4-1) and (4.4-8), respectively], of which (5.2-3) employs the politeness strategy, while (5.2-4) does not employ it.

(5.2-3)	*gosi-ci*,	*min-de*	*ala-me*	*bu-reo*
	have. mercy-COND	1SG(*bi*/*min*)-DAT	tell-IPFV. CVB	give-IMP

If (you) have mercy (on me), would (you) tell me please? (NSB: 25)

(5.2-4)	*age*	*sin-de*	*aika*	*manju*	*bithe*	*bi-ci*,	*emu*
	sir	2SG(*si*/*sin*)-DAT	if	Manchu	book	be-COND	one

udu	*debtelin*	*juwen*	*bu-reo*
how. many	volume	loan	give-IMP

emu udu：several，some

juwen bu-：to lend

Sir，if you have Manchu books，could you please lend (me) some volumes (of them)? (MFG：41)

A performative (speech-act) conditional contains a performative verb in the main clause; that is, the speaker performs the act denoted by the verb simply by uttering it. The subordinate clause of a performative (speech-act) conditional serves to specify the content of the speech act, though via a negation that appears to be the condition for the speech act. The following example is taken from Section 4. 10 (4. 10-4).

(5. 2-5)	*enenggi*	*fiyaratala*	*tanta-rakū*	*o-ci*，	*bi*
	today	very. much	beat-IPFV. PTCP. NEG	become(AUX)-COND	1SG
	uthai	*gashū-kini*			
	then	take. oath-OPT			

fiyaratala tanta-：to beat someone very badly

If (I) do not beat (him) very badly，let me take an oath. (OJ2：38)

As analysed in Section 4. 10，the conditional relation is actually between the addressee's disbelief regarding what the speaker will do (in this example，of beating someone badly) and the speaker's speech act (in this example，of taking an oath) that implies undesirable consequences for the speaker if he does not keep his word.

5. 2. 3 Concessive Constructions

There are two types of concessive constructions—concessive conditionals and concessives proper. Concessive conditionals can be further divided into three types：(i) scalar concessive conditionals (even if...); (ii) alternative concessive conditionals (whether... or...); (iii) universal concessive conditionals (whatever/whoever/wherever...). Each type of concessive conditional is found in Manchu，as shown by the following examples. [taken from Section 4. 5 (4. 5-15), (4. 5-20) and (4. 5-26)].

(5. 2-6) *sin-i* *tacibu-re* *sain* *gisun* *be*
2SG(*si*/*sin*)-GEN teach-IPFV. PTCP good words ACC
min-i *dolo* *buce-ci*, *inu* *onggo-rakū*
1SG(*bi*/*min*)-GEN inside die-COND still forget-IPFV. PTCP. NEG
mini dolo: in my heart, lit.: "inside me"
Even if (I) die, (I) will not forget the kind words you teach me. (MYK7: 10)

(5. 2-7) *je-ci*, *omi-ci*, *amtan* *baha-rakū*
eat-COND drink-COND taste get-IPFV. PTCP. NEG
Whether (I) eat or whether (I) drink, (I) can't enjoy (any) taste (out of it) [lit.: "... I don't get (any) taste"]. (MFG: 30)

(5. 2-8) *ai* *bi-ci*, *ai* *be* *tukiye-fi* *ulebu-mbi*
what be-COND what ACC hold. up-PFV. CVB feed-IPFV. FIN
Whatever (food) (he) has, (he) will offer it with both hands and treat (his guests to it) [lit.: "What there is (at his house), that (he) will offer..."]
(AGA1: 141)

Like ordinary conditionals, concessive conditionals express suppositions about the states of affairs represented in the subordinate clauses and do not entail them. In contrast to ordinary conditionals, however, concessive conditionals usually do entail the states of affairs represented in the main clauses. (König 1986) Additionally, concessive conditionals appear to lack or negate the conditional relation between the two states of affairs concerned. Still, as König (1986: 231) points out, all the types of concessive conditionals "relate a set of antecedent conditions to a consequent", which is realised by different means. That is, according to König (1986: 231), a "focus particle" (even) in the case of scalar concessive conditionals, a disjunction (whether... or...) in the case of alternative concessive conditionals, and a universal or free-choice quantifier (whatever, whoever, and so forth) in the case of universal concessive conditionals.

Concerning scalar concessive conditionals, previous studies (e. g., König 1986; Sweetser 1990) point out that even if introduces an extreme state of affairs that is the most unfavourable for the occurrence of the consequent. Thus, by affirming this relation, a scalar concessive conditional gives rise to the understanding that all states of affairs that are not as extreme as the one introduced by even if will also bring out the consequent in question.

It is shown in Section 4. 5 that a universal concessive conditional such as (5. 2-8) can be interpreted as an abstraction of a series of ordinary conditionals *X bici*, *X be tukiyefi ulebumbi* (X stands for a nominal structure) that differ from each other only in the content of X. Following this train of thought, it is plain to see that an alternative concessive conditional such as (5. 2-7) can also be interpreted as an abstraction of two conditionals. Thus, all the types of concessive conditionals are linked to ordinary conditionals.

It seems that in a language like English only scalar concessive conditionals morphosyntactically resemble ordinary conditionals—there is the conjunction "if" in even if—while the other two types do not. In contrast, all the three types of concessive conditionals in Manchu can share part of the morphosyntax of a prototypical conditional—the presence of conditional-converb structures in the subordinate clauses. This does not mean, however, that conditional-converb structures are the only means for concessive conditionals. In fact, other morphosyntactic patterns exist as well, especially concessive-converb structures (V-*cibe*), as shown in Section 4. 5. the Qing Dynasty Manchu grammars (UH: 30; AMH: 38) demonstrate that the converb V-*cibe* always expresses concession: either concessives proper or concessive conditionals. Therefore, the concessive converb V-*cibe* (and the complex structures it forms) can be seen as the core mechanism of expressing concession.

Distinct from concessive conditionals, concessives proper entail both clauses. Nonetheless, in Manchu the two types of concessive sentences comprised by the converb V-*cibe* are not distinguished morphosyntactically but are largely determined by the context. On the other hand, as shown in Section 4. 5, the conditional converb V-*ci* can also occur in concessives proper.

It has been demonstrated that the conditional converb V-*ci* can occur in all semantic types of concessive constructions: both concessive conditionals and concessives proper. In these constructions the conditional converb V-*ci* seems to serve as an alternative for the concessive converb V-*cibe*. The morphological similarity between the two converbs may also account for this phenomenon. Gorelova (2002: 280) points out the possibility that the concessive converb V-*cibe* originated from the concessive converb V-*ci*. If this supposition is true, it would then be reasonable to assume that in expressing the concessive meanings, the converb V-*cibe* has emerged as a marked form while the converb V-*ci*, which allows a number of semantic possibilities, remains unmarked. On the other hand, it may be true that since the conditional converb can occur in concessive conditionals, and since Manchu does not distinguish between concessive conditionals and concessives proper morphosyntactically, the conditional converb would also be expected to occur in concessives proper. König (1986: 243) points out that, of concessives proper, concessive conditionals and conditionals, "conditionals are the most flexible in meaning", since they are the most open to different interpretations if "given the right contextual conditions". This is indeed also true of the Manchu constructions containing the conditional-converb structures.

To sum up, as König (1986: 231) points out, concessive conditionals involve a many-to-one correspondence between two states of affairs represented (a set of antecedent conditions to a consequent), and different types of concessive conditionals use different methods in expressing this relation. In contrast, prototypical conditionals involve a one-to-one correspondence. Yet it is in this aspect that concessive conditionals and prototypical conditionals are connected. As for concessives proper, specifically in Manchu, they are not morphosyntactically distinct from concessive conditionals. Since concessive conditionals can be formed by conditional-converb structures, concessives proper also allow this possibility.

5.2.4 Parallel Constructions

The sentences analysed in Section 4.6 share a semantic parallelism between the two component clauses: the states of affairs represented in both clauses of a sentence concern the same topic and differ from each other in a certain respect. In general there are four types: (i) contrastive conditionals; (ii) comparison conditionals; (iii) disjunction conditionals; and (iv) degree conditionals. They can be exemplified by the following sentences [all taken from Section 4.6 (4.6-3), (4.6-9), (4.6-12) and (4.6-17) respectively].

(5.2-9) *julergi alin de emu dobori dedu-ci, amargi*
south mountain DAT one night stay-COND north
alin de emu dobori dedu-ø
mountain DAT one night stay-IMP
While (you should) stay one night in the south mountain, stay one night in the north mountain (as well)! (MYK5: 6)

(5.2-10) *si ere se-de uthai uttu oibo-ko*
2SG this age-DAT then so become.decrepit-PFV.PTCP
o-ci, se baru o-ho manggi adarame
become(AUX)-COND age toward become-PFV.PTCP after how
boo boigon be jafa-me baita be icihiya-ci
house family ACC hold-IPFV.CVB matter ACC manage-COND
o-mbi
become(AUX)-IPFV.FIN
se baru o-: to become aged, to get old
boo boigon: household
V-*ci o-*: complex structure expressing possibility/permission
If you are already so decrepit at this age, how could you manage your household and handle matters after you get (really) aged? (MFG: 59)

(5.2-11) *balai fiyente-me gisun eye-bu-rakū*
unreasonably spread.rumours-IPFV.CVB words flow-CAUS-IPFV.PTCP.NEG
o-ci, uthai niyalma de gebu ara-mbi
become(AUX)-COND then people DAT name make-IPFV.FIN

fiyente-me gisun eyebu-: to spread rumours around, lit.: "spreading rumours, make (them) flow"

gebu ara-: to call (someone) names

(He) either spreads rumours around or calls people all kinds of names [lit.: "if (he) does not spread rumours around, (he) will then call people names"].

(AGA4: 75)

(5.2-12)	*ele*	*juhe*	*muke*	*omi-ci*,	*ele*	*kangka-mbi*
	more	ice	water	drink-COND	more	be. thirsty-IPFV. FIN

The more iced water (I) drink, the thirstier (I) become. (OJ2: 152)

Despite the interclausal relation in each of the sentences (contrast, comparison, disjunction or relevance of degree), the conditional or causal relation can always be found in a certain domain. In (5.2-9), the issuing of one command necessarily enables or causes the issuing of the other command, both commands constituting an entirety. Here conditionality exists in the speech-act domain. In (5.2-10), the speaker's observation that the addressee is decrepit by now causes his concern about the addressee's future life. The conditional relation presents itself in the epistemic domain, since the speaker makes an inference based on his observation. In (5.2-11) the conditional relation is less obvious, involving a syllogistic reasoning process: the major premise is that of the two states of affairs, one and perhaps one only is true; the minor premise is that the first state of affairs (this person's spreading rumours) is held to be untrue; and the conclusion is that the second state of affairs (this person's calling people names) is true. Thus, conditionality is in the epistemic domain, since the negation of one state of affairs enables/causes the affirmation of the other state of affairs. In (5.2-12) a conditional relation is straightforwardly present between the two states of affairs: the speaker's drinking more iced water causes his feeling thirstier, though this may sound contrary to what one would expect. Furthermore, the degree of the former state of affairs is proportionate to the degree of the latter state of affairs.

5.2.5 Evaluative Conditionals: Reduced Conditionals

Section 4.7 analyses some conditional sentences in which the subject of the main clause, usually implicit, does not refer to any entity in the outside world but denote the state of affairs represented in the subordinate clause. Semantically (rather than syntactically), the subordinate clause serves as the subject of the sentence as a whole, and the main clause serves as the predicate of the sentence, "evaluating" the state of affairs of the subordinate clause. The subordinate predicate can either be simple, consisting of the conditional converb of a lexical verb (5.2-13), or complex, consisting of the conditional converb of an auxiliary verb which combines a lexical verb. In (5.2-14) the auxiliary verb *bi-* combines the imperfective converb of a lexical verb, *tebu-* "to put", that is, *tebu-me*. Additionally, evaluative conditionals can be either factual conditional [(5.2-13) and (5.2-14)] or counterfactual (5.2-15). The following are some examples [all taken from Section 4.7 (4.7-1), (4.7-8) and (4.7-11)].

(5.2-13)	*jurgan*	*giyan*	*be*	*gai-me*	*yabu-ci*,	*beye-i*
	righteous	principle	ACC	take-IPFV.CVB	act-COND	self-GEN
	teisu					
	responsibility					

It is (one's) own responsibility to act in accordance with righteous principles. (AGA1: 117)

(5.2-14)	*damu*	*ishunde*	*mujilen*	*de*	*tebu-me*	*bi-ci*,
	only	mutually	mind	DAT	put-IPFV.CVB	be(AUX)-COND
	teni		*gucu-i*	*doro*		
	only.then		friend-GEN	way		

gucu-i doro: the way of (being true) friends

Only if/when (people) put each other in (their) mind can it be the way of (being true) friends. (MFG: 7)

(5.2-15)	*ine mene*	*gama-ha*	*bi-ci*,	*sain*	*bi-he*
	willingly	take-PFV.PTCP	be(AUX)-COND	good	be-PFV.PTCP

ine mene: willingly, as one wishes

If (you) had taken that away as you wished, it would have been good.
(OJ2: 150)

The distinguishing characteristic of evaluative conditionals is that semantically there is one overall subject-predicate structure. In contrast, ordinary conditionals, which have a subject-predicate structure in each clause, can be semantically represented by the formula "{Subj1+Pred1}↔{Subj2+Pred2}". Evaluative conditionals can be regarded as reduced or degenerate forms of ordinary conditionals and can be represented by the formula "Subj2 {Subj1 + Pred1} ↔ Pred2". Besides, like ordinary conditionals, evaluative conditionals do not entail the states of affairs represented in the subordinate clauses.

5.2.6 Topic Constructions

Section 4.8 discusses the conditional-like sentences that serve as topic constructions, in which the conditional clauses serve to introduce topics. The verb in the form of the conditional converb V-*ci* is mostly the copular verb *o-* "to become/be", or the quotative verb *se-* "to say". In a few cases the verb can be some other lexical verb. The following are some examples of topic sentences [all taken from Section 4.8 (4.8-2), (4.8-14), (4.8-7), (4.8-10) and (4.8-22) respectively]:

(5.2-16)

Manju	*bithe*	*hūla-ra*	*niyalma*	*o-ci*,
Manchu	book	read-IPFV.PTCP	people	TOP (< become-COND)

urunakū	*hergen*	*tome*	*gemu*	*getukele-me*	*sa-ci*
definitely	word	every	all	make.clear-IPFV.CVB	know-COND

aca-mbi
suit(AUX)-IPFV.FIN

V-*ci aca-*: complex structure expressing obligation

Concerning the people who read Manchu books, (they) should make clear (the meaning of) each and every word (of the books). (MFG: 3)

(5.2-17)

te	*min-de*	*o-ci*,	*min-i*	*jalin*	*de*
now	1SG(*bi*/*min*)-DAT	TOP(< become-COND)	1SG(*bi*/*min*)-GEN	sake	DAT

gūwa *be* *geli* *gabta-rakūbi-o*
other ACC also shoot-IPFV. FIN. NEG-Q
Now as for me, would I not shoot (arrows) at other people for my (own) sake?
(MYK2: 2)

(5.2-18) *ineggi* *se-ci*, *moo-i* *abdaha* *ci* *hono* *fulu*
day TOP (< say-COND) tree-GEN leaf ABL still many
kai
PTL
Speaking of (our) days (in the future), (they are) indeed more numerous than the leaves of a tree. (MFG: 21)

(5.2-19)(a) *buda* *je-mbi* *se-ci*, *bi* *yargiyan i* *sin-de*
meal eat-IPFV. FIN TOP (< say-COND) 1SG really 2SG(*si*/*sin*)-DAT
isi-rakū;
reach-IPFV. PTCP. NEG
(b) *nure* *omi-ki* *se-ci*, *si* *min-ci*
wine drink-OPT TOP (< say-COND) 2SG 1SG(*bi*/*min*)-ABL
cingkai *eberi*
completely weak
Speaking of eating, I really am no match for you (lit.: "I cannot reach your level"); (but) speaking of drinking, you are completely too weak (a match) for me (lit: "you are much worse than I am"). (MFG: 52)

(5.2-20)(a) *je-ci*, *jete-re-ngge akū*;
eat-COND eat-IPFV. PTCP-NMLZ NEG
(b) *etu-ci*, *etu-re-ngge* *akū*
wear-COND wear-IPFV. PTCP-NMLZ NEG
As for eating, there is not anything to eat; as for clothing, there is not anything to wear. (OJ1: 64)

The present study argues that, as shown in Section 4.8, the conditional converb V-*ci* in Manchu can serve as a topic marker because the conditional relation can be retrieved within these topic constructions. However, conditionality is not presented in the content domain, but in the speech-act domain. In the sentences where *o-ci*, a conditional converb, topicalises a nominal structure or a case structure, an abstract subject that can be inferred that does not denote an entity in the outside world but refers to the current conversational topic or the state of affairs under discussion. Thus, topic sentences using *o-ci* as a topic marker can be interpreted as: "if the state of affairs under discussion is X, I offer the following comment Y" (X and Y stand for the topic and the comment in a topic sentence). The conditional relation can be represented as: the state of affairs under discussion being X enables or causes the speaker's offering the comment Y.

The sentences where *se-ci*, the conditional converb of the quotative verb *se-* "to say", serves a topic marker are more straightforward than the topic sentences containing *o-ci*, since the implicit subjects of *se-* denote people (who hold the current conversation). The topic sentences containing *se-ci* can be interpreted as: "if I speak of X, I offer the following comment Y". In the topic sentences where neither *o-ci* nor *se-ci* is used, lexical verbs themselves occur in the form of the conditional converb and serve as topics. However, they should be interpreted in a similar way as are the topic sentences containing either *o-ci* or *se-ci*: "if the state of affairs under discussion is X/if I speak of X, I offer the following comment Y".

5. 2. 7 Constructions Containing Perception or Cognition Verbs, and Inferential Conditionals

Section 4. 9 analyses conditional-like sentences in which verbs denoting perception, obtainment of information or cognition verbs occur in the form of the conditional converb in the subordinate clauses. The main clauses of these sentences either specify the content of perception or the conclusions drawn via mentally processing the obtained information. Such verbs include *tuwa-* "to look", *donji-* "to listen/hear", *amtala-* "to taste", *baica-* "to investigate", *gūni-* "to think", and *bodo-* "to consider/think". The conditional-converb structures formed by these verbs have become somewhat fixed expressions in Manchu. In particular, all of them (except *amtala-* "to taste") frequently occur alone in the leftmost position of sentences (or sometimes with first-person pronouns), introducing the main clauses. Theoretically, the grammar of Manchu would not forbid any other (lexical) verb to occur in this position, but such use of verbs denoting perception, obtainment of information or cognition seems to prevail.

In these sentences under discussion, when the subject of the verb denoting perception or obtainment of information (but not cognition verbs) also refers to the speaker; that is, when their subject is in the first person, such a verb (in the form of the conditional converb) can be regarded as a lexical evidential strategy in Manchu. As for the cognition verbs, they do not indicate the source of information, but the epistemic process of the speakers.

Many (even if not all) of these sentences represent acts of perception (or obtaining information, or thinking) that have been performed by the speakers, rather than express suppositions about the acts. In this sense, conditionality, which has a hypothetical nature, cannot exist within these sentences. However, causality can still be found, though not in the content domain. Specifically, if the main clause of such a sentence represents the content of direct perception, the causal relation is presented in the perceptual domain. If the main clause represents an inference (or a conclusion, etc.) based on the information perceived or obtained, the causal relation is in the epistemic domain. Therefore, the domain in which the causal relation is presented (perceptual or epistemic) does not necessarily conform to the type of the verb in the subordinate clause, whether it denotes perception or cognition.

Finally, inferential conditionals deserve a brief remark. They are another type of construction that involves the conditional relation presented in the epistemic domain. As shown in Section 4.10, an inferential conditional involves the process of deductive thinking, from an observed phenomenon (represented by the subordinate clause) to a reasonable conclusion (represented by the main clause). Thus, the conditional relation is not presented in the content domain, but in the epistemic domain.

Chapter 6 Conclusion

This chapter concludes this book and consists of two sections. Section 6. 1, in view of the analysis in Chapters 4, compares the functions of conditionals of other Altaic (or Altaic-like) languages with the functions of Manchu conditionals, placing Manchu within a larger typological picture. Section 6. 2 summarises the contribution of the present study. Both sections suggest future research that can be conducted, concerning the research of conditionality in other Altaic languages and Manchu linguistics respectively.

6. 1 Typological Comparisons between Conditionals in Manchu and Those in Other Altaic (and Altaic-like) Languages

In previous studies some Altaic (and Altaic-like) languages have been shown to share similar semantic or syntactic patterns with Manchu conditionals that have been analysed in the present study. The following provides examples of conditional constructions from previous studies as well as from materials of other languages, in which no systematic research on conditionals has been done. These examples are not meant to—and are not, by any means, able to—present the functions of conditionals in the languages concerned exhaustively, but are only intended to illuminate what I consider to be the most relevant features as far as the present study is concerned.

6. 1. 1 Japanese (Altaic-like)

Alpatov and Podlesskaja (2005: 636) note that conditional-converb (V-ba) structures can express the contrastive relation, which presents "two situations that differ in some particular point, but are otherwise similar". This function is also found in Manchu "contrastive conditionals" as discussed in Section 4. 6. 1. The following is a Japanese example. ①

(6. 1-1)

usu	*ya*	*kine*		*o*	*ur-u*	*mise*	*mo*
mortar	as. well. as	pestle		ACC	sell-PRS. PTCP	shop	also
ar-eba,	*yama*	*kara*	*matsu*	*o*	*ki-tte*	*ki-te*	*u-tte*
exist-COND	mountain	ABL	pine	ACC	cut-CVB	come-CVB	sell-CVB
i-ru	*hito*	*mo*		*i-mashita*			
be-PRS. PTCP	people	also		exist-PST			

There were shops with mortars and pestles, as well as people who came down to sell pine trees cut in the mountains. (Alpatov and Podlesskaja 2005: 636)

Alpatov and Podlesskaja (2005) also discuss "observational" conditionals, as shown by (6. 1-2) and (6. 1-3), explaining (2005: 640) that in (6. 1-2) the conditional relation exists "not between the 'turning round the corner' and 'the shop's location', but rather between the 'turning round the corner' and the possibility for the listener to see the shop". Although not explicitly stated, this relation involves precisely what the present study terms as the perceptual domain (see Section 4. 3. 2. 4 and Section 4. 9).

(6. 1-2)

sono	*kado*	*o*	*magar-eba*,	*mise*	*ga*	*ar-u*
that	corner	ACC	turn-COND	shop	NOM	be-PRS. PTCP

If (you) turn round the corner, there will be a shop.

(Alpatov and Podlesskaja 2005: 640)

---

① The glosses (as well as translations) of some examples in Section 6. 2 from previous studies are modified to suit the format adopted in this study.

(6. 1-3)

mado	*o*	*ake-reba*,	*soto*	*wa*	*ame*	*da-tta*
window	ACC	open-COND	outside	TOP	rain	be-PST

I opened the window to find it was raining [lit. : "As I opened the window, (I found that) it was raining outside"]. (Alpatove and Podlesskaja 2005: 641)

Moreover, some of the conditional complements in Japanese represent the states of affairs "as desirable or undesirable" (Alpatov and Podlesskaja 2005: 646). Such sentences are comparable to the evaluative conditionals of Manchu, in which the main clause serves to "evaluate" the state of affairs represented by the subordinate clause (see Section 4. 7). The following is an example from Japanese.

(6. 1-4)

jidō	*furikae*	*deki-reba*	*benri*	*desu*	*ne*
automatic	transfer	be. able-COND	convenient	be. PRS	PTL

Well, it would be convenient (for me) if (I) could make an automatic transfer. (Alpatov and Podlesskaja 2005: 646)

It seems that in Japanese the quotative verb structure *to iu* "to say that" can serve to mark the topic of a sentence when the verb *iu* "to say" takes the form of the conditional converb, *i-eba* [see (6. 1-5)].

(6. 1-5)

futsū	*yokin*	*to*	*i-eba*,	*nihon*	*de*	*wa*	*riritsu*
ordinary	deposit	QUOT	say-COND	Japan	LOC	TOP	interest. rate
ga	*zuibun*	*hikui-n*	*desu*	*ne*			
NOM	very	low-NMLZ	be. PRS	PTL			

Speaking of ordinary deposits, in Japan the interest rate is very low. (Alpatov and Podlesskaja 2005: 640)

This function is encountered in Manchu in the case of the conditional converb of the quotative verb *se-* "to say", *se-ci* (see Section 4. 8).

6. 1. 2 Even, Evenki and Negidal (Tungusic)

The Even, Evenki and Negidal languages are all genetically closely related. (Janhunen 1996: 67, 73) Thus conditional sentences from these languages are discussed together here whenever appropriate.

Sentence (6.1-6) is a counterfactual conditional in Even. In the subordinate clause, the complex predicate consists of a perfective participle and the conditional converb[①] of the verb *bi-* "to be". In the main clause, the complex predicate consists of another perfective participle, which is followed by the subjunctive form of the verb *bi-*.

(6.1-6) Even

ak-mu	(*tiniv*)	*mučw-ča*	*bi-sek-e-n*,
brother-1SG	(yesterday)	return-PFV. PTCP	be(AUX)-DS. COND-EPN-3SG
bujuh-ne-če		*bi-mč-u*	
hunt-DIRN-PFV. PTCP		be(AUX)-SBJV-1SG	

If my brother had come back (yesterday), I would have gone hunting.

(Malchukov 2005: 536)

Evenki has a counterfactual conditional with a similar morphosyntax (6.1-7): the subordinate clause has a complex predicate consisting of a perfective participle and the conditional converb of the verb *bi-* "to be" (used as an auxiliary verb). The main predicate consists of the subjunctive form of a lexical verb. However, it is not clear whether an Evenki counterfactual conditional can have a complex main predicate as in the Even example (6.1-6), or whether an Even counterfactual conditional can have a simple main predicate as in the Evenki examples (6.1-7) and (6.1-8).

(6.1-7) Evenki

si	*min-dule*	*eme-če*	*bi-sik-i-s*,
2SG	1SG(*bi/min*)-ALL	come-PFV. PTCP	be(AUX)-DS. COND-EPN-2SG
bi	*sin-du*	*purta-va*	*bu-mče-v*

① Even, Evenki and Negidal all have two forms of conditional converbs, depending on whether the subordinate and the main clause of a conditional have the same subject or have different subjects. The same-subject conditional converb has the form V-*mi*, while the different-subject conditional converb has the form V-*rAk*-. The latter form has multiple morphophonemic variants and is followed by personal endings (which in many cases require epenthesis).

1SG 2SG(*si/sin*)-DAT knife-ACC. DEF give-SBJV-1SG
If you had come to me, I would have given you the knife.
(Nedjalkov and Bulatova 2005: 560)

(6. 1-8) Evenki
bi *ekin-me-s* *aj-ča* *bi-mi*,
1SG sister-ACC. DEF-2SG cure-PFV. PTCP be(AUX)-SS. COND
ahi-ja-vi *ga-mča-v*
wife-ACC. INDF-REFL. POSS take-SBJV-1SG
If I could cure your elder sister, I would take her as my wife.
(Nedjalkov and Bulatova 2005: 560)

Conditional-converb structures in both Even and Evenki can express temporal relations, which is a function also found in Manchu (see Section 4. 3). Such temporal relations include simultaneity and anteriority. The following examples are taken from Even and Evenki expressing anteriority and simultaneity. Both languages can express both temporal relations.

(6. 1-9) Even (anteriority)
ömen *anngani* *ielten-eke-n*, *kunga* *balda-ča*
one year pass-DS. COND-3SG child be. born-PFV. PTCP
When one year had passed, a child was born. (Malchukov 2005: 545)

(6. 1-10) Evenki (anteriority)
mo-va *una-ri-var* *ete-mi*, *mit* *ungtu*
firewood-ACC. DEF saw-PTCP-POSS. PL finish-SS. COND 1PL. INCL another
avala *ngene-d'enge-t*
work go-FUT-1PL. PRED
When finishing sawing the firewood, we shall go (to do) some other work.
(Pevnov 1980: 12)

(6. 1-11) Evenki (simultaneity)
bira-li *d'avra-d'a-rak-i-n*, *girki-n* *homoty-va*
river-PROL boat-IPFV-DS. COND-EPN-3SG friend 3SG. POSS bear-ACC. DEF
pertyren-e-n
shoot-NFUT-3SG
While he was boating along the river, his friend shot a bear.
(Nedjalkov and Bulatova 2005: 557)

A type of sentence in Evenki mentioned in Pevnov (1980) is comparable to an evaluative conditional in Manchu (see Section 4. 7). Similarly, Malchukov (2005: 540) discusses "evaluative-hortative" conditionals in Even, pointing out that such conditionals "have an indirect illocutionary function", which is "to prescribe the listener to perform" the act represented in the subordinate clause. Nedjalkov and Bulatova (2005) demonstrate that conditionals in Evenki can also have the same "evaluative-hortative" function. Here are some examples.

(6. 1-12) Even

nulge-sn-ek-u	*aj*	*(bi-mče)*
nomadise-INCH-DS. COND-1SG	good	(be-SBJV. 3SG)

(It) would be good to set out. (Malchukov 2005: 540)

(6. 1-13) Evenki

min-du	*d'avra-d'a-mi*	*urge*
1SG-DAT	go. by. boat-IPFV-SS. COND	difficult

It is difficult for me to go by boat. (Pevnov 1980: 16)

(6. 1-14) Evenki

Kodakčon-akaj,	*edu*	*d'ulle-ve*	*bi-sik-i-s,*	*aja*
PN-brother	here	two. days-ACC. DEF	be-DS. COND-EPN-2SG	good

bi-mče
be-SBJV. 3SG

Brother Kodakča, it would be good if you spent two days here. (Nedjalkov and Bulatova 2005: 572)

In both Even and Evenki, conditional-converb structures are able to express concessive meanings, just as in Manchu (see Section 4. 5): concessives proper and concessive conditionals are equally possible.

(6. 1-15) Even (concessive proper)

am-mu-da	*gasči-rak-a-n,*	*növ*
father-1SG. POSS-EMPH	ask-DS. COND-EPN-3SG	brother-1SG. POSS

e-h-ni	*emep-te*
not. do-NFUT-3SG	stay-NEG. CVB

Although (my) father asked (him to do so), my brother did not stay.

(Malchukov 2005: 547)

(6.1-16) Even [(universal) concessive conditional]

ngi-vul-de *gasči-rak-a-n*, *e-te-m* *bör*

who-ever-EMPH ask-DS.COND-EPN-3SG not.do give-NEG.CVB

Whoever asks (for this), I will not give (this) away.

(Malchukov 2005: 548)

(6.1-17) Evenki (concessive proper)

sun-da *bi-rek-i-n* *bi* *upkačin* *ulaip-ča-v*

coat-EMPH be-DS.COND-EPN-3SG 1SG whole get.wet-PST.1SG

Although I had a coat, I got all wet. (Nedjalkov and Bulatova 2005: 571)

(6.1-18) Evenki [(scalar) concessive conditional]

tygde-d'e-rek-i-n-ket, *eme-d'enge-vun*

rain-IPFV-DS.COND-EPN-3SG-CLT come-FUT-1PL

Even if it rains, we shall come. (Nedjalkov and Bulatova 2005: 571)

Nedjalkov and Bulatova (2005: 563) describes conditionals "of logical conclusion" in Evenki, which correspond to sentences termed "inferential conditionals" in the present study (see Section 4.10). The following is an example.

(6.1-19) Evenki

songo-d'or *bi-mi*, *teli* *ku-si-ve*

cry-PTCP be-SS.COND that.is fight-PTCP

If (he) is crying, that means that he has had a fight.

(Nedjalkov and Bulatova 2005: 564)

Gorelova (2006: 159-160) discusses the use of the conditional converb as a topic marker. These include *bi-mi* [be-COND] in Evenki/Negidal, and *gun-mi* [say-COND] in Negidal. The following are examples.

(6.1-20) Evenki

omolgī *bi-mi* *tiken* *gūn-cē*

youth TOP (< be-SS. COND) such. way say-PST. PTCP
As for the youth, (he) said in such a way... (Gorelova 2006: 160)

(6. 1-21) Negidal
ge, tay Buγa bi-mi o-l-ca, beynge-l-be
well that PN TOP (< be-SS. COND) create-INCH-PST. PTCP animal-PL-ACC
o-ca-n
create-PST. PTCP-3SG. PRED
Well, that Buga began creating, (and he) created animals. (Gorelova 2006: 160)

(6. 1-22) Negidal
Omnankan gun-mi, deγin-ji-da hul-le-n,
PN TOP (< say-SS. COND) bird-INS-PTL go-PRF-3SG. PRED
gehuktami-da hul-le-n
on. foot-PTL go-PRF-3SG. PRED
Omnankan: a mythical creature of the Upper World
As for Omnankan, (he) flies like a bird and walks on foot. (Gorelova 2006: 160)

6.1.3 Mongolian (Mongolic)

In Mongolian,[1] the particle *bol*, orthographically identical with the stem of the copular verb *bol-* "to become/be",[2] can serve as a conditional marker in sentences where the conditional converb (V-*bal*) is not used. The following is an example of a counterfactual conditional, in which the particle *bol* follows a perfective participle in the subordinate clause. The main predicate is an imperfective participle followed by a multifunctional particle that can be used to express modal and other meanings.

---

① The Mongolian language discussed here is the standard written variety used inside the People's Republic of China, rather than the Khalkha Mongolian, which is the standard language of Mongolian People's Republic. Accordingly, the transcription is based on the traditional Mongolian script, which is the norm in China.

② Gorelova (2006: 162-163) mentions two views concerning the origin of the particle *bol*. According to one view (e. g., Sechenbaatar 2003: 187-188), the particle *bol* may be a shortened form of the conditional converb of *bol-* "to become/be", i. e., *bol-bal*. The other view (e. g., Sanzheev 1953-1964) hypothesises that *bol* came from the conditional converb of an existential verb **a-* "to be", i. e. **a-bol*, which has disappeared in the course of time.

(6.1-23) *či* *min-ü* *beye* *bol-oγsan* *bol*, *nada* *ača*
2SG 1SG(*bi/min*)-GEN self be-PFV.PTCP COND 1SG(nada) ABL
ilegüü *bačimda-xu* *yum*
more worry-IPFV.PTCP PTL
If you were me, you would be more worried than I (am now).①
(Chenggeltei 1991: 384)

Besides its role in forming conditionals, the particle *bol* can also serve as a topic marker as well (Gorelova 2006). The following is an example in which *bol* topicalises a demonstrative.

(6.1-24) *ene* *bol* *man-u* *nutuγ-un* *γarulta*
this TOP 1PL(ba/man)-GEN hometown-GEN product
Speaking of this, (it is) a product of our hometown. (Chenggeltei 1991: 401)

Apart from following nominals, the particle *bol* is can also occur after oblique case structures (and can topicalise them). Sechenbaatar (2003) notes this function in the Chakhar dialect of Mongolian. The function is comparable to that of the Manchu conditional converb *o-ci* when it topicalises case structures (see Section 4.8). The following are two examples from standard written Mongolian. In (6.1-25) the particle *bol* follows a noun in the locative case, and in (6.1-26) it follows a nominal phrase in the ablative case. In both examples the conditional meaning is expressed, while the case structures can be regarded as topics.

(6.1-25) *teimü* *nom* *begejing-dü* *bol* *bai-xu* *maγad* *ügei*
like.that book Beijing-LOC TOP be-IPFV.PTCP certainly NEG
maγad ügei: probably, lit.: "not certainly"
If we are talking about Beijing, there are probably books like that [lit.: "Such books if in Beijing, there are probably (such books)"].
(Chenggeltei 1991: 401)

① Since the examples in Section 6.2.3 are originally provided with Chinese translations in Chenggeltei (1991), the author is fully responsible for their English glosses and translations here.

(6.1-26)

tere	*xümün-ü*	*aman-ača*	*bol*,	*eimü*	*üge*
that	person-GEN	mouth-ABL	TOP	such	word
ɣaru-mar	*yum*				
come. out-POT. PTCP	PTL				

If we are talking about that man, such words can indeed come out of his mouth [lit.: "If out of that man's mouth, such words can (indeed) come out"].

(Chenggeltei 1991: 401)

6.1.4 Uyghur (Turkic)

In expressing the counterfactual conditional meaning, Uyghur uses a complex structure in the subordinate clause, which is a recurrent pattern among the languages discussed above. Again, the subordinate predicate consists of the perfective participle (either affirmative or negative) and the conditional converb of the verb *bol-* "to become/be" (used as an auxiliary verb). The main predicate may be either simple or complex. When it is simple, it may take either the past imperfective form (6.1-27), or the present indirect form (6.1-28). When the main predicate is complex, it usually consists of the perfective participle and the past imperfective form of the verb *bol-* (6.1-29).

(6.1-27)

säl	*kechik-ip*	*käl-gän*	*bol-singiz*,	*män*
a. little	be. late-CVB	come-PFV. PTCP	be(AUX)-COND. 2HON	1SG
sirt-qa	*chiq-ip*	*ket-ättim*		
outside-DAT	go. out-CVB	leave-PST. IPFV. 1SG		

If you had come a little bit later, I would have gone out.

(Zäynäp and Wang 2001: 198)

(6.1-28)

baldur-raq	*de-gän*	*bol-singiz*,	*orun-din*
early-DIM	say(*dä/de*)-PFV. PTCP	be(AUX)-COND. 2HON	bed-ABL
tur-may-dikän-män			
get. up-NEG-PRS. IDR-1SG			

If you had said (that) a little earlier, I wouldn't have got up from bed.

(Cheng et al. 1996: 393)

(6.1-29)

ägär	*biz*	*yaxshi*	*ägän-mi-gän*	*bol-saq*,	*bu*
if	1PL	good	study-NEG-PFV. PTCP	be(AUX)-COND. 1PL	this

qetim-qi	*imtihan-ni*	*yaxshi*	*ber-äl-mi-gän*
time-ADJ	exam-ACC	good	give(bär/ber)-ABIL-NEG-PFV. PTCP

bol-attuq
be(AUX)-PST. IPFV. 1PL

imtihan bär-: to take (lit.: "give") an exam

If we hadn't studied well, we couldn't have performed well in the exam.

(Cheng et al. 1996: 393)

Conditional-converb structures in Uyghur can also express temporal relations. The following are two examples.

(6.1-30)

män	*kino*	*kör-üwat-sam*,	*mu'ällim*	*meni*	*chaqir-ip*
1SG	movie	see-PROG-COND. 1SG	teacher	1SG. ACC	call-CVB

chiq-ip	*kät-ti*
go. out-CVB	leave-PST. 3SG/PL

When I was watching a movie, the teacher called me to go out.

(Cheng et al. 1996: 394-395)

(6.1-31)

u	*käl-sä*,	*silär*	*ämgäk*	*qil-iwatqan*	*ikän-silär*
3SG	come-COND. 3SG/PL	2PL	labour	do-PROG. PTCP	COP. IDR-2PL

When he came, (he found that) you were doing physical work.

(Cheng et al. 1996: 443)

Just as in Manchu, Even, and Evenki, the Uyghur conditional converb can express the concessive relation, indicating "that the subject matter of the sentence is spoken in opposition to another matter or state" (Hämit 2003: 311). The following is an example.

(6.1-32)

aka-m	*bar-sa*,	*u*	*nahayiti*	*qopalliq*
elder. brother-1SG. POSS	go-COND. 3SG/PL	3SG	very	rudeness

qi-ptu
do-PST. IDR. 3SG/PL

qopalliq qil-: to act rudely

My elder brother went, but s/he apparently acted really rudely.

(Hämit 2003: 311)

Contrastive conditionals also exist in Uyghur [see Section 4.6.1 for

Manchu examples; see also the Japanese example (6.1-1)]. The following is an example.

(6.1-33)	*bir*	*qetim*	*uyghurchä*	*kino*	*kör-säk*,	*bir*	*qetim*	*xänzuchä*
	one	time	Uyghur	movie	see-COND.1PL	one	time	Chinese
	kino		*kör-äyli*					
	film		see-OPT.1PL					

Let's see a Uyghur movie one time, and see a Chinese film some other time (for a change). (Zäynäp and Wang 2001: 252-253)

Again, it is not surprising to find that the Uyghur conditional converb can not only serve as a topic marker but also governs a case structure. The following is an example where the conditional converb *bol-sa* topicalises a locative structure.

(6.1-34)	(*tagh*	*üst-i-dä*	*ap'aq*	*qar*, ...)	*töwän-dä*
	mountain	top-3POSS-LOC	pure.white	snow	below-LOC
	bol-sa,		*küpkük*	*muz*	
	TOP (< be-COND.3SG/PL)		clear.blue	ice	

On the mountain top—pure white snow, ... and below—clear blue ice.

(Hämit 2003: 111)

6.1.5 Summary

The comparison between conditional constructions in Manchu and those in some other related or typologically similar languages involve most of the categories analysed in Chapter 4. These include counterfactual conditionals (Even, Evenki, Mongolian and Uyghur); temporal constructions containing conditional-converb structures (Even, Evenki, and Uyghur); concessives proper and concessive conditionals (Even, Evenki and Uyghur); contrastive conditionals (Japanese and Uyghur); evaluative conditionals (Japanese, Even and Evenki); topic constructions (Evenki, Negidal, Mongolian and Uyghur); sentences with the conditional converb of perception verbs (Japanese); and inferential conditionals (Evenki). Table 6.1 summarises the comparison.

Table 6.1 A Cross-linguistic Comparison between Conditionals in Manchu with Those in Other Altaic or Altaic-like Languages

		Counterfactual Cond.	Temporal	Concessive	Contrastive	Evaluative Cond.	Topic	Perc. /Cog. Verbs	Inferential Cond.
Tungusic	Even	√	√	√		√			
	Evenki	√	√	√		√	√		√
	Negidal						√		
Mongolic	Mongolian	√					√		
Turkic	Uyghur	√	√	√	√		√		
Altaic-like	Japanese				√	√		√	

As pointed out at the beginning of Section 6.1, this comparison is only partial, and it does not necessarily mean that the conditional constructions in these languages are only comparable to the Manchu constructions mentioned here. However, starting from the shared characteristics under discussion, and with a proper corpus, one can further investigate the conditional constructions in any of these languages (which have not yet been systematically studied) using the approaches of previous studies as well as that of the present study. On the other hand, based on such individual studies, a more comprehensive study of conditional constructions can be conducted. In this process, numerous other issues relevant to conditionals (such as the tense-aspect-modality system, among others) will have to be addressed, which will be beneficial to the overall understanding of the languages in question.

6.2 The Contribution of the Present Study

The present study aims to provide a comprehensive description of conditional constructions in Manchu. In defining "conditional constructions", the present study adopts a prototype-theory approach (Taylor 1995). That is, the category "conditional constructions" consists of central members (prototypes) and peripheral members (non-prototypes) both semantically and morphosyntactically. While each of the various peripheral members shares a certain characteristic with the prototypes, no single characteristic is shared by all members of the category: all peripheral members are connected with each other through the prototypes. Semantically, prototypical conditionality is defined as a relation between two states of affairs (A and B), represented by two clauses—a subordinate clause and a main clause. While neither A nor B is entailed by the sentence, A is a cause of B: as explained by Mackie (1975), A is an insufficient but necessary state of affairs out of a set of unnecessary but sufficient states of affairs that causes B. Morphosyntactically, prototypical patterns of Manchu conditionals are identified based on the Qing Dynasty Manchu grammars and on actual use attested in the corpus. The non-prototypes, distinct in various ways and to different degrees from the prototypes in morphosyntax or semantics, are analysed in relation to the prototypes.

In analysing all the constructions, the present study adopts the approach used by Sweetser (1990) and Dancygier (1998), which recognises multiple domains where certain aspects of conditionality are likely to be presented. These domains include the content domain, the speech-act domain, and the epistemic domain. In addition, the present study also refers to "the perceptual domain" when analysing constructions that contain the conditional converb of certain perception verbs (see Sections 4.3.2.4 and 4.9). Table 6.2 summarises the constructions analysed in Chapter 4 and discussed in Chapter 5.

Table 6.2 A Summary of Conditional Constructions in Manchu

<table>
<tr><th></th><th>Conditionality or What Aspect of It</th><th>Domain of Semantic Presentation</th><th>Additional Remark</th></tr>
<tr><td>Prototypes</td><td rowspan="2">Conditionality</td><td>Content</td><td rowspan="3"></td></tr>
<tr><td>Non-prototypical Conditionals</td><td>Content</td></tr>
<tr><td>Temporal</td><td>Temporality only</td><td>Content</td></tr>
<tr><td>Speech-Act Conditionals</td><td rowspan="2">Conditionality</td><td rowspan="2">Speech-act</td><td>Protasis used as politeness strategy</td></tr>
<tr><td>Performative Conditionals</td><td>Protasis specifying content of speech act</td></tr>
</table>

Continued

		Conditionality or What Aspect of It	Domain of Semantic Presentation	Additional Remark
Concessives Proper		Not applicable	Content	
Concessive Condition-als	Scalar	Conditionality	Content	Conditionality as a many-to-one correspondence
	Alternative			
	Universal			
Parallel Construc-tions	Contrast	Conditionality	Content/speech-act/epistemic/perceptual	
	Comparison			
	Disjunction			
	Degree	Causality/conditionality	Content	
Evaluative Conditionals		Conditionality	Content	Main subject referring to protasis state of affairs; "reduced conditional"
Topic Constructions		Conditionality	Speech-act	Topic → Comment
Perception/Cognition Verb Constructions		Conditionality/temporality/causality	Epistemic/Perceptual	
Inferential Conditionals		Conditionality	Epistemic	Phenomenon → inference

The contribution of the present study can be viewed from two perspectives: that of the research of linguistic conditionality and that of Manchu linguistics. First, the present study is based on a corpus and investigates the conditional constructions in a particular language (Manchu) in which no such research has been conducted before. It supplements the existing body of studies on conditional constructions with new materials. The present study identifies morphosyntactic prototypes for factual and counterfactual conditionals (Section 5. 1), and explores the range of functions of conditional constructions (Chapter 4) in terms of semantics, morphosyntax and pragmatics (Section 5. 2). It is of the same type as numerous previous studies and its research approach has benefited from them [Dancygier (1998), Declerck and Reed (2001) on English conditionals; and studies included in Xrakovskij (2005) on conditionals in a wide range of languages that exhibit different grammatical systems]. In particular, the present study is relevant to, and inspired by, studies conducted on the conditionals in languages such as Even (Malchukov 2005), Evenki (Pevnov 1980; Nedjalkov and Bulatova 2005), and Japanese (Alpatov and Podlesskaja 2005), which are genetically (Even and Evenki) or typologically (all of the three languages) close to Manchu (see Section 6.1 for details).

Second, the present study is a contribution to Manchu linguistics. This is not to claim that conditionals have been entirely neglected in previous studies. Indeed, the Qing Dynasty Manchu grammars record examples of conditionals, and later works of Manchu studies address conditionals (especially when discussing the conditional converb), but the present study has the advantage of collecting data from a corpus of a considerable size and of providing an in-depth analysis of the conditionals.

Various linguistic issues of Manchu involved in the present study can be further explored. It is demonstrated in Chapter 4 that the non-prototypical conditional constructions of Manchu overlap with other constructions, such as temporal, concessive, and topic constructions, all of which allow more than one morphosyntactic pattern and deserve separate research in their own rights. Furthermore, the tense-aspect-modality system of Manchu verbs, which in certain respects still perplexes researches despite the existing studies, requires a thorough analysis based on a sufficiently large corpus. Corpus linguistics, then, is quite likely to help answer some old questions as well as leading to new discoveries.

Bibliography

1 Manchu Materials Used

AGA Ihing. *An i gisun i amtan be sara bithe* [庸言知旨，The book for knowing the taste of ordinary language (in four books)]. Peking，1802.

AMH Uge Šeoping (舞格寿平). *Manju bithei gisun de aisilara mudan i hergen* (清文助语虚字，Functional words in the Manchu language). [*Cing wen ki mung bithe* (清文启蒙，An elementary textbook of Manchu) 3]. Peking：Sanhuaitang，1730.

IMN Hu，Z. (ed.). *Ice manju nikan gisun kamcibuha buleku bithe* (新满汉大词典，A new manchu Chinese dictionary). Ürümchi：Xinjiang Renmin Chubanshe，1994.

LQD Chuang，C-F. (ed.). *Qing yu lao qi da* (清语老乞大，Lao qi da：a Manchu translation). Taipei：Wenshizhe Chubanshe，1984.

MFG Uge Šeoping (舞格寿平). *Nikan gisun kamciha manjurara fiyelen i gisun* (兼汉满套话，Passages of Manchu Dialogues with Chinese Translation). [*Cing wen ki mung bithe* (清文启蒙，An elementary textbook of Manchu) 2]. Peking：Sanhuaitang，1730.

MYK *Manjui yargiyan kooli* [满洲实录，Veritable records of the Manchus (in eight books)]. Beijing：Zhonghua Shuju，1985.

NSB *Nišan saman bithe* (The tale of the Nišan Shaman). A manuscript presented to Alexander V. Grebenshchikov by Dekdengge.

OJ1 Chang，H-K. *Sume hūlara manju gisun i oyonggo jorin i bithe*

(清文指要解读，Essentials of the Manchu language with Chinese annotation). Taipei: Wenshizhe Chubanshe, 2005.

OJ2 Chang, H-K. *Sume hūlara sirame banjibuha nikan hergen i kamcibuha manju gisun i oyonggo jorin i bithe* (续编清文指要解读，Recompiled essentials of the Manchu language with Chinese annotation). Taipei: Wenshizhe Chubanshe, 2005.

SG Ji, Y., L. Bai and B. Zhao (translation and annotation). *Shi yu gushi* (尸语故事，Stories of the bewitched corpse). Beijing: Zhongyang Minzu Daxue Chubanshe, 2002.

UH Heotiyan Wanfu and Liu Fengshan. *Dasame foloho manju gisun i untuhun hergen i temgetu jorin bithe* (重刻清文虚字指南编，Essensials of the functional words in Manchu: A reprint). Peking: Longfusi Juzhentang, 1894.

2 References

Aikhenvald, A. Evidentiality in typological perspective. In Aikhenvald, A. and R. Dixon (eds.), *Studies in evidentiality* (*Typological Studies in Language* 54) (pp. 1-31). Amsterdam and Philadelphia: John Benjamins Publishing Company, 2003.

Aikhenvald, A. *Evidentiality*. Oxford: Oxford University Press, 2004.

Aisin-Gioro, Y. *Manyu zashi* (*A comprehensive handbook of the Manchu language*). Beijing: Xueyuan Press, 2004.

Akatsuka, N. Conditionals are discourse-bound. In Traugott, E. C., A. ter Meulen, J. S. Reilly and C. A. Ferguson (eds.), *On conditionals* (pp. 333-351). Cambridge: Cambridge University Press, 1986.

Alpatov, V. M. and V. I. Podlesskaja. Conditionals in Japanese. In Xrakovskij, V. S. (ed.), *Typology of conditional constructions* (*LINCOM Studies in Theoretical Linguistics* 25) (pp. 629-655). München: LINCOM GmbH, 2005.

Amiot, J. M. *Grammaire tartare mantchou*. Paris, 1788.

Austin, J. L. *How to do things with words*. Cambridge, Mass.: Harvard University Press. 1962.

Avrorin, V. A. *O kategorijax vida i vremeni v man' č žurskom jazyke*

[*Izvestija AN SSSR VII*(1)] [On categories of aspect and tense in the Manchu language: Proceedings of the Academy of Sciences, USSR, VII(1)] (pp. 60-66). Moscow, 1949.

Avrorin, V. A. *Grammatika pis'mennogo man' č žurskogo jazyka* (Grammar of the written Manchu language). Saint Petersburg: Nauka, 2000.

Bennett, J. *A philosophical guide to conditionals*. Oxford: Clarendon Press, 2003.

Chafe, W. L. Givenness, contrastiveness, definiteness, subjects and topics. In Li, C. N. (ed.), *Subject and topic* (pp. 25-55). New York: Academic Press, 1976.

Chafe, W. and J. Nichols (eds.). *Evidentiality: The linguistic coding of epistemology* (*Advances in Discourse Processes* 20). Norwood, N. J.: Abex, 1986.

Cheng, S., A. Yaqub, M. Kärim, Zhang D., Zhang L., Hu Y., Talant, and Jin C. (eds.). *Xiandai weiwueryu yufa/Hazirqi zaman uyghur tili grammatikisi* (A grammar of modern Uyghur). Ürümchi: Xinjiang Renmin Chubanshe, 1996.

Chenggeltei. *Mengguyu yufa* (A grammar of Mongolian). Hohhot: Nei Menggu renmin chubanshe, 1991.

Cherkasova, E. T. *Russkie sojuzy nemestoimennogo proisxoždenija* (Russian conjunctions of non-pronominal origin). Moscow: Nauka, 1973.

Comrie, B. *Aspect: An introduction to the study of verbal aspect and related problems*. Cambridge: Cambridge University Press, 1976.

Comrie, B. Conditionals: A typology. In Traugott, E. C., A. ter Meulen, J. S. Reilly and C. A. Ferguson (eds.), *On conditionals* (pp. 77-99). Cambridge: Cambridge University Press, 1986.

Dahl, Östen. The relation between past time reference and counterfactuality: A new look. In Athanasiadou, A and R. Dirven (eds.), *On conditionals again* (*Current Issues in Linguistic Theory* 143) (pp. 97-114). Amsterdam & Philadelphia: John Benjamins Publishing Company, 1997.

Dancygier, B. Interpreting conditionals: Time, knowledge and causation. *Journal of Pragmatics*, 1993, 19.

Dancygier, B. *Conditionals and prediction: Time, knowledge and causation in conditional constructions*. Cambridge: Cambridge University Press, 1998.

De Haan, F. Evidentiality and epistemic modality: Setting boundaries. *Southwest Journal of Linguistics*, 1999, 18.

De Haan, F. The place of inference within the evidential system. *International Journal of American linguistics*, 2001, 67.

De Haan, F. Typological approaches to modality. In Frawley, W. (ed.), *The expression of modality* (pp. 27-70). Berlin & New York: Mouton de Gruyter, 2006.

Declerck, R. and S. Reed. *Conditionals: A comprehensive empirical analysis*. Berlin & New York: Mouton de Gruyter, 2001.

DeLancey, S. Mirativity: The grammatical marking of unexpected information. *Linguistic Typlogy*, 1997, 1.

Fillenbaum, S. The use of conditionals in inducements and deterrents. In Traugott, E. C., A. ter Meulen, J. S. Reilly and C. A. Ferguson (eds.), *On conditionals* (pp. 179-195). Cambridge: Cambridge University Press, 1986.

Fleischman, S. Temporal distance: A basic linguistic metaphor. *Studies in Language*, 1989, 13(1).

Friedman, V. Evidentiality in the Balkans: Bulgarian, Macedonian, and Albanian. In Chafe, W. and J. Nichols (eds.). *Evidentiality: The linguistic coding of epistemology* (*Advances in Discourse Processes* 20) (pp. 168-187). Norwood, N. J.: Abex, 1986.

Gerbillion, J-F. *Elementa linguae tartaricae*. Paris, 1696.

Gökse, A. and C. Kerslake. *Turkish: A comprehensive grammar*. London & New York: Routledge, 2005.

Gorelova, L. M. *Manchu grammar*. Leiden: Brill, 2002.

Gorelova, L. M. Grammatičeskie sredstva pragmatičeskogo strukturirovanija predloženija v man'čžurskom jazyke (Grammatical means of pragmatic structuring of sentence in the Manchu language).

In *Gumanitarnye Nauki v Sibiri* (*Humanities in Siberia* 4) (pp. 60-70). Moscow, 2004.

Gorelova, L. M. Typology of information structures in the Altaic languages. In Boikova, E. V. and R. B. Rybakov (eds.), *Kinship in the Altaic world* (*Proceedings of the 48th Permanent International Altaistic Conference, Moscow 10-15 July*, 2005) (pp. 149-171). Wiesbaden: Harrassowitz Verlag, 2006.

Gorelova, L. M. and M. N. Orlovskaja. Informacionnye struktury v srednemongol'skom i man' č žurskom jazykax (tipologi č eskij, êtnoistori českij i areal'nyj aspekty) [Information structures in Middle Mongolian and Manchu (typological, ethno-historical and areal aspects)]. In *Bjulleten' Obš čestva Vostokovedov RAN* (Newsletter of the Oriental Society, Russian Academy of Sciences 17) (pp. 573-622). Moscow: Institut Vostokovedenija RAN, 2010.

Greenberg, J. H. (ed.). *Universals of language*. Cambridge, Mass: MIT Press, 1963.

Haiman, J. Conditionals are topics. *Language*, 1978, 54.

Haspelmath, M. and E. König (eds.). *Converbs in cross-linguistic perspective: Structure and meaning of adverbial verb forms—adverbial participles, gerunds* (*Empirical Approaches to Language Typology* 13). Berlin: Mouton de Gruyter, 1995.

Jacobsen, W. The heterogeneity of evidentials in Makah. In Chafe, W. and J. Nichols (eds.). *Evidentiality: The linguistic coding of epistemology* (*Advances in Discourse Processes* 20) (pp. 3-28). Norwood, N. J.: Abex, 1986.

Jackson, F. *Conditionals*. Oxford: Basil Blackwell, 1987.

Jespersen, O. *A modern English grammar on historical principles V: Syntax*. London: George Allen & Unwin, 1940.

Johnson-Laird, P. N. Conditionals and mental models. In Traugott, E. C., A. ter Meulen, J. S. Reilly and C. A. Ferguson (eds.), *On conditionals* (pp. 55-75). Cambridge: Cambridge University Press, 1986.

Janhunen, J. *Manchuria: An ethnic history*. Helsinki: Finno-Ugrian

Society, 1996.

Keenan, E. L. Towards a universal definition of "subject". In Li, C. N. (ed.), *Subject and topic* (pp. 305-334). New York: Academic Press, 1976.

König, E. Conditionals, concessive conditionals and concessives. In Traugott, E. C., A. ter Meulen, J. S. Reilly and C. A. Ferguson (eds.), *On conditionals* (pp. 229-246). Cambridge: Cambridge University Press, 1986.

Lavrov, B. V. *Uslovnye i ustupitel'nye predloženija v drevnerusskom jazyke* (Conditional and concessive sentences in the Old Russian language). Moscow & Leningrad: Izdatel'stvo Akademii Nauk SSSR, 1941.

Lebedeva, E. P. & L. M. Gorelova. *Sidi kur-sibinskaja versija "volšebnogo mertveca": Teksty v zapisi V. V. Radlova* [Sidi kur-a Sibe version of the "bewitched corpse" cycle: Texts recorded by V. V. Radlov (with transliteration and an English introduction by Giovanni Stary)] (*Aetas Manjurica* 4). Wiesbaden: Harrassowitz Verlag, 1994.

Lehmann, C. Prinzipien für "Universal" 14. In Seiler, H. (ed.), *Linguistic Workshop* II (pp. 69-97). Munich: Wilhelm Fink Verlag, 1974.

Li, C. N. and S. A. Thompson. Subject and topic: A new typology of language. In Charles N. Li (ed.), *Subject and topic*, (pp. 457-489). New York: Academic Press, 1976.

Li, G. Roth. *Manchu: A textbook for reading documents* (2nd edn.). National Foreign Language Resource Center, University of Hawai'i at Mānoa, 2010.

Liu, J., Y. Ji and L. Qu. *Manyu yufa* (A Manchu grammar). Beijing: Minzu Chubanshe, 1986.

Mackie, J. L. Causes and conditions. In Sosa, E. (ed.), *Causation and conditionals*, (pp. 15-38). Oxford: Oxford University Press, 1975.

Meadows, T. T. *Translations from the Manchu—with the original texts, prefaced by an essay on the language*. Canton: Press of S. Wells

Williams, 1849.

Malchukov, A. L. Conditional constructions in Even. In Xrakovskij, V. S. (ed.), *Typology of conditional constructions* (*LINCOM Studies in Theoretical Linguistics* 25) (pp. 527-555) München: LINCOM GmbH, 2005.

Miglioranza, A. Alla ricerca del verbo essere in mancese: La frase nominale, il verbo "bimbi" e il verbo "ombi" tra il mancese classico e il sibe parlato. A paper presented at a workshop in Torino, 2004.

Nedjalkov, I. V. and N. Ja. Bulatova. Conditional constructions in Evenki. In *Xrakovskij, V. S. (ed.), Typology of conditional constructions* (*LINCOM Studies in Theoretical Linguistics* 25) (pp. 556-576). München: LINCOM GmbH, 2005.

Nordström, J. *Modality and subordinators*. Amsterdam & Philadelphia: John Benjamins Publishing Company, 2010.

Pevnov, A. M. *Deepričastie na-mī v êvenkijskom jazyke* (The converb in-*mī* in the Evenki language). PhD thesis. Leningrad: Leningradskoe Otdelenije Instituta Jazykoznanija, Akademija Nauk SSSR, 1980.

Palmer, F. R. *Mood and modality*. Cambridge: Cambridge University Press, 2001.

Podlesskaja, V. I. Conditional constructions. In Haspelmath M., E. König, W. Oesterreicher and W. Raible (eds.), *Language typology and language universals: An international handbook* (Vol. 2) (pp. 998-1010). Berlin & New York: Walter de Gruyter, 2001.

Ramstedt, G. J. *Über die Konjugation des Khalkha-Mongolischen* (*Mémoire de la Société Finno-Ougrienne* 19). Helsingfors: Die finnische Litteraturgesellschaft, 1902.

Sechenbaatar, Borjigin. *The Chakhar dialect of Mongol—A morphological description*. Helsinki: Finno-Ugrian Society, 2003.

Sinor, D. La Langue mandjoue. In *Handbuch der Orientalistik. Fünfter Band: Altaistik. Dritter Abschnitt: Tungusologie* (pp. 257-280). Leiden-Köln: Brill, 1968.

Stalnaker, R. C. A theory of conditionals. In Sosa, E. (ed.), *Causation and conditionals* (pp. 165-179). Oxford: Oxford University

Press, 1975.

Stary, G. *Emu tanggû orin sakda-i gisun sarkiyan-Erzählungen der 120 Alten. Beiträge zur mandschurischen Kulturgeschichte* (*Asiatische Forschungen* 83). Wiesbaden: Otto Harrassowitz, 1983.

Stary, G. *Three unedited manuscripts of the Manchu epic tale "Nišan saman-i bithe": facsimile edition with transcription and introduction*. Wiesbaden: Otto Harrassowitz, 1985.

Sweetser, E. *From etymology to pragmatics*. Cambridge: Cambridge University Press, 1990.

Sweetser, E. Mental spaces and the grammar of conditional constructions. In Fauconnier, G. and E. Sweetser (eds.), *Spaces, worlds and grammar* (pp. 318-333). Chicago: University of Chicago Press, 1996.

Taylor, J. R. *Linguistic categorization* (2nd edn.). Oxford: Oxford University Press, 1995.

Traugott, E. C. Conditional markers. In Haiman, J. (ed.), *Iconicity in syntax* (pp. 289-307). Amsterdam: Benjamins, 1985.

Van der Auwera, J. Conditionals and speech acts. In Traugott, E. C., A. ter Meulen, J. S. Reilly and C. A. Ferguson (eds.), *On conditionals* (pp. 197-214). Cambridge: Cambridge University Press, 1986.

Van linden, A. and J-C. Verstraete. The nature and origins of counterfactuality in simple clauses: Cross-linguistic evidence. *Journal of Pragmatics*, 2008, 40.

Vasmer, M. *Russisches etymologisches Wörterbuch* (4 volumes). Russian translation by Oleg N. Trubachjov. Moscow: Progress, 1986 [1950-1958].

Volkova, M. P. *Nišan samani bitxe* (*predanie o nišanskoj šamanke*): *Izdanie teksta, perevod i predislovie* [Nišan samani bithe (legend about Nishan Shamanness): Publication of the text, translation and foreword]. Moscow: Institut Narodov Azii, Akademija Nauk SSSR, 1961.

Von der Gabelentz, H. C. *Eléments de la grammaire mandchoue*. Altenburg, 1833.

Von Möllendorff, P. G. *A Manchu grammar with analysed texts*. Shanghai: The American Presbyterian Mission Press, 1892.

Vovin, A. The end of the Altaic controversy. *Central Asiatic Journal*, 2005, 49(1).

Wierzbicka, A. Conditionals and counterfactuals: Conceptual primitives and linguistic universals. In Athanasiadou, A. and R. Dirven (eds.), *On conditionals again* (*Current Issues in Linguistic Theory* 143), (pp. 15-59). Amsterdam & Philadelphia: John Benjamin Publishing Company, 1997.

Witt, R. J. Auditory evidentiality in English and German: The case of perception verbs. *Lingua*, 2009, 119.

Wittgenstein, L. *Philosophical investigations* (2nd edn.). Oxford: Blackwell, 1958.

Xrakovskij, V. S. (ed.). *Typology of conditional constructions* (*LINCOM Studies in Theoretical Linguistics* 25). München: LINCOM GmbH, 2005.

Xrakovskij, V. S. (ed.). *Typology of concessive constructions* (*LINCOM Studies in Theoretical Linguistics* 50). München: LINCOM GmbH, 2012.

Zakharov, I. I. Polnyj *man'čžursko-russkij slovar'* (A complete Manchu-Russian dictionary). Saint Petersburg: Tipografija Imperatorskoj Akademii Nauk, 1875.

Zakharov, I. I. *Grammatika man' čžurskogo jazyka* (*Grammar of the Manchu language*). Saint Petersburg, 1879.

Zäynäp N. and Wang Y. *Weiwu'eryu kouyu duben* (A reader for spoken Uyghur). Beijing: Zhongyang Minzu Daxue Chubanshe, 2001.

Zhao, J. *Xiandai manyu yanjiu* (Studies of the modern Manchu language). Beijing: Minzu Chubanshe, 1989.

Zhao, Z. *Nishan samanzhuan quanji*: (Translation of various versions of the Tale of the Nišan Shaman). Beijing: Minza Chubanshe, 2014.